Sinsemilla Tips

DOMESTIC MARIJUANA JOURNAL

The very best of seven years of the nation's only
technical trade journal for the marijuana industry

New Moon Publishing
Sinsemilla Tips Magazine
PO Box 90
Corvallis, Oregon 97339
503-757-8477

Published by:
New Moon Publishing, Inc.
PO Box 90
Corvallis, Oregon 97339

First Printing: April, 1988, United States of America

ISBN: 0-944557-00-7

Compiled by Tom Alexander
Designed and edited by Don Parker
Cover photography: Bill Budd
Index: Nancy Votrain and Eric Ackerson
Data entry: J. Woods
Graphics: Bram Frank

The material presented in this book is intended for informational and educational purposes. The publisher does not advocate violation of existing state or federal laws. However, we encourage readers to continue to work on the local and national levels to secure passage of fair legislation governing the use and cultivation of marijuana and to join the National Organization for the Reform of Marijuana Laws (NORML). Send $25 to:

NORML
2001 S Street
Washington, D.C.
Or call 202-483-5500 and find out what you can do to help.

Table of Contents

Introduction

At no time in the long history of man's relationship with the genus of plants known collectively as Cannabis has the plant been the object of as much attention as it is today. Decades after most of the myths about the harmful effects of marijuana should have been buried once and for all by an abundance of scientific studies showing it to be one of the most benign of all "mind altering" substances, the headlines and commentators continue to drone on.

In the last year alone, so-called scientific studies have "linked" marijuana use to permanent brain damage, psychological changes and genetic damage. Meanwhile, the overwhelming reality of perhaps 50 million healthy, productive and well-adjusted regular users goes undiscussed and unreported in scientific circles and the press. Two generations after "Reefer Madness" thrilled and terrified audiences down at the Bijou, the same old stories— stories of ruined minds, bodies and lives— continue to circulate.

But although the presentation has been given a face lift— a new coat of "scientific" evidence and a carefully applied polish of paranoia— the message remains the same. Nancy Reagan's alcohol-induced blathering about just saying "no" to drugs has nearly the comedic value of the original. It would, that is, were it not for the thousands of otherwise law-abiding citizens who find their way into the nation's prisons every year for the heinous crime of cultivating the forbidden plant— the crimeless victims of government caprice.

It seems almost incongruous that *Sinsemilla Tips* should be a product of the era of Ronald and Nancy Reagan. In 1980 when the first issue of *Tips* rolled off the press— or out of the typewriter, as it was— the pollsters had already elected Ronald Wilson Reagan as the country's 40th president. Unlike so many of the so-called "alternative" or "underground" publications that sprung up during the idealistic 60s only to wither in the cynicism of the 70s, *Sinsemilla Tips* has continued to grow despite the increasingly oppressive political and cultural atmosphere of 1980s America.

And yet, it often takes oppression— the kind of ruthless disregard for human dignity and personal liberties exemplified by CAMP and copy-cat efforts in other states and mandatory drug testing in the workplace— for individuals to find their own voices and cry out together against injustice. *Sinsemilla Tips* is only one of those voices. There are others and there will be more. As long as the government makes the harmless and private activities of its citizens the object of criminal prosecution, there is no separating private lives from public policy.

That is and always has been one of the driving forces behind *Tips*. Of course, the magazine is primarily a technical journal. But as long as the simple act of planting a seed in the ground with the intent of allowing it to grow is a criminal— even subversive— act, the very existence of *Sinsemilla Tips* will remain a political statement. This book is intended to make the same statement— that the Bill of Rights and those basic liberties assumed to be a part of what it means to be free still live, if not in the corrupted centers of government, at least in the hearts and minds of the people.

Like the magazine, this book is dedicated almost exclusively to the art and science of marijuana cultivation. This volume might well have been titled, "Some Good Stuff From Past Issues of Sinsemilla Tips," rather that sticking with the standard "best of" form. No sooner had we begun sorting through the stacks of past issues than it became obvious that picking out the very best, even for a volume twice the size of this book, would be an impossible task. Still, long-time readers of *Sinsemilla Tips* should be able to find some of their favorite articles from the last seven years in the following pages, even if some are conspicuously missing.

In assembling this volume, we looked first for articles covering a wide range of general topics— lighting, irrigation, pests and nutrients, to name a few. Because of the tremendous advances in growing technology, especially in indoor cultivation, since that first 16-page issue of *Tips* in 1980, some articles were rejected as being too out of date. Others were resurrected, dusted off and given a new polish for inclusion in this edition.

An effort has been made throughout to include as much material as possible from early issues of the magazine, many of which were distributed in limited quantities and have long since gone out of print. Although this book is not intended primarily as a step-by-step grower's guide, many of those early articles contain easy to follow instructions and advice suitable for the novice grower.

More experienced growers, too, should find much of interest in the following pages. Many of the articles by writers like Jorge Cervantes, Ed Rosenthal and others, along with the work of *Tips'* regular columnists, The Bush Doctor, Doctor Hydro, Chief Seven Turtles, and the Farmer in the Sky, represent some of the most advanced work available on the subject of marijuana cultivation.

Don Parker, Editor

"Who overcomes by force hath overcome but half his foe" —John Milton

by Tom Alexander

Although the first 16-page issue of *Sinsemilla Tips* was published in April 1980, the story of the magazine's genesis actually began seven months earlier on a small farm in the coastal mountains of western Oregon.

My career as a marijuana farmer had been nipped in the bud, so to speak, when my wife and I were arrested for cultivating over 1,200 female sinsemilla plants. Neither of us wanted to see the inside of a jail cell again, so we searched for something that would be legal and yet make us some money. Hence, *Sinsemilla Tips* was born.

Actually, the seeds of the magazine were first planted in 1976, when we lived on one of the most beautiful parts of Northeastern United States, Cape Cod. A suggestion by a friend to grow our own seemed like a good idea. With an over abundance of Mexican seeds we planted a small crop of 20 plants in early May in a clearing in a heavily wooded area. Throughout the summer we watered when the plants wilted and didn't add any fertilizer other than the compost we put in the area when we first planted.

Most of the plants grew to be four to five feet tall by September. I immediately acquired an appreciation for the beauty of the marijuana plant, even though it is considered by some to be a weed. At that time, we didn't know anything about male or female plants. The males started flowering in late August and we were delighted!

My friend was moving to Vermont in October, so about a week before he left, we cut everything down and hung the plants upside down in his barn. We split everything up between us and enjoyed the

Courtesy of the Corvallis Gazette-Times

A Benton County (Oregon) sheriff hand-cuffs *Tips'* publisher Tom Alexander in September 1979 at a remote coastal homestead with over 1,200 sinsemilla plants. Six months later, Alexander published 1,000 copies of the first issue of the magazine. The rest was, as they say, history.

slight buzz we got from smoking immature females and full-flowering males.

In the late '70s, the threat of commercial development prompted something of a migration out of the area. With all our friends leaving Cape Cod, Nancy and I decided to leave, too. Rather than stay in the Northeast we selected the great pioneer state of Oregon. We sold practically everything we owned, packed our little Honda station wagon and headed west on the first of November.

When we arrived in Oregon we still had a couple of ounces of our Cape Cod "home-grown." At a New Year's Eve party, I proudly pulled some out and offered some to the new acquaintances at the party. Several people commented, "What the hell you smoking males for, why don't you grow and smoke these," as they pulled out foot-long buds with the sweetest smell I had ever come across.

After smoking and experiencing the high of Oregon homegrown, I knew I had to grow some here in Oregon. In early April of 1977, I started some unknown varieties in a small cold frame outdoors. By mid May, I decided it was time to plant them in a permanent spot. We were living on a river, so I took our small rowboat and went downstream and planted the babies in what I thought was a safe spot. Several days later, I learned that the local wild deer had at least as much appreciation for the tender plants as I did.

Still with high hopes of a harvest, I replaced the devoured plants. I was accustomed to the climate of the Northeast, where it rained throughout the summer— usually torrential downpours followed by hot sunny days. Several 100-degree days without water wilted my second batch of plants. By that time, it was late June. I thought it was too late to plant again, so I wrote off 1977.

But now and then, I would meet someone who would turn me on to more of the sweet smell and taste of Oregon sinsemilla and I became even more determined to grow my own.

During the next year, I met up with some "big" Hawaiian growers who were buying up farms in western Oregon and turning them into pot plantations. They offered me a chance to be an "apprentice manager" of one of their farms near Roseburg, Oregon. I decided with their expertise and money we couldn't fail.

In reality, my wife and I became their human slaves. We started over 2,000 seedlings, using soil that we had to haul with a wheelbarrow from a hillside about 500 feet away. When the seedlings were ready to plant outside, we then had to haul the 2,000 five-gallon grow bags back up the hillside to three different planting sites.

Since the bosses had a bulldozer scrape all of the topsoil into big piles, all that was left in the planting sites was clay subsoil. They decided to rent a 12-inch wide post hole digger which we used to drill out 2,000 planting holes.

The promise of drip irrigation never materialized because of a supposed cash crunch. No problem for them, they had me as their arm-strong irrigation person. Each day I would water by hand the various patches, adding fish fertilizer every 10 to 14 days.

Back in 1978 the authorities were arresting a few growers, but aerial surveillance was almost unknown. Most cultivation busts were the result of dumb luck or tip-offs from narcs or unsympathetic locals. Nevertheless, any low flying aircraft was certain to produce an acute bout of paranoia, complete with sweaty palms and heart palpitations.

The bosses selected a strain of Hawaiian sativa that flowered late and finished by mid-November. By the end of November, most of the crop had been cleaned, packaged and sold. According to our "deal"

One of the 16 police officers who participated in the raid stands guard over the $100,000 crop. It took over seven hours to hand harvest the crop.
Courtesy of the Corvallis Gazette-Times

the bosses sold the crop and gave us a 20 percent share of the profits. They said we grew 15 pounds of bud and they sold it at the "going rate" of $800 per pound (1978 prices!). So, for our efforts we received a paltry $2,400.

Later we found out that they took the pounds to Hawaii, along with their production from other farms, and sold it for over $2,000 per pound. Twice burned, first by the weather and then by the boss man, we decided it was time to strike out on our own and go for the big crop.

Since we had "apprenticed" under these big Hawaiian growers, we didn't know any other way to grow marijuana than on a large scale. We looked around the Roseburg area for another farm to rent but couldn't find anything. In April of 1979 we found the "perfect" place. Way out in the coastal mountains, 35 miles from the small college town of Corvallis and a couple of miles from the nearest neighbor, we found an old homestead with a one room cabin without electricity, hot water or indoor plumbing.

We moved onto our farm in early May with seedlings ready to be planted. We started preparing the soil with a Troy-Bilt rototiller. The half-acre site proved to be too big for this small machine so we went to the local Kubota tractor dealer and purchased a four-wheel drive tractor, with financing graciously provided by the International Harvestor Credit Corp. We plowed and rototilled the soil before spreading over 100 truck loads of compost on the planting site.

Over 2,000 small seedlings were transplanted from flats into four-foot raised beds. It was an organic grower's dream! Our dreams of achieving financial independence seemed to be coming true.

In late June, we had the first of many trespassers. The man said he was training his dog to track bears when the animal bolted down a trail that just happened to lead directly to our garden. I had no choice but to stop the man half way down the trail and tell him he couldn't go any further. This obviously raised his curiosity. After I brought the dog back, he asked us some personal questions which we answered as vaguely as possible. We asked him his name and he mumbled something and was on his way. Looking back, I wish we had pulled all our plants then and started planning for the next growing season!

Other people strayed onto our land during that summer. A local lumber company began making plans to cut down some of the old growth timber on the 160 acres we were renting. They sent out a timber cruiser whose job was to estimate the board feet of timber standing on the property. He stumbled onto our patch in early June, told the county sheriff and a summer-long observation began.

In early August, logging operations started farther up our dead end road. The entrance to the farm had a locked gate, but the company owned some land up the road and had an easement through our property.

It was autumn and the nights were getting quite cool. We were looking forward to the end of our own venture into the commercial marijuana business. We had dreams and fantasies as to how we were going to spend the money that our one-half acre patch would produce.

We felt a little paranoid throughout September after a series of busts in the county. We just kept repeating to ourselves, "We live so far out in the hills, that they won't bother busting us." How wrong we were!

The locked gate raised some suspicion with some of the local folks. We confronted hunters at the gate who claimed their families had always hunted on the property. As anyone familiar with the rural lifestyle knows, property rights cease to exist during the hunting season. The hunters wanted the gate unlocked and they got their wish. Once the log trucks started hauling out timber, the gate was always wide open during the day. Anyone, for any reason, could walk down our driveway. Throughout all of this, we were convinced that our scheme was going to succeed.

The harvested crop would need to be dried so we decided to build a drying shed. The skeletal frame was as far as we ever got.

Thursday, September 27 was one of those beautiful Indian Summer days. Work on the drying shed was proceeding and we were planning the first harvest of buds in about a week. Most of the plants appreciated the care we had given them and had grown to be bushes. Some as tall as 12 feet! We did things right when it came to fertilizers, pruning and maintaining our crop. The love we had given to our plants throughout the summer was being returned. The maturing buds would have probably produced between 50 and 100 pounds of sinsemilla— the legendary $100,000 crop!

The temperature was quite warm for this early fall day. I took off from work on the shed early and had a leisurely walk to our cabin, a half a mile away. My wife was getting lunch ready in the cabin and there was nothing to warn of what was about to take place.

After lunch, I got up and walked to the door. The bust was already in progress. Eight heavily armed goons were slinking behind bushes up the path to our quiet cabin.

It stunned me for a few seconds, but then I went out to meet them. I realized immediately we had lost big in the marijuana game. We had no guns and one of the first things they said was, "We don't want anyone to get hurt." I told them that they were the ones with all the

Hamming it up for the news photographer, this cop seemed particularly proud of his catch. These beauties were a Hawaiian Sativa hybrid and were two weeks from full bloom. Some of the plants produced over a pound of manicured bud.

Courtesy of the Corvallis Gazette-Times

weapons and we didn't want to get shot either.

Some people have asked me why I didn't run? I do not believe in running from things, especially from something that is not wrong in my mind. They ordered my wife out of the cabin, frisked us both, and told us we were under arrest. We all started a procession down the path to the patch. It felt like a parade, we were at the head of the parade as the grand marshals leading everyone behind.

After handing me the search warrant, the ringleader of the goons said, "OK boys, start over there," pointing to our six-foot high staked tomato plants. I laughed and said they didn't even know the difference between pot and tomatoes. He told me that he bought all of his tomatoes at Safeway.

In fact, the affidavit the police used to get the search warrant from the judge said that there were between two and three acres of marijuana observed growing on our farm. We had about two acres of

**"All in a day's work,"
mumbles a sheriff's
deputy as he shoulders
out part of the crop. The
cops would later com-
ment on how beautiful
the plants were—and no
males!**

Courtesy of the Corvallis Gazette-Times

vegetables and one-half acre of marijuana. Much of what they had seen were staked tomato plants. But all they saw was green.

There was some confusion following the march down to the patch, but soon enough, we were read our rights and stuffed into waiting squad cars for the free ride to our new home— the county corrections facility.

A number of things flashed through my mind on the way to the jail. The farm that we hoped to buy was now impossible even to dream about. People would stare at us and think that we were hardened criminals. I smiled at the officers in the car, but they looked away, fast.

The automatic door swung open and we drove inside. The jailers were expecting us. We were processed and bail was set at $10,000 each. I had a total of $57.78 in cash and about $100 in the bank— a little short on the bail money. So we had to wait until our arraignment hearing the next day to try and get the bail lowered. I repeated to myself, "What did I do that was so wrong?"

The sound of the heavy metal cell doors clanging shut still sticks in my mind. The microwaved TV dinners also made an impression. Being a vegetarian, I refrained from eating the stuff that looked like Kentucky Fried chicken beaks. By the next morning, though, I was starved and ate a few of the things that they brought in.

All the while, they refused to let me out of my cell to mingle with the other prisoners. A new prisoner is not usually let out of his cell until he has been indoctrinated by the staff in the niceties of jail etiquette. They kept telling me that we would be arraigned the next day and probably be let out on our own recognizance.

During the 28 hours that I sat in that cell, I had a lot of time to think about and see for myself just how screwed up the system really is. While I was in jail, a man charged with second degree rape was brought in. His bail was set at $1,000 and he was out on the street in less than an hour. Another man was brought in, charged with pouring gasoline on two women and threatening to set them on fire. His bail was also set at $1,000. My sense of the injustice of it all grew by the hour, and with it my rage. Certainly a system with those kinds of priorities was doomed in the long run, I thought.

Before our arraignment, an interrogator came to see me and ask me incriminating questions. He promised to treat me like a human being. "Thanks for the favor, pal," I thought as he read me my rights. I should have demanded that a lawyer be present during the questioning, but one hadn't been appointed by the court yet. So I answered some of the questions and incriminated myself. He used all of the standard lines, even promising that if I would cooperate, the judge would take that into consideration. That was, of course, a bunch of bullshit.

We were brought before the judge late Friday afternoon. It was the last time available for an arraignment before Monday morning. We tried to persuade the judge to let us out without bail. He apparently decided that we weren't going to skip town and let us go. What a relief. Living in an eight-by ten-foot cell is not healthy for the mind or body, even for a single day.

After getting out of jail, I sat down and finally read the search warrant that was handed to me when the cops invaded our lives the day before. I noticed what seemed like a typographical error in the wording describing the location of the patch. There was a "NW" where a "SW" should have been.

My court appointed attorney did not believe me at first. I had to persuade him to check it out at a real estate company to find out where the wording would have placed the patch. It was, in fact, on another section of Bureau of Land Management land, far from our patch.

The police in their haste to catch us with the goods, neglected to get the wording right on the search warrant. That would allow us to seek suppression of all evidence obtained in the search in court. Without that evidence, there was no case.

It took the district attorney only a couple of hours to drop all of the charges and we were free.

I was, of course, elated to be off the hook. But the bankruptcy of the system and the corruption of the police left a bad taste that remains with me today. As we were collecting our things back at the jail, an officer said to us, "My, you took good care of those plants. You pruned them real well and out of 1,230 plants, you only left 20 males." Then he added with a grin on his face, "Now we get a Christmas bonus." He continued, "Don't make waves and be grateful that you are out of jail."

At first, I wanted some kind of revenge for this injustice. But after one night behind bars, jail was the last place I wanted to see again.

It was that frustration that led ultimately to the creation of *Sinsemilla Tips*. Were it not for the cops, I would still be a peaceful hippy, up in the woods manicuring buds. Maybe someday I will be, but I won't grow again until the present oppressive laws are changed.

When I started *Sinsemilla Tips* it was intended to be a sort of bulletin board for the domestic marijuana industry. Much to my surprise, it has become that and more! It has a life of its own. People send me all types of articles, pictures, drawings, letters, news clippings and other assorted items relating to America's number one cash crop.

The magazine has also become a symbol—a latter-day David against the Goliath of an all-powerful system, a system based on the sometimes ruthless enforcement of laws that have, at best, lost all relevance in the 1980s.

My determination to continue to publish *Tips* and to speak out against the system is based on the spirit of truth. We will not back down from taking on the government and its idiotic policies regarding marijuana.

Those polices are, in fact, not much different from many other government policies. The best often lack goals or clear direction, the worst seem to exist only to convey the simple message: "Your life is not your own to live as you see fit."

Sinsemilla Tips was born as a reaction against that notion that the government ultimately knows what's best for the individual and that conformity is always the best policy. To be certain, *Sinsemilla Tips* was born out of frustration. But the only sure cure for frustration is action, and we will continue to take whatever action is needed until a better cure comes along.

"God has granted you the privilege of knowing the secret of these leaves. Thus, when you eat it your dense worries may disappear and your exalted minds may become polished" —Abu Khalid, 632 A.D.

Seed Selection

There are three distinctly different but closely related strains of marijuana. They are Cannabis Sativa, Indica, and Ruderalis. Most people know of only Cannabis Sativa while the other two varieties are beginning to get a name for themselves.

Cannabis Sativa originated in the orient but is now grown world-wide, primarily for its fiber in rope production. During World War II the U.S. government had farmers in our country grow large quantities for rope. The seeds from these plants have propagated new plants, year after year, to the point that plants grow wild along roadsides in the Midwest.

Cannabis Indica is the species grown for its psychoactive resins. A few growers in this country have acquired seeds of this variety, but it is mainly grown in Iran, Iraq, Afghanistan, and parts of Africa. The THC content of Cannabis Indica is usually between four percent and 10 percent, but concentrations of over 10 percent have been reported.

Cannabis Ruderalis also has strong resins, with a THC content of usually five percent or more. It is grown in Russia and the Middle East, although a few U.S. growers have grown this variety also.

These three species have been crossbred so that it is rare to find a pure species. But they do exhibit distinct characteristics.

Cannabis Sativa has long slender leaves and grows quite tall, sometimes reaching a height of 18 to 20 feet. Cannabis Indica and Ruderalis have short, fat leaves, and inder ideal conditions growing anywhere from four to seven feet tall. Under average environmental conditions, Cannabis Sativa will reach heights of eight to 12 feet, while Indica and Ruderalis grow three to five feet tall.

At the U.S. government's pot farm in Mississippi, researchers have found that seed ancestry is the most important factor in growing good resinous pot. The hereditary background of the seed will make the difference between a plant that would be good for rope and one that gives an excellent high.

A grower must make sure that seeds come from an area of the world whose climate is a lot like that in which it will be grown. South American seed is fine for the equatorial lands, but do poorly here. Hawaiian, Northern Mexican and most Middle Eastern varieties do well here.

Obtaining seeds from someone who has been growing in your area for awhile gives you a head start. Seeds should be one year (two years at most) old. Look for gray, gray-green, or brown colored seeds that have a shine. Reject any that are cracked or dull in appearance. Seeds should be stored in a dry, dark and cool place. Good fresh seeds ensure a high germination rate.

First printed in Vol. 1 No. 1, Spring 1980, page 3.

Improving the Weed

Mankind has already improved and adapted the marijuana plant by the simple process of selection. In this process, the individual plants which most approach the desired ideal are the ones used to provide the seed for the next year's crop.

Selection works whether your crop is pot or parsnips. However, the pot plant isn't as improved as it could be. For one thing, it has only recently been imported into North America as an intoxicant. Selection could better adapt the plant to northern conditions. The plant could also be made more uniformly potent.

Unfortunately, the illegality of pot production makes it difficult to scientifically improve the plant. For good selection and breeding work, large populations of plants are needed to be worked with. This isn't true of all kinds of plants. Plants which are self-fertile, like beans or tomatoes, can be developed with only a few individuals.

However, certain kinds of plants, including marijuana, exchange pollen freely with each other in the process of fertilization of the seeds. Many gardeners who have saved corn seed for example find out that after a few years, their seed "runs out". What has happened is that a line weakens, the plants get smaller, the seed germinates poorly and the yield decreases significantly.

Pot growers find that the same thing happens after a few years of saving seed, and they are forced either to use freshly imported seed, or introduce new genes into their strain by borrowing some male pollen from a friend's line.

Introducing a new strain in this way can add vigor to a fading line, but it can also add a measure of uncertainty to the results. Ideally, a seed grower would want to take an individual strain of pot and continually improve it until it is uniformly good.

It certainly would be more useful to have a field of 50 plants which were uniformly fully mature before frost, and uniformly potent, and uniformly good smoking, than to have 200 plants of which 50 were good, 50 were fair, 50 were poor and 50 were very poor.

Why does a line run out? Basically it is due to having too few plants growing at any one time. Ideally, pollen exchanging plants grow in large communities. A field of only a hundred plants is a very small sampling. This kind of "incestuous" relationship encourages the expression of negative traits in the plants due to their concentration in the gene pool.

Why is this true? Well, it would take a genetics textbook to explain it entirely. However, simply put, inbreeding occurs when a grower selects the best single male plant and uses only this pollen to fertilize the lower branches of his or her best sinsemilla plants. The consequence of this is that every seed has the genes from a single plant. Worse yet, perhaps only the best three or four females from the harvest are the ones whose seed is used for growing next year's crop. Consequently, the 100 or so plants started for the next year contain genes from only four or five individual plants.

By using such a small selection, these bad genes become concentrated in the offspring. With each generation the line weakens and the situation worsens. Eventually the grower is forced to abandon the line or introduce new male pollen.

The solution is to grow a separate patch of pot away from the main sinsemilla patch, and use it only for seed production. A seed patch could contain a great many plants grown closely together. It should be carefully managed. By direct seeding in rows about six inches apart, and thinning later to about 12 inches, many hundreds of plants could be grown in a small space.

The seed patch should be "rogued" very carefully. Roguing means to destroy any plants whose qualities aren't desired. Roguing is the means by which selection is accomplished. What traits should be eliminated from a good line of pot?

the seed patch

traits

Some qualities of the plant are a matter of taste. This difference in aesthetic sense is the reason for so many different looking cabbages, for example. Each is the ultimate in beauty to some plant breeder. Some, however, affect the reason the plant is grown, and there is pretty good agreement about these traits.

Lack of seedling vigor is one trait to remove. If directly sown seedlings are not sprayed, the weak ones will be automatically culled by insects and diseases, The grower could speed the process by thinning the smaller, less vigorous plants.

Tallness would be an undesirable trait. Shorter branching plants are easier to manage. After all, you're not growing rope fibers. Even in pruned plants, you can tell their tendency toward tallness by examining the internode spacing. Plants which grow a considerable distance of stem between leaf groups are usually going to be tall plants. I would remove any overly tall ones as soon as this trait is recognized— probably at about the fourth or fifth leaf group.

Potency in the male is a good trait. Sampling unopened male flowers would be one good way to choose which male will be allowed to pollinate the surviving females. "Impotent" males should be removed before their flowers open. This should help to maintain a higher THC content in the females, as well as giving you something to smoke early in the season.

Late maturity is a bad trait in northern climates. Any plant which is late to flower should be removed after the earliest two-thirds of it has flowered. Do not leave a few very early flowering plants and abandon all the others! This limits your population too much. Over the years, the line will be earlier and earlier as the percentage of very early flowering plants will increase and the percentage of late flowering plants will decrease.

By this time, perhaps one-third to one-half of the plants have been rogued. Then, after all the females have been pollinated, the males may be removed. This leaves more room for the females to gather sunlight and to ripen a good seed. Don't pull the males if the plants are close together, cut them off at the base.

With a starting population of at least 200 plants, only 75 or so should be left to mature. They should be spaced more than 12 inches in all directions. (It would be better if the starting population were 1,000).

After harvest, hang each female plant separately. After drying, take a sample from each plant and set aside the seed from the best plants for next year's crop. Keep seed from at least one-third of your female plants.

The seeds from these remaining plants are your selected seed crop for next season's patches—both seeded and sinsemilla. Several years of this kind of selection will improve the health of your plants and the quality of the smoke.

Because fields of only 200 or even 1,000 plants are small populations for breeding work, everything possible should be done to reduce the danger of inbreeding. Avoid selecting the strain to be too uniform. If you are selecting for height, taste and potency, as well as early maturation, don't also be concerned about leaf shape or color or other variations of the plant's structure which are less important. Allow the strain to be as variable as you can in those areas which are of little concern.

A seed strain which is uniformly vigorous, potent, and good to smoke would be worth a great deal. Additionally, once strains like this exist, a seeds person could take them and perform "miracles" through intentional inbreeding and hybridization. However, it is unlikely that professional breeders will work with the plant until its cultivation is made legal. Too much investment has to be made to take the risk of being ripped off when growing inbred lines and working on hybrids. This is why the growers who are developing hybrid lines now are going to be rich people later, when legalization occurs.

One last thing to remember, always grow your seed patch far enough away from your sinsemilla patch so that the pollen from the seed plants does not pollinate the females in the sinsemilla patch. The pollen from a male plant can travel a mile or more depending on the velocity of the wind.

First printed in Vol. 1, No. 3, page 18.

inbreeding in small populations

Plant Breeding

by Chief Seven Turtles
A thorough understanding of the biology of a species is essential to succesful breeding. For this reason, it is suggested that the breeder read *"Marijuana Botany"* by Robert Connell Clarke. In Chapter 3, Clarke outlines the goals necessary to preserve and improve the gene pool of Cannabis.

This article will deal with many of the preliminary considerations which face someone who is starting a breeding program. These considerations include goals, germplasm collection, and preparations for the evaluation of germplasm. Subsequent columns will deal with evaluation methods, collection of field data, pollination control, genetic and statistical analysis, and selecion of superior germplasm.

setting goals

One of the most important facets of any breeding program is the establishment of goals which your efforts are directed toward. Without well defined goals, a breeding program quickly degenerates into a collection of unrelated, sub-projects which require more attention than the breeder can handle.

First of all ask yourself: "Why do I want to conduct a breeding program?" The reasons may be many, but be sure that it will be worth the trouble. If your present Cannabis variety suits your needs, keep it. If not, exactly what traits would you like your Cannabis variety to have? Be very specific and write down the specifications. For example your "ideal variety" or "ideotype" must have the following traits:

desirable traits

• Highest cannabinoid level possible
• Early maturing
• Shorter than your neighbor's favorite corn hybrid
• Tolerant to your neighbor's favorite herbicide
• High yield
• Disease resistence
• Good taste (like hash)
• Grows well in slightly acidic soils
• Has cute red hairs protruding from the flower buds

The next consideration is to rank these traits in order of importance. For example, if you live in North Dakota, early maturity may be the main objective. If you grow indoors, cannabinoid level may be a top priority. The fewer your priorities, the better your chances of achieving your goals.

Plant breeding can be visualized as a poker game. Each card represents a specific gene and each possible hand represents one of the many possible gene combinations that a plant can have. Think of a full deck as the total pool of genetic variation available within the species. The cards are shuffled during meiosis and dealt out into hands during pollination. Let a Royal Flush represent the "ideal" gene type. The chances of dealing a Royal Flush are rare, but there are several ways to find one. First of all we can take thousands of random chances until we come up with the flush. This would be time consuming. A second strategy would be to eliminate inferior hands and save hands which come close to our ideal hand. When we save and recombine the better hands, we have restricted the number of cards in the deck but we have increased our chances of getting a flush in subsequent hands. Our new deck is therefore a sub-population of the old deck.

Likewise, a Cannabis breeder must look at as much of the available gene pool as possible. The available gene pool is split up into many sub-populations (such as randomly mating varieties and inbred varieties from various sources). The breeder must first eliminate inferior populations to improve the gene pool. The gene pool is then re-evaluated, re-selected, and if necessary, re-combined.

You may be wondering what a population or sub-population means in practical terms. A population can be any collection of plants (usually represented by a batch of seeds) which have some common ancestry. This could mean a sample of seed from a good bag of herb, seed of another breeder's prize variety, a half-sib family (seed from a single female plant which was randomly pollinated), a full-sib family (seed from a controlled cross between two plants) or a partially inbred line.

collecting germplasm

Your first job will be to collect seed from as many different populations (which are supposedly superior) as possible. Keep each population separate and record any traits that the donor has claimed. It is a good idea to purchase an accounting or engineering notebook to keep such records. Keep the notebook organized, subdivided, and updated. For example, you may have a section for recording notes on special techniques you learn. A binder is handy since pages can be added, deleted and rearranged.

During the winter months, it is a good idea to test a sample of each population for percent germination and record results in the notebook and on the seedbag. This will allow you to adjust your planting densities or eliminate poor seed batches. There is no sense in wasting nursery space on seeds that won't germinate.

Another preparation that can be done during winter months is to select a female plant (which is growing indoors) and clonally propagate it until you build up a fairly large population of small plants. These clones will then be transplanted into the field during the summer. By measuring the variation among these clones, you can estimate the amount of experimental error which is associated with measurements that you make. Since there are no genetic differences among plants of a certain clone, the differences you observe are due to experimental error. An alternative to using clones would be to use a variety that is inbred or selected to the point that all traits of interest are true-breeding. However, I would seriously doubt that there are many such varieties available.

the test site

The site or sites which you choose for selection can have a profound effect on the progress you can make. If possible, test and select at the same site at which you will be growing your crop in future seasons. This applies to indoor growing. Geneotypes which do well under one set of environmental conditions, do not necessarily do well elsewhere. If you cannot use the same site, use one that is similar to the ultimate production site.

Your breeding site should also be far enough from other Cannabis patches to prevent pollen contamination. If your goal is to produce sinsemilla, you should evaluate your populations based on the performance of unfertilized female plants. In other words, keep the testing site male-free. Seed of each population should then be maintained at a separate site by making controlled pollinations. These pollinations should be made with a mixture of pollen from many males (within each population) to maintain the genetic diversity within each population.

Attempt to make each selection site as uniform as possible. The goal is to minimize environmental variation so that the variation observed is mainly due to genetic differences among plants. This makes selection more efficient and allows the breeder to quickly shift gene frequencies in the desired direction. If you have only one available testing site which is highly variable, variation can be controlled by replication or "blocking." Blocking means splitting the field up into subfields or blocks which differ in some physical attribute. Each block should be uniform within. If, for example, one-half of your field is shaded by trees, split the field into a shaded and non-shaded area. Your experimental design can then be replicated once in each area. This will give you an idea of how each population performs in each area.

nursery layout

Once you have identified and procured a suitable testing site, then determine the most efficient planting design. The overall layout will depend on the number of populations to be tested and the amount of labor available to plant, maintain the nursery, and make observations. If large numbers of populations are to be tested, it may be best to plant only one plot of each. Most of the inferior populations can be eliminated with visual examination by an experienced grower. Actual measurements— THC content, maturity and yield— should be made only on those plots which look acceptable.

If a small number of "elite" populations will be tested, the breeder may want to split the field into uniform blocks and plant one plot of each population per block. Performance of each population can then be averaged over several replications for a more reliable estimate of performance. The allocation of populations to field plots should be randomized a second time for each block to eliminate any systematic error due to field conditions or interactions among adjacent populations.

The diagram below shows an example of a nursery plan which could be used to evaluate maturity, THC content and plant yield in 10 populations of Cannabis. Notice that the field is divided into two large blocks which differ in drainage ability. Each population is randomly assigned to a plot within each block. Plants within each plot will be thinned to a constant density which reflects the needs of the grower. Notice also that each block contains a plot which will be

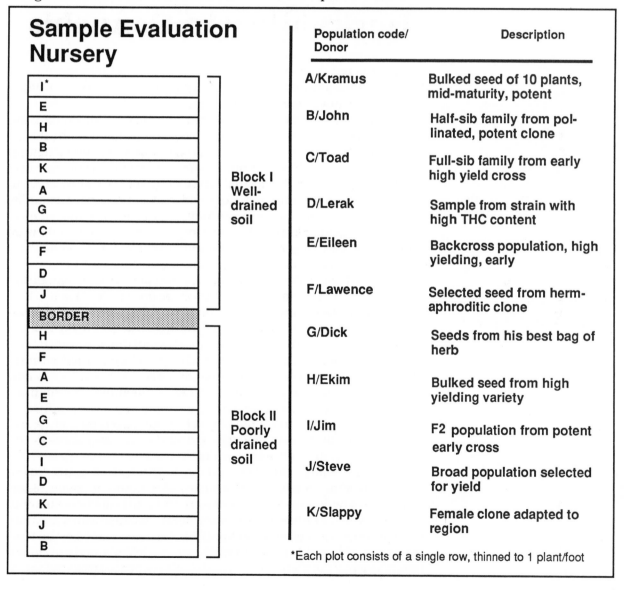

Sample Evaluation Nursery

I*	
E	
H	
B	
K	
A	Block I
G	Well-drained soil
C	
F	
D	
J	
BORDER	
H	
F	
A	
E	
G	Block II
C	Poorly drained soil
I	
D	
K	
J	
B	

Population code/ Donor	Description
A/Kramus	Bulked seed of 10 plants, mid-maturity, potent
B/John	Half-sib family from pollinated, potent clone
C/Toad	Full-sib family from early high yield cross
D/Lerak	Sample from strain with high THC content
E/Eileen	Backcross population, high yielding, early
F/Lawence	Selected seed from herm-aphroditic clone
G/Dick	Seeds from his best bag of herb
H/Ekim	Bulked seed from high yielding variety
I/Jim	F2 population from potent early cross
J/Steve	Broad population selected for yield
K/Slappy	Female clone adapted to region

*Each plot consists of a single row, thinned to 1 plant/foot

planted with a clonal female line. The clonal line will be used to estimate the environmental variation which exists among plants within a plot and among plots within the field.

First printed in Vol. 5, No. 3, page 27.

Heritability in Cannabis

By Chief Seven Turtles

There are basically two types of traits that plant breeders work with: qualitative traits and quantitative traits.

A qualitative trait is one which can be classified discretely, for example, the presence or absence of a certain pigment in the flower parts. It is very easy to differentiate a red flower from a green flower. Many qualitative differences are unaffected by environmental variation and selection of the desired type can be accomplished without concern for the environment from which it is selected. Generally speaking, most qualitative traits have rather simple inheritance patterns (usually controlled by one or two genes). Segregation of such traits can be easily monitored and used to deduce the underlying inheritance patterns.

Unfortunately, most traits of economic importance are quantitative in nature. Quantitative traits cannot be discretely classified but show a continuous range of variation. Examples are yield, cannabinoid level, and plant height. Quantitative traits can be greatly influenced by the plant's environment. It is sometimes assumed that quantitative traits have a complex (multi-gene) inheritance pattern. This is certainly true for a trait such as yield, however, this is not always the case. High plant-to-plant environmental variation may be responsible for the failure to detect simple inheritance patterns and prevent breeders from making selections based on Mendelian genetics. For this reason, breeders use statistical procedures to aid in the selection of quantitative traits.

Yield is the prime example of a quantitative trait. A plant grown under optimum conditions will yield more than the same plant grown in a shaded field with poor soil. Even the soil and shading variation which exists within a single field can cause wide variation in the response of a given genotype. This variation can be estimated by measuring individual plant yields within a field planted to a clonal variety in which all plants are vegetatively propagated from the same source plant and have the same genotype. Any variation observed will be strictly environmental. On the other hand, a randomly intermating Cannabis population is composed of plants with different genotypes (heterogeneous). Some populations have more genetic variation than others. When observing such populations, the total observable variation, phenotypic variation, is composed of genetic and environmental variation. To make sound and predictable decisions about selection, you must be able to determine how much of the phenotypic variation is due to genetic causes.

Variance is a statistical measure of variation. The equation at right illustrates the components of phenotypic variance for a given trait.

For strictly qualitative traits, the environmental variance is close to zero. The magnitude of V^2e is not constant since it depends on the amount of variation which exists in a given environment. However, for a given trait in a given population, V^2g is constant (until factors such as selection or mutation change the amount of genetic variation).

The components of variation (V^2g and V^2e) must be determined separately for each trait within each population and, ideally, within a number of different environments. For example, a certain population (e.g. a random mating variety) may show a lot of genetic variation for plant height but not for date of maturity. Likewise, the environmental variation within your field plots may be greater than that within your greenhouse.

The most progress from selection is made when genetic variation (V^2g) is high and environmental variation (V^2e) is low. Heritability (H^2 at right) measures the proportion of the total variation (for a given trait) which is due to genetic variation (within a given population).

H^2 is always between 0 and 1, or 0 percent and 100 percent. For example, if the heritability of THC content in a given population equals 60 percent ($H^2=0.60$), then that 60 percent of the variation you observe within that population is due to genetic differences among the plants. The other 40 percent of the variation in THC content is due to environmental variation within the testing site. Environmental variation includes lighting, nutrient distribution, soil structure, drainage and disease severity (anything that affects plant growth). Errors in sampling and measurement of THC content are also a component of environmental variation (experimental error is actually a more appropriate term).

As you might guess, high heritability is desirable to breeders since this permits more efficient selection of desirable genes. To increase heritability of a trait, a uniform environment and consistent, accurate methods for measurement of the trait are necessary. If you learn

$$V^2p=V^2g+V^2e$$

Where V^2p is the total phenotypic variance, V^2g is the genetic variance, and V^2e is the environmental variance

$$H^2=V^2g/V^2p=$$
$$V^2g/V^2g + V^2e$$

where:
X=an individual plant's data
N=number of plants measured
E=summation of values (individual data or squares)

mean=EX/N
variance=EX²-EX²/N divided by N-1

calculations for heritablitiy of THC content

nothing else from this article, remember these last two points:

• **Select in a uniform environment**. This means providing all plants with the same amount of space, light, nutrients, etc.

• **Measure as accurately and consistently as possible.** This includes consistent sampling and a repeatable method of measuring the response of each plant.

The following case is an example of how to calculate heritability of a specific trait (THC content) in a seed-propagated Cannabis population.

Assume data has been collected from a field experiment similar to the one diagrammed in the previous article. Also assume that we have been using a reliable method for determining the percent THC in air-dry flower tops of individual plants. Remember that variation within the clonal variety will be used to estimate environmental variation because no genetic variation exists within a population of clones.

Plot No. 1 was grown in the well drained half of the field and plot No. 2 was grown in the poorly drained half of the field. We will calculate means and variances within each plot and then obtain overall means and variances. Formulas for mean and variance are given at left.

If you are not good at math, have a statistics whiz help you with these calculations. An error can really screw up your conclusions

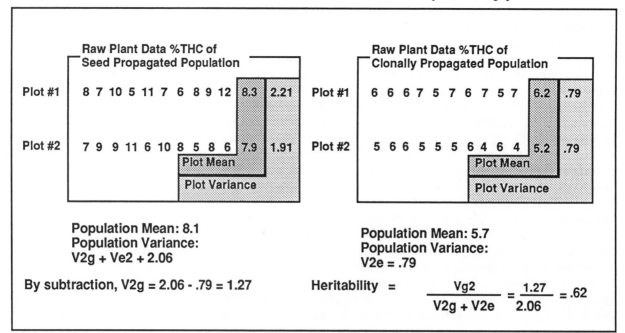

Raw Plant Data %THC of Seed Propagated Population

| Plot #1 | 8 7 10 5 11 7 6 8 9 12 | 8.3 | 2.21 |
| Plot #2 | 7 9 9 11 6 10 8 5 8 6 | 7.9 | 1.91 |

Plot Mean — Plot Variance

Population Mean: 8.1
Population Variance:
V2g + Ve2 + 2.06

By subtraction, V2g = 2.06 - .79 = 1.27

Raw Plant Data %THC of Clonally Propagated Population

| Plot #1 | 6 6 6 7 5 7 6 7 5 7 | 6.2 | .79 |
| Plot #2 | 5 6 6 5 5 5 6 4 6 4 | 5.2 | .79 |

Plot Mean — Plot Variance

Population Mean: 5.7
Population Variance:
V2e = .79

Heritability $= \dfrac{Vg2}{V2g + V2e} = \dfrac{1.27}{2.06} = .62$

about the experiment.

From this series of calculations we can conclude several things:
• The seed propagated population had a higher average THC content than the clonal population under the environmental conditions of the test— 8.1 percent versus 5.7 percent.
• The genetic variation within the seed-propagated population accounted for 62 percent of the total observed variation for THC content ($H^2=0.62$).
• We should be able to improve the THC content of the seed-propagated population by saving seed from a few of the most potent plants and using them to propagate the next generation, assuming that we had made controlled pollinations on one branch of each plant.
• If the heritability of THC content had been low (less than 20 percent), very slow progress could be expected from selection because most of the variation would have been due to environment.
• It is useless to select within a clonal variety because no genetic variation exists in a population of true clones, vegetative descendents of a single source plant.

In the preceding article, I presented an example of a field nursery in which 10 populations were being evaluated for variation in THC content, maturity date, and plant yield. It would be wise to collect individual plant data for each of these traits and then calculate the mean and heritability of each trait within each population. Means can be used to tell which populations will serve as good breeding stock. Heritabilities can be used to determine whether enough variation is present in the population to make selection worthwhile. Set up a table like the one below.

According to the population means, population "C" would be a good source of high THC and yield while population "A" would be a

Population	A	B	C	K (clone)
THC%	8.1	6.52	9	5.7
Mean H2	.62	.5	.2	0
Maturity (days)	80	102	110	95
Mean H2	.3	.5	.4	0
Yield (oz.)	4.1	3.5	6	4.5
Mean H2	.2	.15	.25	0

good source of early maturity.

On the other hand, it would be hard to increase the mean THC content of population "C" due to the low heritability of THC content in that population ($H^2=0.20$). Since population "B" has low THC, intermediate maturity, and low yield, you may not want to bother with it at all.

Remember these closing comments:

• Heritability values are only estimates and can vary when measured in different environments.

• Heritability values should be calculated separately for each trait since variation for one trait may be greater than for another.

• Heritability of a specific trait should be calculated separately for each population. Population No. 1 may have more genetic variation for a certain trait than population No. 2.

• The example presented here gives only a rough estimate of heritability which can be used in making selection decisions. If you are seriously interested in quantitative genetics, I would recommend getting a copy of "Introduction to Quantitative Genetics" by D.S. Falconer, Ronald Press Company, New York.

First printed in Vol. 5, No. 4, page 50.

Reciprocal Recurrent Selection

by Chief Seven Turtles

Although many breeding strategies can be used to improve plants, I'd like to outline a strategy that would be particularly suited to Cannabis. "Reciprocal Recurrent Selection" (RRS) is a strategy in which two different populations are maintained separately but improved so that a better "hybrid" population is created when the two populations are crossed. This is done by evaluating and selecting plants within each population that produce superior progeny when crossed with pollen from the opposite population. RRS has been used to improve corn populations that will eventually be used in crosses with each other. The RRS system that I'm proposing for Cannabis is slightly different but should accomplish the same goal.

Assuming that RRS is conducted properly, the following advan-

tages should be realized:
- The hybrid population will improve with each cycle of selection.
- Although each selection cycle takes two growing seasons, the breeder will have quality herb to market after each season.
- Selection can continue until the breeder satisfies his objectives or destroys too many brain cells.

The following limitations should also be realized:
- The populations to be hybridized should flower simultaneously so that crosses can be made between them. Selection itself may converge the maturity of the two populations.
- The breeder should have access to a separate location for each distinct population to prevent pollen contamination and maintain the identity of each population. Each location should have enough room to grow at least 50 plants if possible. This will conserve genetic diversity and minimize inbreeding within each population.

Establishing goals and choosing the appropriate germplasm are essential to a successful breeding program. Assuming that you will work with only two populations, choose two that have good qualities but differ enough so that they will complement and hopefully display hybrid vigor when crossed.

Let's assume that plants in population "A" tend to have compact structure and dense flower set but average potency, while plants from population "B" tend to be lanky but very potent. We can obviously select for the "ideal" compact and potent plants within each population but are limited by the amount of genetic diversity within those populations. By crossing the two populations (with controlled pollinations), we should be able to expand the genetic diversity. This will increase our chances of finding ideal plants and allow us to take advantage of "hybrid vigor" (see *"Marijuana Botany,"* pp. 69-71). Although we may see some hybrid vigor without selection, RRS will allow us to optimize the expression of hybrid vigor.

The figure on page 36 shows a diagram of one complete cycle of RRS. "A" refers to population A before selection. "A" refers to population A after one cycle of selection, "A" after two cycles of selection, and so on. Although the figure only shows eight females from each population, at least 10 to 20 vigorous looking females should be selected for "topcrosses" (TCs) with the other population. To make a topcross of B onto an A female, collect a random sample of pollen from population B males (by shaking some pollen for each male plant into a bag and then mixing) and dust a receptive branch on each female in population A. Read chapter 2 of *"Marijuana Botany"* for a detailed account of pollination techniques. Make sure that branches to receive controlled topcrosses are bagged before and

strategy

after pollination to prevent pollen contamination. If population A and B are planted in separate locations, crosses of A females with random pollen of A males can be allowed to occur naturally and without bagging (likewise with population B).

In Season 2, plant a sample of seed from each topcross progeny or "topcross family" (at least five to 10 plants of each family and at least 20 families, 10 from females of population A and 10 from females of population B). This means that at least 100 to 200 plants should be evaluated in Season 2. Some families can be eliminated based on seedling vigor if space is limited. Topcross families are then used to evaluate the female plant they came from but are not saved as a seed source. For this reason, pollination control is not necessary in Season 2.

Decide which of the A and B females are superior based on the "average" performance of each topcross family, but do not save seed

diagram of one cycle of reciprocal recurrent selection

Season #1: Each female is crossed with random pollen from Ao males and Bo females (on separate buds) to obtain topcross families and remnant half-sib families.

Season #2: Plant all 16 topcross families in a uniform environment with each family in a separate row.

Eight separate topcross families from Ao females

Remnant half-sib family

Eight separate topcross families from Bo females

Evaluate each family for desirable traits.
Decide which females out of populations Ao and Bo produced the best topcross families (maybe three out of eight).
Reconstitute population A1 by mixing remnant seed from selected Ao females.
Reconstitute population B1 by mixing seed from, selected Bo females. Plants from populations A1 and B1 can now be crossed to make seed of the improved hybrid population. (TC in diagram means topcross)

from the topcross families. Instead, go back to the remnant Season 1 seed from the selected A females— seed that resulted from random matings with A males. Now mix together the remnant seed from only the selected A females. This could be seed from 10 to 50 percent of the A females evaluated depending on how many A females you have evaluated.

In this way, you will not mix genes from population A with genes from B but will concentrate A genes that do well when hybridized with genes from B. Do the same with seed from selected B females. The newly reconstituted populations will now be referred to as A and B respectively, meaning that one cycle of selection has occurred.

It is possible to improve the rate of progress from RRS by using a slightly different strategy, but this would require many more controlled pollinations. The procedure presented here requires minimal controlled crosses and can be conducted rather easily if enough space is available to evaluate 100 to 200 plants.

Remember that the final product of this breeding program is not the improved populations A and B, but the hybrid seeds produced from random matings among A and B plants. The quality of the hybrid can be further improved with additional cycles of selection.

Let's say that we conducted three cycles of selection (six seasons). We would then have the improved populations A and B and, if satisfactory, they can be maintained as such in isolation from each other. To make a population cross (to get hybrid seeds), pick a location where you plant both populations in alternating rows. Then, as soon as flower buds form, rogue out all males from the population A rows. Allow the B males to randomly pollinate the A females and collect the seeds from the A females. This will be seed of the hybrid A/B. If you produce a large supply of hybrid seed and store it in a cool dry place, you can use this seed every season to produce your hybrid plants. Do not collect seed from the hybrid plants themselves since you will eventually observe a decline in hybrid vigor. Always go back to the original seed of the A/B cross.

Several people have asked what the hell turtles have to do with breeding. The answer, as we all know, is that all people have seven. I certainly have no monopoly on these creatures and feel compelled to inform the uninformed. Yes, we all have seven!

As once stated by J. McEno (a devout Poohist), "Lest we take ourselves too seriously."

First printed in Vol. 6, No. 4, page 42.

Germination

by Tom Alexander

Once you have obtained some potent seeds, you are ready to germinate and start the whole process. Soaking the seeds in a liquid seaweed solution helps them to germinate and gives the plants a boost in the early stages of growth.

For large plantings, sow a wooden or plastic flat (One foot by two feet, four inches high) with about 50 or 60 seeds one inch deep in a rich potting soil and vermiculite mixture. The flat should be watered thoroughly and the soil left moist but not overly wet.

If you are only planning on a few plants, obtain some three-inch formed peat pots and fill with starting soil mixture. Cover the seed with one-half to one inch of soil. Set the peat pots in water until saturated. The peat pots absorb and evaporate water readily. Check frequently on warm, sunny days.

A bunch of peat pots can be grouped in a flat. If you are starting more than just a few seedlings, flats are needed to keep things organized. It is best to keep records on planting, watering, germination and growth. The record will help you keep track of what works and what doesn't.

When the top one-half inch of soil dries out, place the flat or peat pots in a container of water so that the water is drawn up from the bottom but at the same time doesn't flood over the sides.

Temperature of the soil should be between 60 to 80 degrees (70 degrees is perfect). Germination usually happens four to 10 days after planting. At germination, the seed coating separates and sometimes the two halves stay connected to the tips of the cotyledon leaves. The cotyledon leaves are the first leaves to appear, with round, smooth edges and are only temporary leaves. The primary tap root emerges from the seed and grows rapidly.

Three days after germination, the tap root should be two to three inches long. The first true serrated leaves appear between five to eight days after germination. The node where the cotyledon leaves are attached to the stem should be between one and two inches from the soil surface. If it is much more, this is an early sign that the plant is not getting enough light and will stretch and get spindly. This is often a problem with old lights that do not produce the full spectrum of light.

Another cause of spindly plants is placing the lights too high above the plants. Lights should be three to four inches above the tops of the plants. Placing plants on a window sill will also cause spindly growth.

Seven to 10 days after germination is the time to transplant into either a permanent outdoor spot or a five-gallon (or more) bucket of rich soil. The plants may be transplanted outdoors without protection by late spring, depending on your climate.

Water the flat of small seedlings thoroughly before attempting to transplant. At this stage of their growth they have a long tap root without many root hairs. When you are ready to put the plants in their new home, place two or three fingers underneath a seedling and lift out. Make a hole in the dirt with your finger and place the tap root perfectly straight in the hole. Push some dirt around the seedling and water thoroughly.

If the seedling is in a peat pot, it is necessary to gently break the outside of the pot. Plant the broken peat pot about one inch below the surface of the soil. Water gently but thoroughly.

Always do any transplanting in the evening or on a cloudy day to prevent the plant from wilting.

If you have had your seedlings inside before transplanting, you should harden them off before planting them outside. In other words, let your plants get used to natural sunlight, heat, coolness, and the wind. For the first few days, only expose them outside for a short time (one hour or so). Gradually increase the time spent outside until after two weeks, they are staying out for eight to 10 hours each day.

If you are relying on natural sunlight and have protection (a greenhouse or cold frame) from the elements, it is best to start your plants in March. Without the addition of artificial lighting, the sun doesn't shine enough during the day until March. With supplemental lighting the plants can be started practically anytime. They should have between 18 to 20 hours of light daily. The plants have a life span of six to nine months, depending on the variety that is grown and how the photoperiod is manipulated during flowering.

The plant does lose potency after maturity even though it still may be growing. Cuttings may be taken from existing plants to start new plants. Put the cuttings in vermiculite until rooted and then treat like a seedling.

First printed in Vol. 1, No. 1, Spring 1980, page 5.

transplanting

Step By Step

Cloning

Cloning is simple and easy. A consistently 100 percent survival rate may be achieved by understanding what happens to a plant during cloning and following the simple step-by-step instructions given below.

The "mother plant" should be at least two months old and can be grown from seed or propagated by cloning from another mother plant. During cloning, the plant's entire chemistry changes. The stem that grew the leaves must now grow roots in order to survive. Chemical sprays should be avoided during cloning and attention paid to providing plants with the best possible environment.

Research has proven that plants tend to root better when the stems have a high concentration of carbohydrate and low nitrogen. By leaching the soil with copious quanitities of water, all nutrients, including nitrogen, are washed out of the soil. The mother plant's growth slows as the nitrogen is used up, and carbohydrates have a chance to accumulate. Carbohydrate content is usually higher in older, more mature branches. A rigid branch that will fold at a sharp angle rather than bend is a sign of high carbohydrate content and a good candidate for cloning.

There are several products available designed to stimulate root growth. These root hormones come in powder or liquid form. Professional horticulturists prefer the liquid type because of penetration and reliability. The powder types are avoided because they adhere to the stem inconsistently, reducing the survival rate.

procedure

Most of these products are not recommended for use on food crops.
1. Leach the soil surrounding plants to be cloned. Apply one gallon of water per five gallons of soil every morning for seven days before taking cuttings.
2. With a sharp knife, take cuttings from several firm, healthy branches, 1/8 to 1/4 inch in diameter, and about eight inches long. Trim off two or three sets of leaves from the lower end of the cutting. There should be at least two sets of leaves above the soil line and one or two sets of trimmed nodes below. When cutting, make the slice half way between two sets of nodes. Cutting too close to one of the nodes could cause mutations. Immdiately place the cut end in fresh tepid water. This helps prevent an air bubble from lodging in the tiny hole in the center of the stem, blocking the transpiration stream and killing the clone. Leave the cuttings in the water overnight in

subdued light or no light.

3. Fill small containers or a flat with coarse, washed sand, fine vermiculite, soilless mix or, if nothing else is available, sterilized potting soil. Saturate with tepid water. Use a pencil or chop stick to make a hole in the rooting medium that is a little larger than the branch. The hole should be at least 1/2 inch from the bottom of the container to allow for root growth.

4. Lightly water with a mild solution of vitamin B1 or Ortho Upstart until the surface is evenly moist. Continue watering as needed but do not overwater.

5. Clones root best under 18 hours of fluorescent light. If no fluorescent light is available, set the traumatized cuttings three to four feet below a halide lamp with a cloth or screen shade above the plants. The shade will prevent shock to the tender clones.

6. Keep the temperature near 80 degrees. A soil heating cable may be placed under the clone to maintain the proper temperature.

7 Keep the humidity near 80 percent. Place a humidity tent over the rooting clones. The tent may be made out of baggies or plastic. this helps to retain moisture since there are no roots to supply the leaves with water.

8. Some cuttings may wilt for a few days; they should bounce back and look normal by the end of the first week. Plants that are still wilted after one week will probably not make it.

9. In two to four weeks, the cuttings should be rooted. The leaf tips will turn yellow and roots may be seen growing out of the drain holes. By this time, a successful clone should begin to show signs of vertical growth.

Excerpted from "Cloning and the Mother Plant," Vol. 3, No. 4, page 16.

Air Layering for Clones

by Professor T. H. Custer

When I start my clones, I use an air layering technique. I suspect that like myself, many growers don't clone because of a high failure rate. Therefore, I have found that keeping the prospective clone attached to the mother plant during root development increases success to almost 100 percent. I adapted my method from the book *"Marijuana Botany"* by Robert Connell Clarke.

1. Choose a branch at least 18 inches in diameter that has not turned hard and woody. Support the branch above and below the area to be rooted using support sticks and tape. Masking tape works well. Be sure that you have etiolated the actual area to be rooted, by covering about a two-inch portion of stem with a dark tape, like electrical tape for about two weeks. This prepares the biochemistry in the stem for adventitious root initiation.

2. With the knife or razor, slit the branch lengthwise for one to two inches completely through the stalk, being careful to keep it as intact and attached to the mother plant as possible.

3. With the dry brush, paint the hormone over all of the cut and etiolated surfaces, inside and out.

4. With forceps, stuff a mixture of fine peat moss and hormone into the cut.

5. Using flap and tape, wrap a jiffy mix (or Terra Lite's "Redi Earth") filled baggie around the air layer, making sure the cut is completly surrounded by moss or jiffy mix.

6. Using an eye dropper, keep the whole assembly wet. In five to 14 days, enough roots will have formed to cut the stem below the newly formed roots. Then plant!

Generally, I have found that all of this can be done under halides with no hardening off period required, due to minimal shock.

First printed in Vol. 5, No.1, page 3.

Materials for air layering (left to right): plastic bag corner cut into square with one flap removed; X-acto knife or clean razor blade; clean, dry paint brush; eyedropper; hemostats or forceps; straight, thin sticks; jiffy mix for bag envelopes; tape; and rooting hormones.

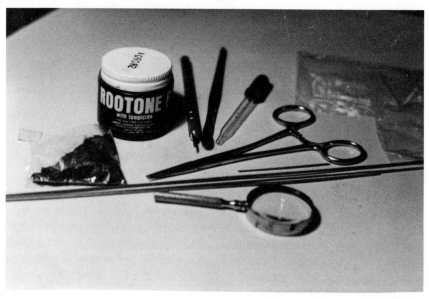

The selected branchs are carefully slit with an X-acto knife and supported by thin sticks and tape (left). The plant hormone is painted onto the branch with a dry brush (lower left). Baggie with Jiffy Mix wrapped around air layer (lower right).

Pruning

by Tom Alexander

Pruning is important in the development of well formed numerous buds in the fall. The amount of pruning and the way it is done affect the later formation of buds. The objective in pruning is to force the plant into growing four to 12 main stalks and to grow bushier.

There are three kinds of branches. The leader is the main branch, a continuation of the stem or trunk of the plant. Side branches growing from the leader are called primary branches and secondary branches grow from the primaries.

The normal growth pattern for marijuana is one main leader branch with many primary and secondary branches, all growing tall. The purpose of pruning is to change some of the primary branches into main leader branches. The reason for wanting a lot of main branches is that the biggest and best buds form on them.

The first prune should be done after the emergence of the third or fourth set of true leaves. This would be some time around the fourth to the sixth week. The incorrect way to prune is to just pinch the emerging new growth above the nodes of the uppermost large leaves. A node is the place where a leaf branch meets the stem.

method

The correct way to prune is to gently grasp the main stem just below the nodes of the uppermost leaves. With the finger of your other hand push the emerging new growth sideways and downward. It will break at just the right spot with no injury to the new growth which will become two new main branches. Within a few days the two new main branches will be growing out and up. When these two new branches have two or three sets of leaves, it is time to prune them. Continue this pruning process on all subsequent main branches once they have two or three sets of leaves up until the end of July.

Stop all pruning after the end of July as the plant enters the flowering stage. Any pruning done after this date will reduce bud size.

On indoor plants, pruning can continue until a few weeks before the light cycle is reduced to eight to 10 hours to promote flowering. When the first pruning is done the plant is only ankle to knee high. As the plant grows, so does the spot that the pruning was done. It could be well over a person's head by the fall. Prune only main branches because overpruning secondary branches can cause the plant to stunt or slow its growth rate considerably.

Some people think that by picking the big fan leaves from the plant

Grasp the main stem just under the uppermost leaves (top). Push the emerging growth sideways and downward (below, left). It should break off with no damage to the two new main branches.

The prune is completed when the little budlet is severed from the plant (below).

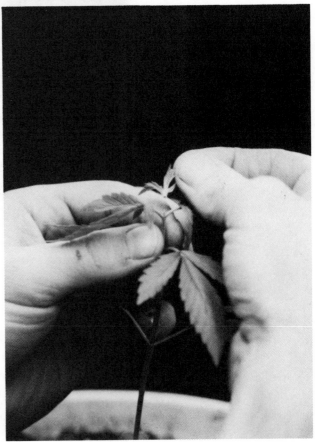

The photo at right shows the wrong way to prune. Simply pinching the new growth could injure the new branches that are formed just above the nodes of the top leaves. This plant (below) is too small for pruning. It should be left for a few more weeks to gain strength and size.

that they are helping the plant in its development. That is not true. Every leaf is a solar collector, gathering the sun's rays for use in the photosynthesis process. Every leaf that is picked off is one less unit of energy that the plant has available for growth. Even when the big leaves turn yellow, the plant is extracting energy from them. The plant will drop or discard yellow or brown leaves when the time is right to be rid of them.

A friend did an experiment a few years ago on two separate patches. On one patch he picked off the big leaves during the growing season. On the other patch all the leaves were left on. The patch that had its leaves left on flowered two to three weeks earlier than the other patch.

In the fall, all the big unwanted leaves may be picked off the plant two to five days before expected harvest date.

Another technique used by some growers is to tie the numerous main branches down horizontally during August and September. This forces all the secondary branches on that main branch to grow up to the light making them longer. Experiment until finding the right distance to tie the branches down so that they do not break in the bending process.

Pruning in moderation will help the plant produce the optimum number of flowering tops. When pruning is done incorrectly or too drastically, harm is done to the plant reducing the number of large buds produced. Know the correct way to prune before attempting to do it. If unsure, wait and obtain more information.

First printed in Vol. 1, No. 2, page 27.

chapter

3

nutrients

"The faces of the past are like the leaves that settle to the ground...They make the earth rich and thick, so that the new fruit will come forth every summer."
—Chief Dan George

Basic Nutrients

by Tom Alexander

Foliage growth is dependent upon nitrogen. A plant deficient in nitrogen will have yellow leaves and will grow slowly. Excessive amounts of nitrogen can damage a plant's root system, stunt or eventually kill it.

Marijuana needs large amounts of nitrogen in the early stages of growth. Stop using nitrogen fertilizers outdoors by the end of July because the plant is slowing down in growth and putting energy into bud production. If your plants have a dark green color and grow rapidly in the summer months, you probably have added the proper amount of nitrogen. Nitrogen deficiencies can be corrected by adding blood meal, manure (especially poultry, rabbit, sheep or horse), compost, and/or fish waste.

Phosphorous

Phosphorous is important to plants for growth and proper bud production. A plant deficient in phosphorous will take on a purplish appearance on its leaves (edges, veins or undersides).

A good source of phosphorous is rock phosphate. Rock phosphate has 28 percent to 30 percent phosphorous content. However, only a small percentage of that total is available to the plants the first year. Rock phosphate is a slow-release nutrient, taking three to four years to be totally absorbed. It is best to apply rock phosphate with manure in the fall, mixing it with the top 12 inches of soil, especially if you plan on using lime in the spring.

Both rock phosphate and lime contain calcium. Plants take up calcium more easily from lime than from rock phosphate. The phosphate can only be absorbed after its calcium is absorbed. Therefore, applying lime and rock phosphate at the same time causes the rock phosphate to be "locked up" until the calcium in the lime and in the rock phosphate has been absorbed. Legumes, such as alfalfa, sweet clover, etc., are aggressive calcium feeders that use rock phosphate well in its raw, insoluble form. For this reason, planting a cover crop in the fall will help your plants absorb phosphorous more easily.

Another good source of phosphate is bone meal. There are several types of bone meal, such as raw, steamed and charred. The best type is steamed bone meal because it has been heated at high temperatures to remove the fats. Fatty materials found in raw bone meal cause a delay in its decomposition. Bone meal is a quick-release source of phosphorous. You may want to apply rock phosphate in the fall and bone meal in the spring. This combination will give your plants plenty of phosphorous during the growing season and give the rock phosphate time to break down for the next season.

potassium

Potassium helps in the formation of plant sugars, protects the plant from the cold, and generally improves plant growth. Plants deficient in potassium produce low yields of buds. The leaves may have a burned, yellow appearance around the edges if there is a potassium deficiency. These plants are stunted, have poor root systems and weak stalks. Sources of potassium that are available include: wood ash, seaweed, hay, leaves, manures and compost.

First printed in Vol. 1, No. 1, Spring 1980, page 10.

Organic, or Chemical?

by Tom Alexander
There seems to be no such thing as a middle-of-the-road position when it comes to discussing the benefits and costs of organic vs chemical cultivation.

Blinded by the desire for short-term profits, large-scale corporate farmers long ago opted for the speed and convenience of chemical fertilizers and pesticides. But the price, in the long run, has been high.

In any agricultural venture, be it raising vegetables, fruit or marijuana, the only sane and sensible way to accomplish your goals is through organic methods. With organic practices, the soil is vibrant and full of earthworms and other organisms that keep adding, not draining, the life to the soil. It becomes a recycling network in your soil.

Chemical agriculture concerns itself with present yields at the expense of future consequences. When the future becomes the present, the answer is to dump more chemicals. These chemicals render the soil lifeless; earthworms are either killed or driven away and other beneficial organisms suffer the same plight.

Growing organically is hard work, however. Much of the first year or so is spent hauling animal manure, compost, seaweed and other soil additives to the growing site. But the quality of your crop, especially taste, will be much superior if organic methods are used. All the hard work in the beginning will be well worth it. Your crop will have a much sweeter taste and aroma than one grown using some quick-fix chemical.

getting started

During the first year, large amounts of manure and compost are applied to the growing area. This is an invitation to earthworms to digest this material into nitrogen-rich humus. They also will make this area their home. Maintenance after the first year or two is cut down considerably. Using cover crops (rye, oats, clover, vetch) after the growing season and then tilling them in in the spring is a positive soil-building technique.

If you have the space, alternate growing areas each year by leaving one or more plots fallow. Apply manures and compost to these areas so nutrient levels for the next year will be high.

Unlike organic fertilizers, chemicals will actually drive many beneficial organisms away from your plot. Pesticides and insecticides kill both the target pests and beneficial bees, birds and ladybugs.

Proper soil management creates a soil with good humus content and a good texture, easily penetrated by roots and rainfall. It supplies sufficient drainage so that excess water gradually seeps away to the water table. If a soil doesn't have a good structure and texture, too much rainfall is lost by runoff which is also the cause of soil erosion. Humus improves the moisture holding capacity of the soil which provides a constant reservoir of moisture for the plant.

In organic agriculture, the soil is full of life, Mother Nature's balance is maintained. People should learn to work with nature rather than try to control or conquer it. Once the cooperative bond is made between nature and human beings, wonders spring forth from the soil. Try it!

First printed in Vol. 1, No. 1, Spring 1980, page 11.

Here We Go Again!
Another Organic Explanation

by Simeon Murren

Whether you are an outdoor, seasoned grower or a newly converted indoor grower, organics makes your business more profitable and your product more enjoyable (tastier and more potent in all respects) for your customers.

Rumors abound about organics. Some say there is no difference between natural plant foods (natural fertilizers) and their chemical counterparts. I say bullshit! And, by the way, bullshit when properly composted is one hell of a natural plant food! Better than any bag of petrochemically devised NPK you can buy. It is more available, and a very good microbial stimulator besides. However, bullshit is not the top of the line.

To get to the top of the line in organics you will either have to work your way through a few processes (like I did when I first started) or take someone's word for it (like mine) and start out at the top. Sort of like the old Chinese proverb, "old way/new way!"

I don't care how you are growing. The method may vary. You may grow indoors, under lights, in pots or hydroponically, outdoors in trees, in greenhouses or in the ground. It doesn't matter, if you follow the simple directions that I'm going to lay out for you, you will profit greatly. You will be able to grow the very best, healthiest plants you have ever grown in your life.

This stuff is phenomenal! Excreted from the lowly earthworm, it turns out that it is the most highly water-soluble plant food possible to obtain on this planet. It is what we earthlings refer to as "humus." The protoplasmic stuff of the earth, containing all the right biological "timeclocks" and chains necessary to ensure life's uninterrupted genetic progression and evolution. With chemical cultivation, the "timeclocks" often turn out to be "timebombs."

Earthworm casts are known to be at least five times richer in available nitrogen, seven times richer in available phosphorus, 11 times richer in available potassium, 1.5 times richer in exchangeable calcium and three times richer in available magnesium than any other growing medium (natural or chemically concocted). In addition, they contain all the trace elements and live enzymes a plant could ever hope for. Terra firma, period!

earthworm casts

bat guano

Another natural phenomenon! Think of this: there are millions and millions of bats; there always have been. Year after year, in another time-honored tradition, they swoop down nightly in nearly every corner of the earth, each bat devouring thousands of insects. A researcher in Texas recently discovered that the bats that fly into southern Texas skies each evening from Mexico, eat over 10,000 lbs. of insects each year. That is a lot of bugs! Bats are an important cog in Mother Nature's machine. They are not carriers of rabies or dreaded lung diseases as previously thought.

It is sufficient to say that bats and bat guano are top of the line. Especially dry cave bat guano which has had thousands of years to fossilize, making the nutrients "available" for growing plants.

It isn't that the stuff dissolves into the "mouths" of plants. It doesn't mysteriously slip through the cracks in the plant's roots. It is transferred and transmuted (passed on) through a living chain of micro organisms and living enzymes, not by some magical process as some petrochemical companies would like to have you believe.

When you use bat guano— a natural microbial stimulator— you are enhancing the transfer and transmuting process. Elements and nutrients are easily and quickly "taken in" by plants. Guano stimulates! It activates! It really promotes growth and heartiness. And of course, being high in phosphorus and magnesium, it enhances the reproductive process in all plants.

When guano is used in conjunction with earthworm casts, look out! This is the wonder stuff of the 1980s! It is the stuff that will turn out to be a gift in helping us restore soil fertility everywhere on this planet. This brings me to the ultimate plant food:

super tea mix

This might seem like something from a science fiction story, but the truth is that it has been used for centuries. However, due to the efforts of certain money-hungry warlords to spread chemical doom no matter what the ultimate ecological costs (with only the almighty dollar in mind), this organic truth has been nearly blotted out of human memory systems by constant promotion and teaching of the chemical theory. Our schools are full of minds teaching other minds these untruths: that chemicals are where it is at.

To make "Super Tea Mix", simply mix bat guano (the dry cave kind) with some dry, sifted earthworm casts (minus the worms). The ratio is something like five to 10 lbs. of bat guano for every five cubic feet of earthworm casts. The more guano you use, the more of a blooming agent you come up with.

Once mixed, you simply dissolve one tablespoon of this Super Tea Mix in one gallon of water and feed it to the plants you love once a week. You can't over do it. It's organic! Chemicals are the only thing that ever burn or stunt a plant's growth.

When using this tea, you will have to filter it well (through in-line filters) if you plan to run it through a drip system, foliar feed system or in a hydroponic system. Take the residues that are left from this process and spread them around the base of your favorite plants.

Fill up your holes or growing containers with pure earthworm casts mixed with some perlite to improve aeration. About one cubic foot of perlite to every five cubic feet of earthworm casts. When you plant using the hole method, put about 10 pounds of bat guano in each hole. Fruit trees especially dig this. They will bear incredibly sweet fruit!

Sprinkle a handful of earthworm casts, a teaspoon of guano or a handful of Super Tea Mix on each of your house plants and water immediately.

Once you have given these methods a try, I guarantee that your days of using Miracle-Gro, Bloom or any other chemical product will be over. And thank God. Chemical products are at the root of our soil problems (and cancer problems) in this country and the world. It is the indiscriminate use of chemicals throughout our growing systems that is causing the soil to become lifeless and "locked up." The soil microbes and earthworms are perishing in a sea of chemicals. That, my friends, is a crime.

Here we go again, organically! Happy Growing!

First printed in Vol. 3, No. 4, page 30.

more hints

Foliar Feeding

The mechanism by which foliar nutrients are absorbed remains something of a mystery.

Foliar feeding was discovered in 1844 and introduced into modern agriculture some 20 years ago, when it was held by some people as a revolutionary method of fertilization. It was thought that foliar feeding would replace all established methods of plant nutrition. More realistic people made less spectacular claims for this new technique and have been rewarded by seeing foliar feeding become an established part of crop cultivation, being complementary with, rather than replacing established base fertilization, pest and disease control techniques.

Foliar feeding is a method by which plant nutrients are supplied to the plant via the leaves, rather than the roots.

It was originally observed as early as the 1880s that plant metabolites could be leached from the leaves by rain. So it was proposed that if plant substance could move out of the leaf, could they not equally move in the reverse direction, that is, into the leaf.

Studies with fluorescent materials, which act as dyes, and radioactive tracers enabled research workers to follow the passage of plant nutrients through the leaves and into the plant system, and also to determine the rate at which they travel. In this way the absorption of nutrients by the leaves has been established. These techniques, not only showed that plants can absorb nutrients through their leaves, but also gave an indication of the rate at which nutrients are absorbed therein.

There appears to be no conclusive evidence as to the manner in which nutrients enter the leaf. Entry is thought to be possible by two routes. One is through the imperforated cuticle, or alternatively, through breaks in the cuticle, such as the stomata and the hydrathodes.

The upper and lower surfaces of leaves are covered initially by single layers of flattened epidermal cells. The main purpose of these cells is protection. The epidermis (this layer of epidermal cells) is so thin that transpiration can take place through it, but before the leaf is very old, a layer of a substance called cutin forms over the surface of the leaf and prevents further transpiration. This continuous covering of cutin, which is a resistant fatty material, renders the outer walls of the leaves more or less water and gas tight. Very often the cuticle is coated with wax which increases this water and gas resistance. This wax is present to a high degree in evergreens and

cross sectional view of epidermal layer

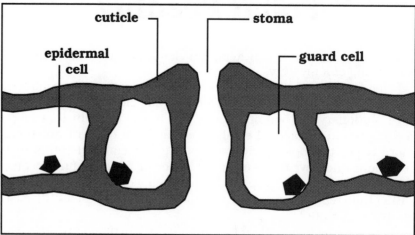

gives these leaves their characteristic shiny appearance.

It is thought that plant nutrients sprayed on to the leaf might be absorbed to some extent through this triple protective layer— first the wax, then the cuticle and then the epidermal cells. This could occur by the process of diffusion as this protective layer exhibits a degree of permeability. Permeable membranes are those which allow certain materials to pass through them. This occurs when such materials are present in greater concentration on one side than the other; they pass through to the side in which they are present in less concentration. It is possible that this is one way in which plant nutrients could be absorbed by the leaf.

However, it is more likely that nutrients are absorbed through natural breaks in the leaf. The most common of these are the stomata, which are slit-like openings between two guard cells. The guard cells enable the stomata to be opened and closed. The purpose of the stomata is gaseous interchange; carbon dioxide finds its way into the leaf through the stomata, but there is one obstacle in the path of this argument. The guard cells which surround the stomata are so shaped as to make the entry of water impossible unless it is forced under pressure. The guard cells give the stomata such a shape that drops of water are unable to pass through.

If it were the case that plant nutrients were being absorbed by the stomata, then anything which reduced the size of the water droplets should increase the absorption of the foliar nutrients. However, research workers are still debating whether or not this is the case. One piece of supporting evidence comes from the use of ultra low volume sprayers which use very fine droplets and seem to be the most effective method of applying foliar feeds.

There are other openings in the leaf surface, for example, the hydrathodes which are water secreting glands, which are present on the edges and tips of the leaves. However, these are not present nearly as frequently as stomata and not in sufficient numbers to be the route for the considerable absorption of foliar sprays that takes place.

So the mechanism by which foliar nutrients are absorbed remains something of a mystery. What is known, however, is that they are absorbed and that they are absorbed quickly.

Despite the paucity of fundamental understanding, a considerable amount is known about the absorption of various nutrients. For instance, urea nitrogen is absorbed, transported and metabolized as quickly as any plant nutrient. Uptake of urea is most rapid at night or in the early morning. This could be due to the higher relative humidity of the air at this time. The elements sulphur, chlorine and

pathways

iodine are known to be very rapidly absorbed. Whereas the rate of absorption of magnesium varies during the day, it is better absorbed at night. Magnesium, calcium, strontium and beryllium have a rapid initial absorption, but this is followed by the failure of the plant to absorb anymore. Iron, manganese, zinc, copper, molybdenum and cobalt act the same way. This is thought to be because these elements have a limited mobility within the plant and become accumulated in the leaf, thus precluding further absorption. Cobalt is only absorbed under the action of light and in the presence of sugars.

In more general terms, absorption rates are greater for younger leaves than older leaves and usually absorption is greater on the underside of the leaf than on the exposed surface.

Finally, it should be mentioned that urea, potassium, phosphorus, sulphur and iron have all been shown to be absorbed through the bark of deciduous fruit trees, and zinc has also been shown to be absorbed through the bark of citrus trees. It would appear that the leaf is not the only area which is capable of absorbing foliar nutrients.

recommended applications

Only in specific instances are foliar applications of NPK mixtures to be recommended. H.S. Wittwer of the Department of Horticulture at Michigan State University has said categorically, "Foliar application of most commercially available NPK mixtures is an expensive and unnecessary operation for most crops." NPK can be much more cheaply applied as a base dressing and when given in a foliar feed it may well diminish the absorption of the more important constituents of the foliar feed. All proprietary foliar feeds sold in this country usually contain large proportions of NPK.

It must be emphasized that in certain situations foliar applications of NPK are of extreme benefit. The obvious example of this is in hydroponically grown crops, the most common of which is tomatoes. Another example is the use of high nitrogen foliar sprays on apples post-harvest to build up nitrogen reserves to ensure good bud development for next spring to reduce scab. However, these are isolated cases.

trace elements

Trace elements are the major constituents of most foliar feeds and are the plant nutrients most economical to administer by foliar feeding. Trace elements are acquired by the plant more widely than most people realize. Magnesium, calcium, sulphur, iron, boron, manganese, molybdenum, zinc and copper all have known roles within the plant, but many more trace elements can be found in plants and although deficiencies cannot be seen in gross terms in the absence of these elements, it would appear that they are necessary for the health, vigor and maximum production of any plant. So any really effective foliar feed must attempt to supply as many trace elements as possible.

The trace elements in the foliar feed must be present in the right proportions, since an excess of one trace element can inhibit the absorption of the other trace elements.

One of the advantages of making a foliar feed with a soluble solution of seaweed is that not only does one obtain a complete range of trace elements— over 50— but these trace elements are present in the proportions in which they are found in the plants and thus this is the ideal proportion for absorption.

The role of trace elements within the plant is varied and complex. In general terms they are primarily involved as constituents of complex chemicals known as enzymes. Enzymes are catalysts which speed up the vast number of different chemical reactions involved in plant growth and development, including respiration, transpiration, starch synthesis, etc. They are also involved in the hormones which control the various processes which go on within the plant and they have individual roles of their own, very often of fundamental importance to the plant.

Most foliar feeds contain small but significant amounts of growth hormones. Dried and liquid seaweed contains auxins and gibberellins in addition to a wide range of growth hormones which are naturally preserved in the extraction process. Work at Aberdeen University has showed that these growth promoting substances are effective at even a 1:100,000 dilution. One of these compounds, for example, stimulates and maintains growth of both the stem and the root. The hormone gibberellin has been shown to be important in stimulating the synthesis of certain enzymes. But above all, the effect of the auxins and gibberellins is to increase the growth of the plant as long as they are not administered in excessive amounts.

growth hormones

When seaweed is used as a foliar feed, a wide range of organic compounds variously classified as sugars, starches, mannuronic and other organic acids are introduced. The sugars and organic acids are especially important in that they have what is known as a chelating property together with the trace elements. In their commonly occurring form, trace elements are poorly absorbed by the plant, but the sugars and organic acids in the liquid extract of seaweed associate themselves with the trace elements and so make them proportionately more absorbable by the plant.

seaweeds

These organic substances also have the property of wetting agents, that is they reduce the droplet size of the carrying solution. It will be remembered from the discussion on foliar feeding that one of the factors against the theory that foliar feeds are absorbed through the stomata is that the guard cells of the stomata are so arranged that normal droplets are unable to enter via this route. This ability of the organic substances in seaweed to reduce droplet size could be a considerable aid to absorption.

Foliar feeds have a wide and diverse range of activities which are listed below.

benefits

• **Increases in yield.** The main reason for any treatment given to a crop is, of course, to increase the yield. Foliar feeds do increase yields. It is difficult to generalize quoting figures, but in almost all crops, economic increases in yields are seen. That is to say, the use of a foliar feed is profitable.

The main effect on yield is thought to be due to the effect of the trace elements. Just as plants are unable to absorb from the soil, under normal conditions, sufficient NPK to achieve maximum yields, likewise they are unable to absorb sufficient amounts of the trace elements. By supplying trace elements via the leaves, one increases the crop carrying ability of the plant, whatever it may be.

• **Improved quality.** Foliar feeds have been observed to increase the quality of a wide range of crops on which they are used.

• **Increased resistance to pests and disease.** One of the surprising things to come out of the use of foliar feeds containing trace metals was the observation that they reduced the incidence of pest and disease infestations. Experiments using seaweed have demonstrated this effect upon such diverse conditions as powdery mildew in turnips, botrytis in strawberries, damping-off in seedlings and black bean aphids on broad beans.

Subsequent work done by M.D. Austin has also shown significant effects upon the fruit tree red spider mite and upon glasshouse red spider mite. This, and a vast amount of other work, seems to suggest a general inhibitory effect of seaweed against pests and disease. At the moment the mechanism is not understood, perhaps in general terms the foliar feed not only increases the health and vigor of the plant, but increases its ability to resist by stimulating its natural defenses against pest attack and disease infection.

• **Fertilizer utilization.** Studies done in several universities have shown that the use of foliar applications of trace elements increases the amount of NPK the plant takes up from its root medium. In other words, foliar feeds have been shown to increase the amounts of NPK that the plants absorb through their roots and increases the efficiency with which they utilize the fertilizers offered to them in the soil.

• **Seaweed and other sprays.** Seaweed can be mixed with almost all other sprays, such as liquid fish emulsion or Superthrive. This cuts down on the time it takes to apply all of the various nutrients and additives to the plant.

First printed in Vol. 4, No. 3, page 21.

Debunking the Numbers Racket

By Simeon Murren

A fellow named Justus Liebig started it all. Back in the 1800s he burned some sunflower plants, examined their ashes with ancient laboratory equipment and determined that nitrogen (N), phosphorus (P) and potassium (K) were always present— therefore, obviously, always the three key parts of growing plants.

The NPK theory was born. The industrial giants of the time, who chummed around with Justus at the local Explorer's Club, saw their chance to make big bucks. They exploited Justus' theory. Justus died poor, while the chemical fertilizer industry ended up, as Paul Harvey would say, "Now you know the rest of the story."

Or do you? Do you know what those numbers mean, what they stand for on a fertilizer bag or bottle? Do you believe them?

The NPK theory is bunk! At best it is only a small part of the big picture. This is a basic truth that must be grasped in order to realize freedom from the petro-chemical treadmill. Don't blame poor old Justus, he used turn of the century lab equipment, and besides, it was the industrial giants of the time who really exploited and perpetuated the myth. They too believed in what they were doing.

There is an old story I gleaned from an old book on organic farming that really points out the facts of farming with chemicals. It seems that around 1910, a young, eager salesman for a newly emerging chemical fertilizer company was passing through the Ohio Valley selling the latest chemical forms of NPK. His sales pitch was direct. He would chide the farmers for not keeping pace with the changing times. "Now you don't have to haul tons of manure to your fields every year," he said.

He told one wise old farmer who had farmed his place for over 60 years using natural fertilizers, "Now you can carry one of these bags out to your field under each arm and spread it over the same area … that's all there is to it." The old farmer looked the young man in the eyes and replied, "In that case, sonny, you'll be seeing the harvest come in your waistcoat pocket."

How prophetic those wise old farmer's words have turned out to be. Today, it is common knowledge in agricultural circles that something is wrong with the chemical system for growing plants. The soil is eroding at an alarming rate, the elements and nutrients are "locked-up" in the soil, or worse, totally gone. The fields are dangerously poisoned from all the toxic chemicals (pesticides, fungicides, soil sterilizers, slimeicides, etc.) that are being used by the ton, year after year in an effort to kill all unwanted life forms.

It is becoming difficult to draw a line between what life forms we want to kill and those we want to keep. A major agricultural disaster faces the world. The old farmer was right! The harvest *is* coming in the waistcoat pocket of the petro-chemical companies. The nutritive value of wheat, for example, is so poor these days that it now takes several bushels of wheat to equal the protein found in one bushel 50 years ago! All of our food supply is in a similar state.

The plants are losing their ability to take up elements, minerals and nutrients from dead soil. They can't transfer anything of life-giving value in the amounts necessary to properly support the food chain. In fact, the food chain is broken.

The land is mineral deficient. The plants are deficient. The animals are mineral deficient. We are mineral deficient! 12-12-12 is not working.

So many people ask me for the numbers on this or that organic fertilizer. "What is the NPK readout for bat guano?" they will ask. Someone will stop me on the street in Arcata and plead, "What are the numbers?" or "Give me a readout.", etc., etc.

I hope I haven't offended any of you when I reply with such stuff as, "What numbers do you want?" or "50-50-50." It is just that I don't believe in the NPK theory at all and I sometimes become a bit cynical about it. I apologize.

'12-12-12- is not working'

If you ever have the experience of trying to get organic materials tested by a professional lab, you will see what I mean. Labs are set up to serve the chemical industry and the chemical using community.

When a lab tests for phosphorus in an organic fertilizer, for example, the beneficial microbes are killed in the process. The material is diluted in a chemical solution and filtered through such things as a 400 micron filtering system which blocks passage of beneficial enzymes. Therefore, it is not possible, using these techniques, to ever come up with a "number" for organic fertilizers. Also, dead microbes and lost or blocked enzymes translate to low numbers when compared to chemical charts. It will always come out looking like the chemicals have it over organics in the numbers game when testing is done this way.

The fact is, that there can never be a number or numbers for organics. Numbers belong with the petro-chemical industry. It is their identity coding system. It has no relation to the real world of motion and to the billions upon billions of beneficial life forms performing ceaseless work transforming and transmuting elements and nutrients to and through our food chain.

So, the next time you are wondering about what numbers to apply to organics, give up! Remember this article and try having a little faith in the natural world. Stop looking for a mathematical solution to life. These numbers exist only to stimulate your mind to buy and to believe in them.

As that wise old farmer said, "The proof is in the pudding." Try some pudding using organics next time. You will see and taste the difference!

First printed in Vol. 4, No. 2, page 38.

Soil Building the Northern California Way

Finished in four to six weeks.
Mix:
1 cubic yard of redwood sawdust.
1/4 cubic yard rice hulls or cocoa bean hulls.
1/4 cubic yard. ground peat moss (Canadian milled spagnum moss is best).
1/4 cubic yard easily composted lawn clippings and non-poisonous leaves, weeds, coffee grounds, washed beach seaweed, wood ash, eggshells, kitchen scraps, green vegetation, etc. Fresh cut or saved weeds, plants, etc. are important to add life to a pile. Important: Don't include Eucalyptus leaves or pine needles.

step 1

The raw uncomposted sawdust will suck nitrogen from the soil. To break down the sawdust, etc. into rich fertile humus, you'll need to compost the above ingredients with the ones below for approximately three months depending on the materials and your particular situation (temperature, humidity, aeration, pH, carbon-nitrogen ratio, etc.) With more sawdust, use more nitrogen.

Now add 1 cubic yard of fresh, hot manures (fresh cow can take too long). Best fresh mixture is 1/4 cubic yard each of horse, chicken, rabbit and goat manure plus 10 pounds of fishmeal and five pounds of bat guano.

If no fresh manures are available, then add instead:

50 lbs. bagged steer manure
50 lbs. fishmeal
20 lbs. hoof and horn meal
20 lbs. bloodmeal
50 lbs. bagged chicken shit
5 to10 lbs. bat guano

If you are a vegetarian and don't like using bloodmeal and hoof and horn meal, try 50 pounds each of fishmeal, steer manure, and chicken manure. Also, 20 pounds each of cottonseed meal, linseed meal, soybean meal and bat guano. In all of these formulas add more nitrogen if you think it is needed. No matter which nitrogen combination you choose to add to the sawdust mixture, you need also to add 10 pounds sodbuster (humates which breaks up heavy soils and makes nutrients available) and five to 10 pounds of any good biodynamic compost starter.

Mix all the above sawdusts, nitrogens, sodbusters, etc. very well and turn the pile with a pitchfork once or twice a week for about one month. Keep the pile covered with a sheet of plastic which will prevent any rain from leaching away the valuable nutrients. Keep the pile moist but not soggy. The pile should start heating up in a few days and be too hot to stick your arm in comfortably. A garden thermometer can give you accurate temperature readings.

If it is not getting hot, and as long as it is not too soggy or too dry, which will delay composting, then the pile probably needs more nitrogen. If it smells like ammonia, then it has too much nitrogen. Add a little, one or two cubic feet, of peat moss and turn very well. Repeat if necessary. Turn the outside of the pile into the inside. All sawdust should be turning black, with any lumps of sawdust broken up.

step 2

Finished in approximately two to four weeks.
Next add to the pile:
20 lbs. of greensand (trace elements & potassium if unavailable, use granite dust).
20 lbs. rock phosphate (phosphorus).

20 lbs. bonemeal (phosphorus) 20 lbs. powdered and unsalted kelp meal (potassium and trace elements).

10 lbs. ground oyster shells (lime), which raises the pH slowly.

1 lb. trace elements (micro-nutrients) such as agricultural frit, chelated minerals, azomite, or TMI.

Mix all of the above very well, turning once a week for one month. Keep covered and moist. Make sure all the ingredients are well mixed, especially those on the bottom next to the ground. Be sure all sawdust is fully composted and well distributed.

step 3

Finished in approximately two to four weeks.

Next add:

1 to 2 cubic yards of sandy loam topsoil.

1 cubic yard of compost which is already well composted. Use either a high quality store bought compost or use your own.

2 cubic yards worm castings (worm casts have five times the nitrogen, two times the calcium, seven times the phosphorus and 11 times the potassium as the soil they're raised in).

25 lbs. plant charcoal (sweetens and purifies the soil)

25 lbs. perlite (to lighten soil and help conserve water) add more if needed.

5 to 10 cubic feet horticultural sand (coarse, sharp, clean, washed and unsalted). Un-tumbled mountain sand is best.

10 lbs. dolomite (lime to raise the pH).

10 lbs. Ringer's Spring Garden Soil Builder.

50 lbs. peat humus (black)

Mix all the ingredients well and let sit for several weeks turning occasionally. Then measure the pH. You'll want a pH of 7 to 7.5 (slightly alkaline). If pH is below 7 (neutral), add 10 lbs. dolomite lime for each point under 7. Mix well. Test again in one week. If soil is alkaline, add coffee grounds, cottonseed meal, or sulphur (sparingly). The finished mix should have a fresh, woodsy, mushroomy, earthy smell, not rotten or shit smelling. You should test the pH of your water and make any necessary adjustment if it has a pH above or below 7. Water often changes pH during the season, so test often.

Finished compost, like rich soil, has a 10 to1 carbon to nitrogen ratio. Carbon is higher in materials like sawdust (500-1) with a high cellulose content. Nitrogen is higher in materials like manures (15-1) or bloodmeal (5-1). An active compost pile should be approximately 30 to one. Less than 25-to-1, and the pile wastes nitrogen by making ammonia. More than 30-to-1 and the pile will take too long composting.

Yield: approximately four cubic yards for 25 to 100 plants.

Cost: approximately $100 to $500 depending on ingredients and how many you can scrounge up and how many you pay for.

second-year supplement

The following mix makes a good second-year soil supplement for approximately four cubic yards of soil:

20-100 lbs. fishmeal, bloodmeal, hoof and horn meal, bat guano, and rabbit, goat, chicken or steer manures. Don't use manure that is too hot or too fresh unless it has at least three months to break down before planting.

20 lbs. greensand

20 lbs. rock phosphate

20 lbs. bone meal

1 lb. trace elements

20 lbs. kelp meal

20 lbs. Ringer's Garden Soil Builder

10 lbs. sodbuster humate

10 lbs. oyster shells (if needed to raise pH)

Compost

The following are several mixes for special purposes:

special mixes

Starting Mix:

A good starting soil can be made from a mixture of one part sifted worm castings (or sifted compost), one part sand and one part sandy loam topsoil. A little dolomite lime and bonemeal can be added if needed. You really don't want a super-rich soil for new sprouts.

Fast Food:

A one-day soil mix can be made using pure worm castings, a non-acidic planting mix, or sandy loam topsoil, mixed with the Second-Year Soil Supplement given above. Do not use fresh manures!

Pre-flowering Compost Mulch:

When each plant gets over two feet tall, work into the top six inches of soil one-quarter ounce each of 1-10-0 bat guano and Ringer's Outdoor Garden Soil Restore. Mulch plants with a mixture of one part cocoa bean hulls, one part alfalfa hay, and one part living compost. Fertilize with liquid fish emulsion and liquid kelp seaweed.

Flowering and Resin Aid:

When plants begin to show sex organs, cut off nitrogen and work in two to four ounces (depending on plant size) of bonemeal black or steamed bonemeal, hard wood ash (black is best) and bat guano into the top six inches of soil. Also liquid kelp seaweed or spirulina can be used until harvest. Extra nitrogen applied after flowering begins can cause leafiness or encourage mold growth.

First printed in Vol. 5, No. 1, page 16.

Monitoring for Salts and Acids

by Jorge Cervantes

There are two ways to monitor soil nutrient content: pH and soluble salts. When the grower is aware of these two conditions, he or she will usually be able to head off any nutrient disorders. If pH and soluble salts are not monitored, a grower must wait for several weeks for slow growth and sickly plants to signal toxic conditions. An unknown amount of crop quality and quantity have already been sacrificed by the time notable physical "salt burn" symptoms appear.

Salt burn will cause leaves to yellow and remain green between the veins. Dark splotches will appear around the leaf edges. Sometimes mistaken as a fungus condition, salt burn usually shows on older leaves first and will retard overall growth.

The pH of a soil or nutrient solution refers to the acid/alkaline balance. It is measured on a scale from one to 14— one being the most acidic, 14 the most alkaline, and seven neutral. The pH scale measures the strength of the acid in the growing medium. This acidity influences both the availability and balance of the nutrients in the growing medium and nutrient solution that surround the roots.

A pH of 6.3 to 6.8 is considered ideal for most varieties of marijuana. When pH fluctuates or lowers as little as one-half point, growth could slow substantially

For example, if the pH in your garden was abnormally high, say 7.5, it would slow the nutrient up-take of phosphorous, iron, manganese, copper, zinc and boron. If you are unaware of the alkaline build up in the soil, it could take up to a month for the plant to resume normal growth after the pH has been corrected.

A low pH, below 5.4, brings about severe calcium and magnesium deficiencies. Marijuana uses more of these two nutrients than most

pH balance

solu-bridge

pH meters are expensive, some more than others. Remember to follow the directions carefully and to measure only moist soil.

other plants. Dolomite lime, a carbonate of calcium and magnesium, will add these two nutrients and assure a balanced pH. Soluble salts is a measure of all soluble mineral residues in the growing medium. It does not refer to "table salt" or "ocean salt water," but rather to everything that exists in the growing medium that will dissolve in water. These chemicals, such as sodium, magnesium and potassium, take the form of salts when they are combined with chlorine, sulfur and nitrogen to form "salts" such as sulfates, chlorides and nitrates. These salts may be added in the form of fertilizer or already be present in the soil and water. The delicate balance these salts form in the soil dictates their availability to the plants.

A "solu-bridge" or soluble salts meter measures the *total available salts* in the soil. If the salt content of the growing medium is too low, the plant will receive insufficient nourishment. If it is too high, toxic salt conditions exist and nutrient absorption is stifled.

Plants receive nutrition by absorbing salts through the membrane in the root hairs in a process called "osmosis." The nutrient salts (fertilizers) are dissolved in water. The level of dissolved salts in water determines its osmotic pressure. When osmotic pressure is low, the flow of nutrients through the membrane is rapid, but the plants do not receive adequate nutrition. The flow of nutrients is actually reversed and flows away from the roots when osmotic pressure is too high. By adding too much fertilizer or letting it build up to toxic levels, you are actually starving the plant!

The soluble salts meter measures the electrical conductivity or the amount of electricity that a solution will carry. Water with no dissolved salts, like distilled water, will not conduct electricity. The higher the salt content, the more electricity the solution will carry.

The soluble salts meter will read in milli-mohos (mmho), or in the newer term, milli-siemens (mS).

To convert the mS reading into parts per million (ppm) of the total dissolved salts, multiply the mS number by 700.

A soluble salts level of between .6 and 1.2 mS is considered "safe." Any time the level fluctuates beyond this "safety zone" nutrient deficiencies or toxic salt levels could

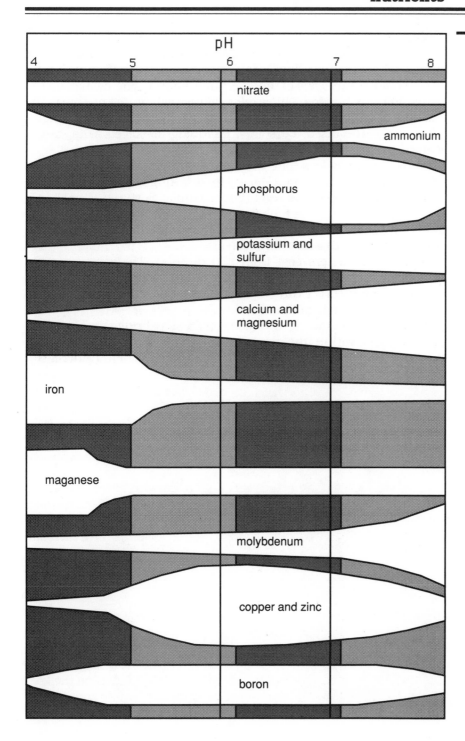

availability of nutrients is limited by pH

safe levels

result.

Tap water that is high in dissolved salts is not suitable for marijuana cultivation. Your local water bureau will be happy to send you a complete analysis of the water they supply. Somewhere on the water analysis printout "filterable residue" will be given. This is the amount of residue that the municipal water bureau is not able to filter out or the dissolved solids, including dissolved salts, in the water.

If this amount is less than 600 ppm (600 milligrams per liter), the water is safe for cultivation. Most city drinking water in the United States is well below this level. For example, Portland, Ore. has a filterable residue of 27.5 milligrams per liter. However, if your water is heavily chlorinated, you may want to let it sit for 24 hours so that the chlorine will dissipate into the air.

Soluble salt meters cost from $70 to $800. The easiest way to maintain a "safe" salt level without purchasing a meter is to flush the growing medium every three to four weeks. Use one or two gallons of fresh water for each gallon of soil.

If the cost seems worth it to you, buy a solu-bridge and keep the soluble salts within the recommended safe zone. If salts are a problem for you, the meter could easily pay for itself in increased production.

First printed in Vol. 6, No. 2, page 67.

"Under the philosophy that now seems to guide our destinies, nothing must get in the way of the man with the spray gun." —Rachel Carson

Aphids or Plant Lice

by The Bush Doctor

At least three species of aphids attack Cannabis. All are small, translucent to light green, soft bodied insects. They have a pear-shaped body, long legs and antennae, and a pair of cornicles— tube like appendages projecting from the rear of the abdomen. Aphids produce several parthenogenic generations (females reproducing without sex) each season. Winged forms also appear and fly to new plants.

Aphids suck plant sap with a long narrow stylet that penetrates into the plant's vascular system. They congregate on the undersides of leaves, causing wilting and chlorosis (yellowing). The entire plant loses vigor.

Feeding aphids exude small drops of excess sap sugar, known as honeydew, from their anus. Honeydew makes the leaves sticky, attracts ants and can support a heavy growth of black, sooty mold. Ants stroke the aphids to milk them of honeydew, and will herd them to new plants as we do Holsteins. Some species attack flowering tops as well as leaves. The tops turn yellow and wilt, and sometimes the male antheridia and female calyxes will exhibit a distorted hypertrophy.

The Bhang aphid is particularly damaging to female buds, where it is found "...sitting between flowers and seeds, sucking plant sap." Aphid populations can explode in tropical environments and warm greenhouses.

They are dangerous vectors of plant disease, spreading viruses and bacteria from one plant to another. The Bhang aphid alone has been cited as a vector for hemp mozaic virus, hemp leaf chlorosis virus, hemp streak virus, cucumber mozaic and alfalfa mozaic (the latter two attack Cannabis as well.)

The scientific name for the Bhang aphid (also known as the hemp louse) is *Phorodon cannabis*. In older literature, it is placed in at least five other genera, *Aphis cannabis*, *Myzus cannabis*, etc. Its body averages 1.5 to 2.2 millimeter long, is flat, described in different places as nearly colorless to bright green with grass-green stripes on its back. Its eyes are black, cornicles are white and up to .5 millimeter long. The head has bristles on it, serving to differentiate it from the Hop aphid.

The winged form is slightly larger, and develops a black brown head and abdomen spots. This species attacks marijuana in North America and southern Asia. It has been suggested as a possible biocontrol weapon against marijuana in the United States.

The second aphid that attacks Cannabis in the United States is the Hop aphid, *Phorodon humuli*. It is yellowish green with dark green strips on its back. Like the Bhang aphid, it is oblong, flat, with similar cornicles. It is slightly larger, 1.7 to 2.2 millimeter long, with little, if any, head bristles. The winged form is green and develops a blackish-brown head, scuttellum and legs. The cornicles lengthen. Hop aphids overwinter on trees and move to Cannabis in the summer. The insect also commonly attacks hops and sunflowers. They serve as vectors for many virus diseases. In California, the Hop aphid has also been shown to spread *Pseudoperonospora humuli*, the fungus causing downy mildew on hemp and hops.

The third aphid attacking marijuana is the Green Peach Aphid, *Myzus persicae*. This species attacks dozens of plants, and is also an effective vector of plant diseases. A native of Europe, it is now distributed all over North America. Green peach aphids have more oval, pear shaped bodies. They are also slightly larger than the above two species, and have darker green bodies. The winged form has a brownish-black body, and holds its wings vertically over its abdomen when at rest.

All three species share similar lifecycles. They overwinter on the bark of trees as shiny black eggs. With spring they hatch into aphids and migrate to nearby Cannabis. Greenhouse aphids may not lay eggs, reproducing parthenogeically all year long. Winged forms are born every couple generations, and migrate far and wide. In autumn, the winged forms give birth to true males and females, which mate and produce the overwintering eggs.

control

There are a number of mechanical and biological controls available to keep aphids in check. The ladybug is the queen of aphid predators. Green lacewings, whose larvae are known as aphid lions, also have a voracious appetite and can be purchased via mail order. There are a dozen other predators and parasites currently being investigated as biocontrol against aphids. None of these insects will attack aphids being protected by ants. Eliminate ant colonies tending aphids near young marijuana.

A dozen fungi also attack aphids. *Entomophthora exitialis* spores have been sprayed in California to control the spotted alfalfa aphid.

Aphids are repelled by growing nasturtiums, garlic, and/or onions near your crop. A spray made from these plants and used as a repellent is effective. Be sure to direct the spray at the undersides of the leaves, where the aphids are.

"Marijuana Growers Guide" by Mel Frank and Ed Rosenthal describes a number of good aphid sprays. One that works great against Illinois aphids: grind up four hot peppers with one onion and several cloves of garlic. Let the mash sit in two quarts of water for several days and filter. Add one half teaspoon of detergent as a spreader. Nicotine sprays or tobacco extract teas have been used for generations against the Bhang aphid in southern Europe. Years ago, the New York Agricultural Society suggested placing a box over infested plants and smoking out the aphids with a cup of burning tobacco.

Plants sprayed with insecticidal soap should be rinsed with water afterward. An Indian researcher reported that ganja protected with fish oil soap in this fashion "...passed the test by veteran smokers."

Aphids are attracted to the color yellow. Yellow dishpans filled with soapy water or yellow cards covered with glue such as the Nature's Control Whitefly Trap, are often recommended. Neither of these have worked for me. Migrating winged aphids will not land on seedlings growing near strips of aluminum foil. The reflection confuses them. On taller plants the foil is ineffective.

Dusting undersides of leaves with diatomaceous earth, although no easy feat, eliminates aphids if thoroughly applied. This talc-like powder, harmless to thick-skinned humans, tears microscopic abrasions in the aphid's soft body. In hot dry weather, they rapidly dehydrate and die.

Several botanical insecticides are effective on aphids. Tea made by boiling quassia wood chips and larkspur seeds kills aphid but spares ladybugs and bees. Rotenone and pyrethrum are also effective, but do not spare beneficial insects. All are harmless to warm blooded animals. If all the above fail, the highly toxic pesticide Malathion serves as the final solution for aphids. On tobacco, malathion residue was reported to be three parts per million only 10 days after application.

First printed in Vol. 5, No. 2, page 22.

Scanning electron micrograph of an aphid, slightly deformed by the microscope's intense vacuum.

Gray Mold

by The Bush Doctor

In 1846, the Rev. M. Berkeley published his convincing theory that fungi could cause disease in plants. He studied the mold that killed untold numbers of potatoes (and millions of Irish citizens) during the Great Potato Famine. With this revolutionary concept, 25 years before Pasteur's germ theory of disease, the science of plant pathology was born. Only eight years later, Dr. C. Massalongo described the organism causing Gray Mold on Cannabis plants growing near Ferraro, Italy.

Gray Mold has grown to become the most widespread and common disease of marijuana. The causal fungus, besides causing Gray Mold in full-grown plants, also causes "damping off" of Cannabis seedlings, and causes a storage mold in harvested plants as well. Gray Mold can reach epidemic proportions and ruin a crop in a week.

Found worldwide, it attacks many other cultivated and weed plants. It thrives in conditions of high humidity and cool to moderate temperatures.

On mature plants, the disease is usually found as a stem rot or decaying buds. Thick white mats of the fungus appear on middle and upper stems, and rapidly turn gray-brown with millions of spores. These are liberated in a gray cloud by the slightest disturbance. At lesion edges, the stems become yellow. The fungus organism's pectinolytic and cellulolytic enzymes quickly turn affected parts into soft shredded mush. Gray mold also attacks flowering tops, especially large mature buds which retain moisture. The tops become partially covered with the characteristic gray mycelium, rapidly turning to gray-brown slime, with any untouched distal portions rapidly wilting.

The organism causing Gray Mold on marijuana is commonly called *Botrytis cinerea*. In older Cannabis literature, it is also called *Botrytis infestans* and *Botrytis fellisiana* (which is what the good Dr. Massalongo erroneously named it). The name *Botrytis cinerea* is based on the organism's spores growing in a gray grape-like cluster, very characteristic if you have access to a microscope.

Please note that the organism occasionally "mates" and then produces completely different sporesina cup-shaped structure 1.5 to 5 millimeters in diameter. Fungal taxonomists, who have a weird sense of humor, name this rare stage *Sclerotinia fuckeliana*. Plant disease books will use one name or the other, *Sclerotinia fuckeliana*

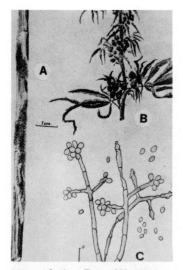

One of the first illustrations of the fungus on stems (left); on female tops (above); and the fungus itself magnified 16.5 times. From *Ann. Epiphyties* 13(2):140.

or *Botrytis cinerea.* Occasionally, they use both. It is only important to know that these are the same organism.

The organism overwinters in dead stems and can persist in the soil for two years or longer. After spring rains, the fungus produces spores which are blown or splashed onto the plant. Infection most commonly occurs via wounds or injured tissue, but young seedlings can be penetrated directly. High humidity or dew is needed for spore germination and infection. After infection, rapid production of spores on diseased plants causes an abundance of secondary infections and leads to epidemic conditions. Fungal growth is optimum at 76 degrees. Ultraviolet light is needed for spore formation, specifically light with wavelengths shorter than 345 nanometers. The fungus may also invade harvested buds, including seeds, destroying them in storage or causing seed-borne infection of seedlings the next season.

In the field, plant on well-drained sites, avoid excessive watering, and plant in wide rows, allowing for air circulation (the latter thwarting "air detection" as well). In endemic areas such as the Pacific Northwest, Alex, in an earlier issue of *Sinsemilla Tips* suggests using early-maturing varieties to avoid heavy fall rains. Closely monitor plants during periods of high humidity and cooling temperatures, like greenhouses at sundown. Do not prune during these periods, except for injured branches, which should be trimmed flush with the stem. Wounds and cuts should be treated with a fungicide, such as captan or dicloran. Alex also suggests scraping gray mold from infected areas and applying tree seal to the wounds. Avoid epidemics caused by a buildup of spores released from diseased plants by removing all infected stems and buds. This may be impossible in a large greenhouse.

Tomato researchers (Gray Mold also attacks tomatoes) prevented secondary infection by installing ultraviolet absorbing vinyl films over their light source. Since *Botrytis cinerea* needs UV light to produce spores, the fungus could not sporulate, and epidemics were prevented. There are two problems with this technique: I don't know of any source of UV-absorbing filters, and UV light may be needed to maximize THC production (although the jury is still out on this, see D.Pate, 1983, *Economic Botany* 37:396-405; and Fairburn & Leibman, 1974, *Journal of Pharmaceut. Pharmacol.* 26:413-419). In any case, harvested material should be cured and dried in dark rooms, the less UV light the better, to prevent Gray Mold storage rot.

Poorly composted organic material worked into the soil just before planting may lead to serious damping-off seedling loses. Plant calcium/phosphorus balance is important. Gray Mold of tomato is

control

reduced when leaf calcium is high and phosphorus is low. Indiscriminant use of phosphorus to promote bud production is dangerous. Liming acid soils to bring soil pH up to seven will help reduce Gray Mold in endemic areas.

The disease rapidly invades senescencing flowers. Promptly harvest buds when sinsemilla hairs begin browning and wilting, while resin glands are still white or light amber, and not brown. In greenhouses, keep the humidity low, keep light intensity high, and temperatures above 80 degrees if having Gray Mold problems. In these conditions, spores find it difficult to germinate and infect plants. Do not overcrowd, avoid overwatering and over-head irrigation.

In greenhouses, turn on heat— electric, propane or natural gas, not kerosene or gasoline— before sundown to prevent a rapid drop in temperature which condenses moisture on plants.

Some fungicides have reported efficacy against Gray Mold on other crops, notably Benomyland Bordeaux mixture. Unfortunately, the fungus develops resistance to the fungicidies quickly, rendering them useless. I emphasize that this insidious disease is controlled by exclusion, not eradication.

First printed in Vol. 5 No. 3, Summer 1985, page 27.

Damping Off

by the Bush Doctor

"Damping Off" is frequently bantered about in Cannabis literature. It is a generic term describing a disease of plant seedlings. Several species of fungi cause damping in Cannabis. Thus, we speak of a damping off fungus, not *the* damping off fungus. Reported pathogens include *Macrophomina phaseoli*, *Sclerotinia fuckelina (Botrytis cinerea)*, *Thanatephorus cucumeris (Rhizoctonia solani)*, three *Pythium spp.*, three *Phytophthora spp.* and several *Fusarium spp.* with Gibberella or Nectria sexual stages, or none at all.

pre-emergent and post-emergent

Before the plethora of Latin names sends us to the slappy farm, some generalizations should be made: There are two types of damping off, pre-emergent and post-emergent. In pre-emergence damping off, the fungus attacks seeds or seedlings before they push their way through the surface of the soil. This situation is often mistaken for poor seed. Post-emergence damping off is more evident, attacking seedlings after they emerge from the soil. In youngest seedlings, with just cotyledons and a pair of true leaves, the fungus invades stems at the soil line causing a brown watery soft rot at that site. Good initial stands fade away, often incorrectly attributed to frost, heavy rains, or other environmental causes. Older seedlings, with up to eight pairs of true leaves, may also be attacked— the plants cease growing, leaves turn pale yellow (sometimes with brown spots) and topple over.

The 14 fungi causing Cannabis damping off have evolved different parasitic patterns over a wide range of conditions. There is a fungus to fit almost any temperature, pH range, lighting condition, or soil type. There is one common denominator in all damping off damage — too much water. Something deep in our human psyche triggers overuse of the watering can. Overwatering is the most common problem for any plant and must be avoided.

Irrigate seedlings infrequently, allowing soil to dry between waterings. When you do water, be sure the moisture penetrates at least six inches. Avoid watering late in the day, or at night, especially in areas with high humidity. Damping off, however, occurs without our help, even in remote guerilla plots far from irrigation sources. Avoid planting in heavy, wet, poorly drained soils which tend to puddle. On questionable sites, try planting in raised beds (four to six inches), or lighten heavy clay and muck soils with perlite. A second choice is vermiculite, which eventually breaks down and contributes to the problem. Damping off damage is increased if seeds are planted deeper than 3/4 inch. Irrigate the soil before planting, watering afterwards will pack soil around the seed. Plant the seedlings far enough apart to allow air circulation between them. Nothing pleases fungi more than an overcrowded seedbed.

Due to all the different fungi involved, damping off can occur at any temperature. Damage is greatest at temperatures which stress the seedlings and are optimal for the fungus. This situation arises when pushing the season— planting in early spring's cold, wet soil. In a recent marijuana article called "Against the Wind," Craig Vetter related a good rule of thumb: "I walked into the middle of my unplanted garden plot, dropped my pants and sat...if the soil is too cold for your bare ass, it's too cold for the seedlings you're getting ready to plant."

Soil mixes can vary. Some authors suggest using a light sandy soil for seedlings. Others say a perlite and peat mix is best. The key characteristic sought is good drainage. I suggest any well textured soil with plenty of organic material (humus). Losses from damping off are reduced by promoting disease-escaping growth habits, such as rapid root development. Hence, nutrient-poor soils, like sand, are

watering for fungus control

other controls

soil salts and acids

undesirable. Balance is the key. Too much nitrogen will increase losses. Excess soil electrolytes of any type can increase damage, so use fertilizer salts carefully on your seedlings. This warning extends to the powerful organics— blood meal and chicken shit— as well as chemical fertilizers.

Damping off is generally worse in acidic soils with a pH less than 7. Full-spectrum lighting above 1,000 foot-candles is beneficial for Cannabis and inhibits the fungi. "Bottom heat" protects seedlings and clone cuttings from most fungi. An insulated horticulture heating table is a good source of bottom heat. This will not work if your damping off is caused by *Macrophomina phaseolina* or *Pythium aphnidermatum,* which prefer warm temperatures.

Some say the only way to control damping off is to sterilize your soil. Small seed bed operators can autoclave their soil in a lab. For large field plots, use of methyl bromide, chloropicrin or other fumigants injected into the soil will eliminate damping off organisms attacking high-value crops. The tactic is expensive, technically difficult, and generally nasty. An old-timer's method is to apply sodium nitrate (four to eight ounces per square yard of soil) several weeks before setting seed. The chemical kills both damping off fungi and nematodes before oxidizing to harmless nitrates by planting time, which may be used as a source of nitrogen by the young plants.

Nematodes in the soil create synergistic damage with damping off fungi, and must be controlled. The root-knot nematode, *Meloidogyne incognita,* burrows into Cannabis roots, providing entry for the fungi. The problem with soil sterilization is re-introduction of pathogenic fungi. Many damping off fungi are ecologically considered "pioneer organisms", their populations will increase logarithmically if placed in a sterile environment devoid of antagonistic organisms. All equipment (including shoes) should be carefully washed before entering a sterilized field or grow room to delay reinfestation. Steam pasteurization using a mix of steam and air at 140 degrees for 30 minutes will kill pathogenic fungi while maintaining a population of competitive bacteria and fungi. This is superior to steam sterilization, using pure steam at 212 degrees, which produces overkill and the biological vacuum a damping off fungus can luxuriate in if re-introduced.

For the rest of this column, we'll take a closer look at the casual organisms of damping off and describe the conditions promoting their pathogenesis.

water molds

"Water molds" are the most common cause of Cannabis seedling mortality in very wet soils. These include three *Pythium spp.* and three *Phytophthora spp.* — difficult to individually differentiate but

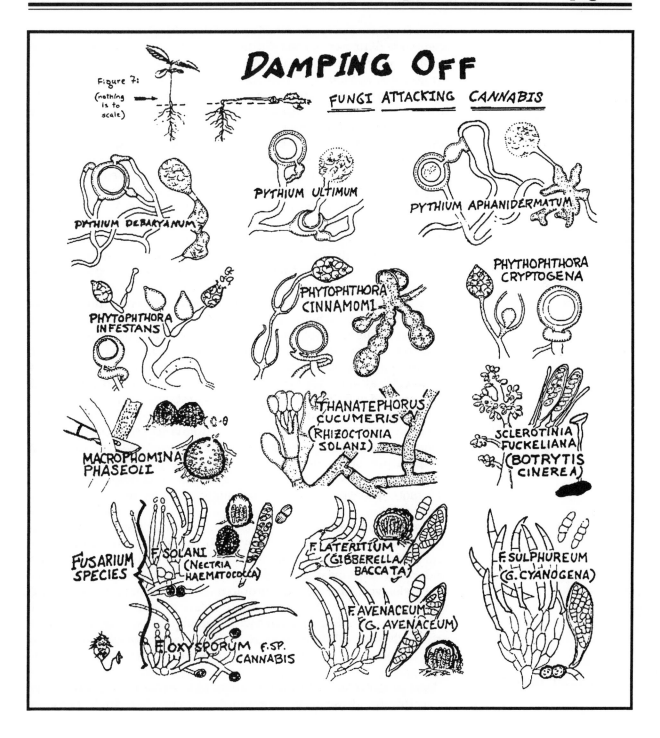

DAMPING OFF

FUNGI ATTACKING CANNABIS

Figure 7: (nothing is to scale)

PYTHIUM DEBARYANUM

PYTHIUM ULTIMUM

PYTHIUM APHANIDERMATUM

PHYTOPHTHORA INFESTANS

PHYTOPHTHORA CINNAMOMI

PHYTHOPHTHORA CRYPTOGENA

MACROPHOMINA PHASEOLI

THANATEPHORUS CUCUMERIS (RHIZOCTONIA SOLANI)

SCLEROTINIA FUCKELIANA (BOTRYTIS CINEREA)

FUSARIUM SPECIES

F. SOLANI (NECTRIA HAEMATOCOCCA)

F. LATERITIUM (GIBBERELLA BACCATA)

F. SULPHUREUM (G. CYANOGENA)

F. AVENACEUM (G. AVENACEUM)

F. OXYSPORUM F.SP. CANNABIS

as a group are easily identified as water molds. Under a microscope their wide diameter "hyphae" (the growing strands commonly called "mold") are white, contain lipid droplets and conspicuously lack cross walls. *Pythium* and *Phytophthora* species produce two types of spore-bearing structures, sporangia and oogonia. The sporangia arise asexually and produce zoospores. Oogonia must sexually fuse with *Antheridia* to produce zoospores. The zoospores have flagella, are strong swimmers, and spread the disease from one plant to another. The oospores are produced in diseased seedling's roots; they do not move, but spread the disease from one year to another as survival structures in situ. I have drawn distinguishing characteristics of the six water molds attacking Cannabis. You may feel a need to precisely diagnose your disease organisms some day, at the slappy farm.

Some comments regarding individual water mold species: *Pythium ultimum* is most commonly encountered in the United States. It attacks many other species of plants, especially at cooler temperatures (60 to 68 degrees). Reports from South America indicate this pathogen causes a high-mortality root rot in mature Cannabis in addition to damping off of seedlings. *P. ultimum* has been demonstrated to follow wireworms, which bore into Cannabis roots at the soil line, causing synergistic damage. *Pythium debaryanum* is found worldwide, attacks 130 different plant species, and has an optimal temperature of 64 to 77 degrees. It was first described on Cannabis by Kirchner in 1906, and causes the most damage in Europe. Snails are implicated in the spread of this fungus in seedbeds. *Pythium aphanidermatum* is the "warm weather Pythium," with an optimum temperature of 98 degrees. It has been reported on marijuana in India. But its occurence in warm greenhouse conditions is probably more widespread than this suggests. The fungus is found worldwide.

If you suspect a *Pythium spp.* is causing your damping off, dig up a plant. Lightly grasp the seedling root between thumb and forefinger and pull away from the stem. If the outer layer of the root (epidermis and cortex) slips away leaving only a thin inner cylinder (endodermis and stele), you have *Pythium* problems. A prophylactic seed soaking with Captan or a dithiocarbamate (Maneb, Ferbam, Zineb) will reduce infection. Soil drenches with Benomyl (a systemic fungicide) are ill-advised. Williams et. al. reported increased disease incidence after benomyl use, attributed to suppression of *Pythium* soil antagonists.

Damping off caused by *Phytophthora spp.* is rare in Cannabis. This is fortunate, these fungi are more virulent than their *Pythium* cousins. Care is needed to differentiate the two genera. Zoospore release and oogonia antheridia fusing differ (see illustrations on page 77). *Phytophthora infestans* causes epidemics in cool (55 to 65 degrees), damp (relative humidity greater than 90 percent) weather. A fungus native to the Americas, it caused the Great Potato Famine when introduced to Ireland in the 1840s. It triggered a wave of Irish immigration to the United States, forever influencing liberal politics in this country (e.g., McGovern, Tip O'Neil, the Kennedys).

Dithiocarbamates and copper fungicides are prophylactically sprayed on seedlings during disease-inducing weather in endemic areas. *Phytophthora cinnamoni* usually attacks woody plants, but has been reported on Cannabis. It occurs in temperate climates with an optimum temperature of 68 to 88 degrees. Disease caused by this pathogen is greater on clay soils. Chemical control is with fenaminosulf seed treatment in endemic areas. *Phytophthora cryptogena* has an optimum temperature similiar to *P.cinnamoni*. They are both capable of causing root rots in mature marijuana as well as seedlings. Chemical control is with fenaminosulf, too. But, I reiterate, the best way to control damping off caused by these water molds is to avoid wet soil. Indoor growers with *Phytophthora* or *Pythium* problems are usually wet behind the ears (or between them). Try germinating seeds in damp paper towels well-squeezed of excess water. Right out of the plastic, paper towels are almost sterile.

Macrophomina phaseolina causes premature wilt in full grown marijuana as well as damping off in seedlings. It is common in the Midwest, especially on or near corn fields. Soils rich in organic matter inhibit the fungus. The organism produces easily identified sclerotia (knots of hyphae serving as survival structures) which look like finely ground pepper. These are found by sectioning the stem. Disease caused by *M. phaseolina* is greatest at warm temperatures (98 degrees).

The fungus causing Gray Mold, *Sclerotinia fuckeliana (Botrytis cinerea)* also causes damping off. *S. fuckeliana* can establish itself in seeds while they are still developing on diseased female plants. Expect a high incidence of pre- and post-emergence damping off in crops set from seed plants infested with Gray Mold the previous season.

Thanatephorus cucumeris (Rhizoctonia solani) is a quintessential damping off fungus. This versatile pathogen attacks at least 230 plant species in all stages of growth at different temperatures all over the world. Constant wetness or 100 percent relative humidity are not essential prerequisites for disease as they are with water molds. In Cannabis, the fungus causes Sore-shin disease in grown plants

gray mold

and damping off of in seedlings. It attacks at the soil line. Tiny bits of soil dangle from the coarse hyphae of *T. cucumeris* attached to the infected marijuana seedlings pulled from the ground. This does not occur in Pythium-infected seedlings, and is fairly diagnostic. *T. cucumeris* rarely produces spores. It is identified by its wide diameter, septate, brown hyphae, which characteristically branch at 45 or 90 degree angles. The hyphae are constricted at origin of these branches, and a cross wall occurs just beyond the constriction at each lateral branch. Damping off by this fungus is most severe in cool, damp (not soaking) conditions. A horticulture heating table would help control *T. cucumeris*. If planting outdoors, drop your drawers before setting seed.

Incorporating organics with a high carbon/nitrogen ratio (straw, corn stover, even pine shavings) reduces the pathogen's viability in the soil. Avoid excessive use of nitrogenous fertilizers. Disease is more severe in acid soils, but it occurs at any pH. Pentachloronitrobenzene (PCNB) at 50 ppm soil weight is quite specific against *T. cucumeris*. The fungicide has also been used as a seed treatment or root-dip for transplanting seedlings into questionable areas. Applying Captan in field furrows and mixing with the covering soil is also reported to be effective. *T. cucumeris* can parasitize *Pythium spp.*, whereas *Fusarium spp.* can inhibit *T. cucumeris*. A lot of competition for your seedlings in that wet muck!

fusarium

The complex of *Fusarium spp.* causing marijuana damping off is difficult to dissect. The symptoms are similiar to those caused by previously discussed fungi-leaf chlorosis, a brown necrosis at the soil line, and the seedling falls over. Additionally, *Fusarium spp.* may cause seedling cotyledons to drop off and/or produce a pink mass of hyphae on sick seedlings with a red discoloration of the roots. All the *Fusarium spp.* produce diagnostic crescent to canoe-shaped spores on Cannabis. If isolated as a pure culture in petri plates, the fungus often produces a sexual stage whose spores are more easily identified to a specific species. The fusaria reported on Cannabis (with sexual stages listed parenthetically) are: *Fusarium solani (Nectria haematococca), F. sulphureum (Gibberella cyanogena), F. avenaceum (G. avenacea),* and *F. graminearum (G. zeae)*. Another species, *F. oxysporum f. sp.* Cannabis, has no reportable sexual stage. These *Fusarium spp.* also cause foot rot, stem canker, and wilt diseases in mature marijuana plants. They deserve, and will receive, a Bush Doctor issue all to themselves.

First printed in Vol. 5, No. 4, page 35.

A Closer Look at Spider Mites

by the Bush Doctor

These insidious arachnids are the most common and destructive pests of greenhouse/grow room marijuana. Outdoor crops in warm regions can also be damaged, with losses in India reported up to 50 percent (Cherian, *Madras Agricultural Journal*, Vol. 20(7):259-265).

Spider mites attack hundreds of different plant hosts, and are found around the world. They suck plant sap, and normally congregate on the underside of leaves. Symptoms initially are not evident, but signs can be seen by careful inspection of lower leaf surfaces for silken webbing, eggs, and the mites themselves. Leaves begin to droop as gray-white speckles appear on the upper leaf surface. With more loss of chlorophyll, these parched areas enlarge and the rest of the leaf turns chlorotic, then dies. In severe infection, the whole plant may dry up, with various portions of the plant webbed together. The pest may or may not attack flowering tips directly.

Mites attacking Cannabis have been called red spider mites, carmine spider mites, two-spotted spider mites, glasshouse spider mites, simple spider mites, and common spinning mites. All these names refer to what is considered two species of spider mites. The two are separated by differences in adult morphology, biology, and distribution. Crossbreeding them results in only male offspring, indicating that fertilization does not occur.

Some 59 taxonomic synonyms of the two species exists, described from different hosts and different parts of the world. Consult Pritchard and Baker for a full synonymy.

The Two Spotted Spider Mite is the more common of the two attacking Cannabis in greenhouses in the United States. It can also attack outdoor hosts in our temperate environment; it is a common pest of fruit trees.

In *"Marijuana Grower's Guide,"* Mel Frank's spider mite photograph is of *T. urticae*. Frank and Rosenthal claim this species will not infest female flowers. In the summer (and year-round for greenhouse populations), two-spotted spider mites are green with two brown-black spots on either side of their dorsal surface. On Cannabis, as well as other chlorophyll rich plants, these spots may grow to almost cover the mite's back. Females grow to .4 to .5 millimeter long.

Males are slightly smaller with a wedge-shaped posterior, and the

the two-spotted spider mite

Tetranychus urticae Koch, 1836 Acariformes
Synonyms:
T. telarius of various authors,
T. bimaculatus Harvey 1898

two trifid spots may not be as evident. For you entomologists, the male's knobbed aedeagi are at right angles to the neck and symmetrical; the Empodium I of the male is claw-like, with other empodia simple and similar to those of the female. Their eggs are spherical, originally translucent to white, turning straw colored just before hatching and .14 millimeters in diameter. They are laid singly on the underside of leaves or in strands of silken web spun by the adults. Larvae are not much larger than the eggs, with six legs and two tiny red eye spots. Protonymphs and deutonymphs are eight-legged and light green. These become quiescent and molt into adults, capable of reproduction.

Outdoor populations have an overwintering stage where females leave the host plant, become yellowish-orange, and hibernate in the ground. Where temperatures remain above 54 degrees (12 degrees centigrade), there is no overwintering stage. Shortening the photoperiod to induce flowering of greenhouse marijuana may also induce some spider mites to enter their overwintering stage.

At optimum conditions for development — 85 degree temperatures with low humidity— the total life cycle takes as little as eight days. Each female can lay as many as 200 eggs (Jeppsen et al.).

the carmine spider mite

Tetranychus cinnabarinus (Boisdural) Acariformes
Synonyms:
Acarus cinnabarinus Boisdural 1867
T. telarius (Linnaeus) 1758

The Carmine Spider Mite is a pest of herbaceous plants in semitropical areas. In temperate zones they are only found in warm greenhouses. The carmine spider mite enjoys a higher optimum temperature than the two-spotted spider mite and can thrive at temperatures above 95 degrees. This species does not overwinter and remains on its host plant, completing nearly 20 life cycles per year. High humidity causes all stages of this species— larvae, nymphs, adults— to stop feeding and enter a quiescent period. Cherian reports that this species is attracted to the female flowering tops of marijuana. He noted that Cannabis varieties that were the most heavily infested were varieties normally producing the largest sinsemilla yields.

Eggs and immature stages of this species are indistinguishable from *T. urticae*. Adults, however, are bright to brick red, with dark internal markings. The male's adeagi are not always symmetrical, having a rounded anterior side and a sharp posterior side. In cooler periods when the adults are not feeding as actively, they turn a darker shade of green and are difficult to distinguish from two-spotted spider mites. Their life cycle and profundity are similar to *T. urticae* as well.

control

Quick action must be taken to keep the two-spotted and carmine spider mites in check. Once established, they are nearly impossible to eradicate, especially in greenhouse situations. Spider mites can be carried into grow rooms on people and pets, in soil, and on transferred plants (including house plants). Be vigilant. Once they are introduced, a grower's constant efforts can at best keep populations low, not eliminate them. In field conditions, natural predators can manage spider mite populations below damaging levels. These include the lady beetle (*Stethorus picipes*), pirate bugs (*Orius tristicolor*), the six-spotted thrips (*Scolothrips sexmaculatus*), lacewings (*Chrysopa carnea*), many predacious spiders and other mites.

In the greenhouse, six-spotted thrips often occur naturally, and many other predators are commercially available for introduction. Much attention has been focused on predacious mites, which can be obtained via mail order in small vials. *Phytoseiulus persimilus* is commonly used to control greenhouse spider mites. Its life cycle has been extensively studied to maximize its role as a biocontrol agent. It is effective at a higher humidity than most predacious mites, but becomes inactive at temperatures over 80 degrees. *Metaseiulus occidentalis* is primarily for orchards and other cool-weather outdoor crops. *Amblyseius californicus* does well with less humidity, and reproduces rapidly in temperatures up to 85 degrees. It is probably the best for most grow rooms and greenhouses. A South American import, *Phytoseiulus longpipes,* works well in temperatures up to 100 degrees, and seems ideal for greenhouses that get hot in the summertime.

To be an effective control, predatory mites must be established at early stages of spider mite infestation. Predatory mite's life cycles are twice as fast as the spider mite's, but if the pest gets much of a head start, plant damage will occur before the predators catch up. Predatory mites must be placed near infested areas, not randomly scattered around a grow room. Oscillating fans help them get around, and manually moving them from healthy leaves to infested plants is advised.

Predators thrive in a ratio of one for every 20 to 25 spider mites. The two populations can establish a living equilibrium, keeping the pests below a level causing crop damage. Often, however, the predators will practically eradicate the pest population, and then die out themselves. When the pests pick up again, it is time to buy a new vial of predators. In an earlier article, the Farmer in the Sky describes an alternative to buying new vials— maintaining a mite colony on African violets, and transferring predators as needed. Insecticides, miticides, and even fungicides should be avoided when utilizing predator mites. Allow previously applied pesticides two to three weeks to break down. Jackson notes that some brands of metal halide bulbs put out a light spectrum that is insufficient for the

predatory insects

predators. He suggests adding a sodium light to the grow room.

As Farmer in the Sky also notes, predatory mites are particularly recommended during flowering, when pesticide sprays can be trapped inside buds, inducing gray mold (*Botrytis cinerea*).

The most innocuous spray you can use to control spider mites is a stream of cold water. As with all sprays, direct it at the underside of leaves, where the mites will get knocked off and their webbing destroyed. Spray several times each week, or until your leaves are shredded by the treatment.

sprays

A mix developed at Purdue University and espoused by Tom Alexander (*Sinsemilla Tips* Vol 2(4):27) is four cups whole wheat flour and 12 cups of buttermilk in five gallons of water. Strain through cheesecloth and spray on plants, repeating in a week. The spider mites become stuck in the glue-like mixture and suffocate.

Cherian reports that sprays made from lime sulphur or fish oil soap were effective against spider mites. Marijuana treated with lime sulphur was "... tested by veteran smokers who gave their verdict against it," while the soap-treated ganja passed the smoker's test successfully. Safer's insecticidal soap spray was reported (*Sinsemilla Tips* Vol. 3 No. 3) to cause 91 percent mortality in two-spotted spider mites and 78 percent in carmine spider mites. Plants should be sprayed at five day intervals, each soap spray followed after several hours by a water spray, especially before harvesting.

Ed Rosenthal, in an interview with *Sinsemilla Tips* (Vol. 3 No. 1) suggests spraying with a nursery tree product, Wilt-Pruf, which suffocates the mites (see "Water Conservation," p.134). Although Wilt-Purf is approved for use on edible crops, I don't like the idea of smoking Saran Wrap (polyvinyl chloride, same stuff). Rosenthal also suggests spraying household bleach, diluted to five or 10 percent, to kill the mites and their eggs. This will break down in a short period of time.

Malathion is recommended by many authorities to control spider mites. Every mite population I've sprayed with this insecticide is resistant. The spider mites come back stronger than ever. Maybe they can now eat the pesticide. Horticulturists and ornamental plant growers use systemic insecticides for spider mite control. These products, such as Science Products Company's "Systemic Spray", are not for food crops. They contain, among other nasties, methyl demeton, an extremely poisonous substance that remains in plant tissues for a long time. If one must spray, use Kelthane, a very effective acaricide.

resistant plant varieties

Genetically resistant plant varieties are the final word in spider mite control. Keep an eye on plants that survive heavy infestations.

Cherian, previously mentioned, compared six varieties of ganja in India for carmine spider resistance. His most resistant varieties unfortunately produced the poorest female blooms. More work needs to be done.

First printed in Vol. 6, No. 2, page 31.

Buyer Beware

Chemicals in Your Stash

by Robert Clarke and James Smith

Marijuana is being cultivated with an alarmingly high increase in the use of hazardous chemicals of which the consumer is totally unaware.

Protection from poisons and possible carcinogens during our daily consumption of food, drink and even tobacco is provided by the United States Food and Drug Administration. But what about the unprotected and generally unsuspecting millions of daily marijuana smokers in the United States?

The only force protecting them is the ethics of the grower who cultivates the plants. However, a tremendous number of growers are themselves ignorant of the dangers inherent in smoking chemically treated marijuana.

Pesticides, fungicides, insecticides, mitecides and herbicides contain various toxic compounds and are usually applied on or near the plants to kill a specific pest.

The most dangerous poisons are systemics; the group of pesticides which are absorbed and diffused throughout the tissues of the plant. When a pest attempts to feed on those tissues that have absorbed the toxic pesticide, it inadvertently eats enough of the poison to prove lethal.

systemic poisons

Systemics are very effective because of the complete and total distribution of the pesticide throughout the plant. They are most dangerous to consumers of the plant because opportunities for dilution, decomposition or vaporization of the poison are greatly reduced. As a result, the pesticides are hidden within the plant and will remain there while the plant is dried, processed and eventually smoked.

Few systemic pesticides are approved by the F.D.A. for use on food crops, and likewise the application of such poisons by growers to their marijuana crops should always be avoided at *any* cost.

non-systemics

Non-systemics, the most common and equally toxic form of pesticides, are usually sprayed or dusted on the plant in an effort to poison the invading pest by contact, ingestion or fumigation. Many of these poisons also remain toxic for years, and most cannot be detected without sophisticated analysis equipment.

Pesticide residues are measured in just a few parts per million (PPM) and very low levels of these toxins are often linked to cancer and disease in research animals.

Some pesticide sprays and dusts are considered safe for application on various fruit and vegetable crops. However, nearly all require a lengthy decomposition period before the produce is considered safe for humans to eat. In addition, there is the probable health risk from smoking the residues of pesticides.

Most experiments to determine the toxicity of pesticides are made with the poison administered orally and not smoked. Even if the oral toxicity of a pesticides may be relatively low, the by- products of their combustion might be much more toxic to the smoker.

It is traditional in modern agriculture to combat pests with chemical warfare, and marijuana cultivators occasionally follow agribusiness' lead. However, serious and conscientious marijuana growers would never dream of applying any potentially hazardous chemicals to their plants.

In fact, a vast amount of domestic marijuana is produced by small, non-commercial home cultivators, most of whom consider their agricultural techniques to be totally organic. In addition, small growers in most areas of the country are fortunate because Cannabis is less susceptible to attack by pests than most other crops and usually require no pesticides.

the greenhouse environment

The advent of extensive artificial light and greenhouse cultivation has added to the problem since pests are much more common in the sheltered indoor environment.

The consciousness of commercial growers unfortunately tends to vary considerably from that of non-commercial growers. Often the situation arises where marijuana is the first crop which an aspiring cultivator has ever attempted to grow, and an organic consciousness is not as easily accessible as chemical solutions.

Commercial growing operations often necessitate the use of more concentrated inorganic fertilizers to support larger gardens of marijuana. Larger areas are also more difficult to maintain free of pests and the commercial grower is more likely to respond with the immediate and thoughtless use of a dangerous pesticide, than to respond by employing preventative or organic control methods.

It is at this point that the general public becomes endangered unknowingly for the financial sake of irresponsible growers. That danger then becomes real when one realizes that inherent in any commercial growing operation is the eventual sale of the final product on the consumer level. By the time a consumer smokes a joint of possibly contaminated marijuana, it has passed through many hands and it is extremely difficult to establish its purity.

Just as prevention is the most successful method of pest control in cultivation, the aim of this article is to inform the consumer of the possible future risks of smoking contaminated marijuana. It must be remembered that most cultivators are both caring and responsible. Only a handful overlook their obligation to protect the consumer, and it is our hope that this information will reach these careless growers.

prevention

Consumers must not support the use of pesticides on domestic marijuana just as consumers did not support the spraying of paraquat on foreign fields. It is now up to the conscious consumer and cultivator alike, to advise others against the use of chemical pesticides on marijuana *before* any serious health problems arise.

First printed in Vol. 4, No. 1, page 24.

chapter

5

lighting

Facts on Artificial Lights

There are four basic types of high intensity discharge (HID) lights. The oldest and most used for general lighting is mercury vapor. Metallic halide and high pressure sodium are basically variations of mercury lamps. Low pressure sodium is similar, but uses no mercury in its arc.

All require ballasts (except for self-ballasted mercury lamps which are worthless for growing because of low light output, high lamp cost and relatively short life). The ballast limits the lamp current and gives it proper running voltage. A ballast for a given wattage can operate lamps of only that wattage.

Mercury vapor lamps are useful only in 400, 750, and 1,000 watt sizes. The 1,500 watt is the same as the 1,000 watt but is over driven by using a special ballast. This raises light output by 20 percent but shortens lamp life by 80 percent. Mercury lamps put out 60 lumens per watt, about the same as VHO fluorescent, but are better because they are longer lasting and the light is concentrated in a three-inch arctube instead of 12 feet of fluorescent tube.

Compared to the standard cool-white fluorescent, Growlight tubes are 30 to 50 percent less efficient. A cool-white fluorescent supplemented with incandescent light is equal to or better than any fluorescent growlight and much less expensive.

The 400 watt and 1,000 watt mercury lamp is available in coolwhite, warmwhite, clear, color improved and natural. The different phosphor coatings improve the spectrum, but certain wavelengths are missing in all coatings. A 400 watt unit hung six feet over the soil lights a 20 square foot area. A 1,000 watt unit lights 50 square feet if hung eight feet above the soil, assuming a good reflector and reflective mulch and walls are used.

Mercury vapor is the cheapest way to go and you do not have to raise or lower the lights. Mercury lights are available in reflector lamp types, eliminating the need for a separate reflector. They burn in any position, but put out less light when horizontal or tilted. The 750 watt type is not readily available.

Metal halide lights, marketed under brand names such as Multi-vapor (GE), Metallic Halide (WESTINGHOUSE), and Metalarc (SYL-VANIA), are mercury vapor lamps with sodium and scandium iodide added to the mercury in precise amounts and a thorium-coated electrode which fills the gap in the mercury spectrum. They put out 90 to 125 lumens per watt and are useful only in 400 and 1,000 watt sizes.

There are 1,500 watt lamps, but they put out hard ultraviolet (UV) radiation and are dangerous to be around when lit. Hard UV radiation causes blindness, cataracts, and skin cancer— so beware! Any metal halide burning more than 15 degrees off vertical center also puts out hard UV.

Metal halide lamps need special ballasts, but won't start if used with mercury vapor ballasts at low temperatures. This doesn't matter for growing in most cases. There are some metal halide lamps made to run on mercury ballasts with some made to operate on one type and others made to operate on another type. Experimenting can be dangerous because the wrong lamp and ballast combination can blow up the lamp.

The metal halide in the 1,000 watt size is an inexpensive way to start an indoor garden. If hung eight feet above the soil surface, it will light 100 square feet and a 400 watt hung six and one-half feet above the surface will light 300 square feet, assuming that there is good reflection.

The one drawback to these lamps is the extremely long restrike time. If turned off after reaching full brightness, it can take 10 to 30 minutes for the lamp to light up again.

High pressure sodium (HPS) is the best single source for growing. It doesn't have as wide a spectrum as metal halide but is much more efficient, producing 110 to 140 lumens per watt. Lamp life is longer and light loss with age is low. In experiments with roses, production was 140 percent greater with HPS and sunlight than sunlight alone.

HPS lamps come in 250 watt, 350 watt self-starting, 400 watt and 1,000 watt. The 250 watt is not as good for growing and more expensive than the 360 watt because of the special ballast required. The 250 watt will light an area of 20 square feet at a height of six feet; the 350 watt, 35 square feet at six and a half feet high; the 400 watt,

metal halides

high pressure sodium

45 square feet at six and a half feet; and the 1,000 watt, 130 square feet at nine feet high.

High pressure sodium lights can be mounted safely in any position, a real advantage in rooms with low ceilings.

low pressure sodium

Low pressure sodium (LPS) is the ugly duckling of the HID family and I mention it because it has been used for successful crops much to everyone's surprise. It is the most efficient commercially used light source, producing 180 lumens per watt in the 180 watt size. The lamp is three feet long, with a significant amount of sodium in it and takes a special socket and ballast.

Its 32,000 lumen output and large size make it a borderline solution because it must be hung too low over the soil. Its spectrum is terrible— orange and nothing else. **The cost is high and if broken, the sodium inside would explode if it came in contact with water.**

In a scientific paper presented to the American Society of Agricultural Engineers in 1975, Dr. Cathy of the USDA labs in Maryland showed the effectiveness of LPS for growing. Even though the spectrum is monochromatic, if low levels of full-spectrum light (daylight or incandescent) were present, the plants grew very well. If the low level of full-spectrum light was missing, the plants still grew but abnormally. The LPS/incandescent combination was slightly better than any other light system in the environmental chambers.

The experiments indicate that spectrum is of less importance than it was once believed to be. If low-level light needs are met, high levels of excess wave lengths will be used by the plants.

using HID lights

A timer is a must with any light system. Random day length hurts plant development as does continuous light. My recommendation is 15 hours maximum for starting, and cutting down to 11 hours for flowering. Plants will not flower with continuous HID light.

A combination of MH and HPS gives a full spectrum from ultraviolet to infrared. The two reinforce each other, one being strong where the other is weak. Since most fixtures that will operate HPS lamps will also run MH lamps of equal wattage, plants can be started with MH for better early growth, and then budded with HPS just by changing the bulbs. Either source of light is excellent alone, too.

Do not try too large a setup. For most residential electric service, 4,000-5,000 watts is the most that should be used without some alterations to the wiring in and out of the house. The transformer feeding the house from the pole is usually good for 10,000 watts total load. Some folks in California tried too big of a system, burned up the transformer and the power company alerted the police. So use common sense!

A 20-amp 120-volt circuit will run a 1,000 watt and a 400 or 360

Lamp	Lumens	Life (Hours)	Light Loss Over Life	Color
LU-360 360W HPS	38,000	16,000	15-20%	Good Gold-White
LU-400 400W HPS	50,000	24,000	10-15%	Good Gold-White
MV400 BU/I 400 W MH	34,000	15,000	50%	Good Silver-White
M5 400 BV 400W High Output MH	40,000	20,000	50%	Good Silver-White
LU-1000 1000W HPS	140,000	24,000	10-15%	Good Gold-White
M1000/BU 1000W STANDARD METAL HALIDE	100,000	10,000 to 12,000	50%	Good Silver-White
M5 1000V or MV1000 BU/I 1000W HIGH OUTPUT METAL HALIDE	125,000	115,000 to 10,000	50%	Good Silver-White

reference table

watt unit. The same circuit will run three 400 or 360 watt units, if each one is started 30 to 60 seconds after the other. Three small units started all at once will trip the circuit breaker sometimes because more power is drawn as they start up than when running. Thousand watt units are just the opposite. Small units operate fairly quietly, and large units make some noise, especially when starting.

Ballasts are better remotely mounted from the light. The weight of a 1,000 watt HPS ballast is 45 pounds. A 400 watt ballast could weigh as little as 10 pounds.

Sometimes a lamp will burn even though the outer glass is broken.

It should be turned off immediately. The bare arc tube could explode and emit a lot of hard UV radiation. Never change lamps with the power on, move them with the power on or burn metal halide lamps tilted with open reflectors. Don't turn HID lights off and on at random. Use a 60 watt regular light bulb on a separate circuit for a walk light in the growing room.

Heat from the lights can be blown away by a fan in the summer, and in the winter, if the lights are operated at night, the heat will keep the space— maybe even the whole house— at a comfortable temperature.

First printed in Vol. 1, No. 3, page 4.

Artificial Light and Its Sources

by Johnny Sativa Hempseed

It has been said before and it can be said again: Light is as important as the other two major environmental factors, nutrients and moisture, which contribute to the maximum growth potential of plants.

Artificial lighting is being used on a massive scale now in this country. Some people use incandescent or fluorescent lights while many people are opting for the top of the line in artificial lights, the high intensity discharge (HID) halide and sodium systems.

Plants can grow and bloom in a situation where artificial light is their sole energy source. Or in a more natural situation, artificial light can be used to supplement sunlight. When the length of the day shortens in autumn and winter outdoors or in a greenhouse, plants will slow down their growth rate and flower under just sunlight. Artificial light can be employed to extend the growing season into a year round hobby or occupation.

Artificial light does not exactly duplicate sunlight because its colors are present in different amounts. Certain types of lights can induce the same natural response in plants. Not all plants will thrive under the same light. The optimum light for marijuana is the HID family of bulbs. Unfortunately, not all growers can afford the expense of HID systems. There are many people using the less expensive incandescent, fluorescent and tungsten halogen.

Incandescent bulbs are the bulbs people use to light rooms in their homes. The tungsten filament wire inside the bulb has a high resistance to electricity and electric current flowing through the high resistance causes the filament to heat up and glow, producing visible light. Incandescent is high in red and far-red light, which is good for flowering. Incandescent light has the same proportion of red and far-red light as does sunlight, although it is much less intense, while having almost none of the blue or violet light necessary for good plant growth.

Reflector bulb incandescents are the best type to use if you're on a limited budget. They have a reflector coating over the ends. They can be obtained in 75, 150 and 300 watt sizes. The 150 and 300 watt sizes will need heavier duty sockets. Larger wattage incandescents give off a considerable amount of heat. It is best to keep plants a foot away from incandescent lighting sources.

incandescents

Fluorescent lamps were commonly used in offices, factories and public buildings until HID lights began to replace them in the past decade. People are constantly buying fluorescents at used or surplus sales at very cheap prices.

Fluorescents were first introduced in the late 1930s and became popular at once because they were long-lasting and distributed light evenly. They are more energy efficient than incandescent lamps, because fluorescent lamps of the same wattage emit up to three times as much light. The lifetime of a fluorescent bulb is up to 20 times that of an incandescent bulb, making the fluorescent more economical in the long run.

The long tubular glass fluorescent bulb is coated on the inside with phosphor. The type of phosphor determines the "color" of the light given off. The mixture of phosphorescent chemicals determines the "mix" of the various color wavelengths. The visible color is not indicative of the proportion of blue and red waves given off.

The bulb also contains a blend of inert gases, including argon, neon, krypton (watch out Superman!) and a minute quantity of mercury vapor, all sealed in a low-pressure vacuum. Electrodes are at both ends of the bulb and when electrical power is turned on, the resulting flow of electrical current between the two electrodes forms an electrical arc which stimulates the phosphor and emits energy in the form of light. This emission is stronger in the center of the tube than at the ends.

Unlike incandescent bulbs, fluorescent bulbs need a ballast in order to fire up and operate. A fluorescent ballast uses about 10 watts of electricity for every 40 watts used by the bulb itself. Ballasts normally last for 10 years. When they burn out they sometimes

fluorescents

smoke and give off a noxious chemical odor. In older ballasts, the very toxic chemical PCB was used. Make sure the ballast is labeled "No PCBs." A pair of 40 watt, cool-white fluorescent bulbs will last about twice as long if burned continuously than if burned three hours a day.

Fluorescent lamps don't turn on immediately like incandescent lamps do. The bulb's cathodes must be warm before an arc can be struck through the lamp. Fluorescent bulbs are available in twelve various shades of white mixed with other colors of the spectrum. Like incandescent light, fluorescent lamps blacken with age and lose efficiency. A flickering lamp is about to burn out and should be replaced.

Most fluorescent bulbs are high in blue light but extremely low in red light which promotes flowering. Special modified fluorescent lamps have been developed and are sold under a wide variety of trade names such as Gro-lux, Agro Lite, Vita Lite, among others.

Since the green and yellow parts of the light spectrum have no known influence on a plant's biological functions, special fluorescent lamps were developed that minimize these rays and concentrate instead on emitting the blue and red rays needed for healthy plant growth. Because of the missing green and yellow light the light tends to be purplish or pink. This light enhances flower colors.

For those growers who can't afford the top of the line halides or sodiums, a combination of incandescents and fluorescents will produce some growth from a plant. And in the end, some produce is better than no produce!

First printed in Vol. 4, No. 3, page 29.

More on Metal Halides

by Tom Alexander

There are three types of lighting which fall under the category of HID lighting (high intensity discharge), mercury vapor, sodium vapor and metal halide. Each type has its own characteristics, but color spectrum is by far the most important to the indoor gardener.

Plants will flourish under a mix of blue light and red light. Mercury vapor lamps emit a high amount of blue light but minimal amount of red light. Sodium vapor lamps on the other hand emit high amounts of red light and relatively low amounts of blue light. The metal halide lamp emits the most perfect balance of blue and red light to create an incredibly effective growing medium.

A lumen is a measurement of the intensity or brightness of a light. An eight-foot two-lamp VHO fluorescent type fixture emits 20,000 initial lumens. The metal halide lamp, depending on manufacturer, will emit 125,000 initial lumens. The high lumen output allows a plant to reach its light saturation level. In other words, it cannot effectively use any more light for growing purposes. By manipulating the photo period (hours of light per day) as well as watering and fertilization techniques, the grower in an indoor environment can control growth rates and induce flowering at will.

lumen output

Mounting

The easiest way to mount the reflector is by hook and chain. The reflector can then be raised or lowered to any desired height. The reflector should never be closer than five inches from the ceiling due to the excessive heat involved. A piece of one-half inch plaster board will act as a good insulator between the reflector and the ceiling. Always allow at least 18 inches of air space around the reflector to ensure proper ventilation. The lamp burns at approximately 400 degrees C. and should not be used in an area of less than six foot square without a fan for cooling.

The lamp should not be operated at more than 15 degrees from straight up and down. Failure to keep the lamp vertical will result in premature lamp failure.

The ballast should be kept on the floor in a protected spot to avoid damage. Ballasts should never be placed less than 12 inches apart. The ballast housing is manufactured with cooling fins but needs ample room for the air to circulate. A properly ventilated ballast will last longer.

Power Consumption

The 1,000 watt metal halide when plugged into a 120-volt outlet will draw approximately 10 amps. Although you may not understand the terminology, what is important to remember is that the lamp should not be plugged into any random electrical outlet. The 10 amps it draws is more than most home appliances draw, and you should be sure that the electrical outlet can handle it.

The circuit breaker or fuse for the outlet should be no less than 15 amps, with no other appliance on that circuit. If you have 20 or 30 amp fuses on that particular circuit, you can operate other appliances, but you simply cannot put a larger fuse in to accommodate the metal halide. The size or gauge of the wire used in the circuit determines what size fuse or circuit breaker is installed.

Here is a test that can be made to determine which appliances are on a given circuit and whether the circuit will be able to handle the metal halide fixture as well. Turn all your appliances on, then turn off a given fuse or circuit breaker. Go around and check to see which appliances or lights have shut off, making a list of these as you go. Example: A fuse or circuit breaker is turned off and the refrigerator drawing 400 watts, the overhead light drawing 200 watts, the TV drawing 300 watts, and the stereo drawing 30 watts all shut off. Totaling the wattage from the above you get 930 watts. Dividing 930 watts by 120 volts (the standard U.S. voltage) you get the amperage being drawn on that circuit. The 7.75 amps being drawn by the appliances, plus the 10 amps that would be drawn by the metal halide if you were to plug it into the circuit, would be too much for a 15-amp fuse or breaker.

Never put a larger fuse or breaker in a given circuit without knowing that the wire in the circuit is large enough to handle it. Doing so could start a fire. Remember: The metal halide may work on a circuit which cannot handle the amperage drawn, but only for a while. If the fixture does not receive enough voltage, the capacitor and the ballast will strain as hard as possible to keep running but will eventually burn out. At this point the fixture will not work no matter where you plug it in. So, be sure from the beginning that the electrical outlet will handle the fixture load.

lamp life

The average life of the metal halide lamp is approximately 10,000 hours. This is dependent on the number of times it is turned on and off. Frequent on/off periods will shorten the lamp life. Fourteen hours on and 10 hours off is a good schedule for most plants. Remember that the light is so intense that plants will reach a light saturation level. At this point more light is of no value to plant growth.

After the lamp has been off, it will not start again until it has cooled enough for the arc to strike. This may take as long as 30 minutes depending on the lamp temperature.

timers and cords

Quite a few timers available are rated at 15 amps, 1,875 watts. These timers are adequate for no more than one 1,000 watt metal halide fixture. Larger timers can be purchased from most electrical supply stores. The Intermatic T-101 timer rated at 40 amps at 120 volts is adequate for up to three 1,000 watt metal halide fixtures.

You may want to consult an electrician when wiring the timer. Always use the correct gauge wire and make sure that all timers and junction boxes are grounded.

If you must use extension cords, be sure they are heavy-duty, grounded cords of the proper gauge. An extension cord of 14-gauge wire should be used on distances of less than 25 feet. For longer distances, a 12-gauge wire should be used. The longer the extension cord, the more resistance in the wire. The more resistance, the greater the voltage drop to the fixture. Too much voltage drop will result in a burned out fixture.

Electric companies charge by the kilowatt hour. The 1,000 watt metal halide draws about one kilowatt per hour. At an average rate of four cents per kilowatt hour, the light would cost $16.80 per month to operate for 14 hours per day.

Consult your local electric company for the exact cost per kilowatt hour.

The MS-1,000 metal halide lamp will only work in approved metal halide fixtures. Make sure you have the correct lamp for the correct fixture. Failure to do so will result in lamp and fixture damage.

When watering your plants remember that the lamp is very hot. If water should come in contact with the glass it may shatter. If the outer glass of the lamp should ever break during operation, shut off the lamp immediately to avoid ultra violet radiation. Although the bulb may work, it should be disposed of.

The lamp should not be used in conjunction with aluminum foil as a reflective surface. Aluminum foil tends to reflect the ultra violet wavelength of light. This reflection may cause spot burning of your eyes. White is the best reflective surface.

If for some reason your growing room should become flooded with water, make sure the circuit breaker or fuse is shut off before entering the room.

caution

First printed in Vol. 1, No. 4, page 21.

Electrical Safety with Older Halides

by Tom Alexander

Many people have owned high intensity lighting systems (HIDs) for two, three or more years. The vast majority of those people don't give any thought to maintaining the electrical connections of these lighting systems.

Both halides and sodiums operate at high voltages and hot temperatures. These two conditions deteriorate electrical wire at the points where connections are made. This is especially true at socket connections. With temperatures from the bulb reaching over 100 degrees, socket connections are easily disconnected. In some earlier manufactured systems, this may mean that the socket and bulb come crashing to the floor and live electrical wires are left hanging where the bulb and socket used to be. A more fortunate situation would be where the electrical current does not move through the loose connections, prompting an inspection by the grower.

The ceramic socket should also be inspected regularly. Any cracks or chips in the socket should earn it a place in the trash barrel. A recent customer came into my store with a halide unit that was malfunctioning. After checking out the ballast and capacitor, which were OK, I saw the socket, which was cracked in half and held together with a large stainless steel radiator hose clamp. With a new socket, the unit operated like new. Also remember that 1,000 watt high pressure sodium units should use 5KV pulse rated sockets. Some people also use the pulse rated socket with the 1,000 watt metal halide, but it is not as critical as with the sodium.

Many earlier systems used wire that was not adequate to handle the large load of HID systems. Wire should be 14 gauge with three wires (two for the electrical current and one for the ground, commonly called 14/3 wire.) The wire should be able to handle high temperatures and high voltages.

ballast placement

Another good idea is to check were the ballast is placed in the grow room. Is it sitting in a puddle of water which is leaking from a hydroponic nutrient tank? If it is, this system is a high risk electrocution hazard. You want to place the ballast part of the lighting system off of the floor, away from any possible contact with water. Many people place the ballast just outside of the grow room and run the lamp wire through the wall to the socket assembly.

If a bug or some residue has come in contact with the bulb, wash off the glass with isopropyl alcohol. Windex isn't advised. When screwing or unscrewing bulbs into the socket, always use a clean, non-oily cloth. If your fingers come in contact with the glass, they can leave oil deposits which can weaken the glass and may eventually cause the glass to shatter.

Above all else, use common sense when operating HID lighting systems. One mistake and your growing career could be terminated prematurely.

First printed in Vol. 5, No. 2, page 21.

Safety Standards for HIDs

by *The Farmer in the Sky*

Sometimes 1,500 watt halides are sold and used with regular open-bottom reflectors. Bulb manufacturers use closed reflectors with 1,500 watt bulbs for a very good reason. If the outer glass shell breaks, there is usually an explosion. This does not happen with lower wattage bulbs.

At least one halide manufacturer has photographs with its ads depicting the socket fixture design and color coding. The white wire from the socket is connected to the white wire from the ballast. The black wires are similarly joined. The white socket wire goes to the outer shell and the black wire goes to the inner shell.

The white wire from the ballast is a common and should be connected to the outer shell. If the hot wire from the ballast goes to the outer shell instead, the danger of electrical shock is increased though the unit will still operate.

Universal ballasts specify a red lamp (hot) wire. Be careful when mixing components from different manufacturers. The National Electrical Code exists to prevent these sorts of problems; it should be followed whenever possible.

The company in the above example does not pretend to have a Underwriters Laboratories (UL) listing. Another company with an even worse design is claiming UL listed for low-ceiling applications. If you have bought a light and the shop said it was UL listed, you know that you were fooled if:

• The unit does not have a strain relief (cord clamp) to protect the junction of the socket wires with the wires from the ballast. Wires joined by wire nuts inside the junction box with no strain relief could come loose, creating a shock hazard.

• The unit is cord-connected, or plug-in type. UL #1572 requires permanent installation.

• The unit has more than six feet of lamp wire that is unprotected by conduit.

• The unit has #16-2 lamp wire and an ungrounded reflector.

If any of these describe your unit, it is not UL listed. It may have a UL stamp on the ballast enclosure, but the original unit has been modified.

UL listing

Be aware that if your house burns down, your fire insurance may be voided if you were using improperly designed electrical assemblies.

First printed in Vol. 5, No. 2, page 25.

Track Lighting

by The Farmer in the Sky
The purpose of track lighting, or the various swing arm versions, is to spread over a large area the light from a small reflector. For that reason, track lighting would probably work best in a greenhouse, where a small reflector is desired to avoid blocking the sun.

There is no provision that I have been able to find in UL #1572 or the National Electrical Code for HID track lighting.

The swing arm system consists of a wall-mounted arm, approximately five feet long that moves rapidly back and forth in a semi-circular arc. The arm can carry one or several lights, depending on the brand and model.

In a totally enclosed growroom, the swing arm system suffers from several disadvantages:

• The plant tops could not grow inside the reflector to receive horizontal light directly from the bulb, or the reflector will brush against the plants.

• Very large reflectors, six-footers, for example, could not be used with a swing arm because they might crash into a wall (more on this later).

• Because of the wall mounting feature, posts would be required for mounting in large grow rooms where many of the plants may be too far from a suitable wall.

• The size and shape of the area covered by the moving reflector might make it impractical or unusable for small grow rooms.

• Phototropism— the bending of the plants toward the light— would not be eliminated because of the semi-circular light pattern.

• The system is expensive and, unlike large reflectors, does consume some electricity.

• Moving the bulb ages it prematurely, resulting in 1/3 less light intensity in some cases.

For totally enclosed grow rooms, I recommend large reflectors for several reasons: They consume no electricity. They are safer. They come all the way to the bottom of the bulb without producing a narrow beam effect.

Some track lighting systems suffer from other problems. Several move so slowly that it takes as much as 40 minutes to travel from one end to the other, reducing the total amount of light reaching the plants. Another type uses a rotating bar with lights mounted on either end, so much of the light goes to the outer edges of the room.

First printed in Vol. 4, No. 4, page 22.

Light Moving Systems

by Tom Alexander

Many growers are using one of two types of light moving systems, both of which move the reflector, socket and bulb around the indoor grow room. The object is to get a more even distribution of light than is possible with stationary units.

As with so many other technical gadgets, growers are divided on the utility of these systems, some preferring highly efficient reflectors to movable lights. Of course, what seems to work for one grower may not work for another. In fact, even among light moving enthusiasts there is division over which type of system— straight track or rotating arm, works best.

The straight tracking system employs a motor, chain and sprocket track up to six feet long with the option of an additional six feet of track. The other type of system uses a motorized unit bolted to the center of the ceiling, with two arms protruding in opposite directions. These two arms rotate in a circular pattern. The straight tracking systems retails for around $100 while the rotating arm systems cost about $150.

Most indoor growers are concerned with their power usage and well they should be. Too many foolish growers have been busted because of an unconcerned attitude toward their electric bills. It would be easy to think of the light moving system as just another power-consuming grow room accessory. But since either system is capable of increasing light coverage, a grower can use fewer lights in some applications, actually reducing power consumption.

In fact, both systems are not only quiet, but use very little power— about the same as a 60-watt light bulb.

The decision as to which system is best for a particular application

Swing arm system (top) and close up of a track system (below).

might depend on the shape of the grow room in which it will be used. Because it distributes light in a somewhat rectangular pattern, the straight line track is usually used in rectangular shaped rooms. Rotating arm systems are used more in square configurations. In some large basements and warehouses or unusually shaped grow rooms, both types of systems are sometimes used together.

The straight line track is rather slow, traveling the six feet in about 45 minutes. The rotating arm moves much faster, making a full revolution in less than 60 seconds. The lights can be closer to the top of the plants with the rotating arm system because it moves much faster, reducing the possiblity of plants being burned by the lights.

When both of these systems were first introduced, there was much skepticism among the indoor gardeners across the country. It didn't take long for either of the systems to prove beneficial, however. Now most advanced grow rooms have either light tracks, rotating arm or at the least, efficient reflectors.

Growing and Blooming

by The Farmer in the Sky

Probably the best light to use for budding (and growing) is the new Ultra High Pressure Sodium (UHPS), This light has enough blue to prevent excessive stem elongation under the right conditions, and more in the beneficial orange/red part of the spectrum. Contrary to popular belief, the regular HPS is primarily yellow/orange, not red. The Low Pressure Sodium is even worse, it is monochromatic yellow. The plant sensitivity curve has a peak in the red portion at 675 nanometers.

Red light is preferable at all stages of growth and a small amount of blue is needed only to prevent elongation of stems. For about 85 percent of all plant varieties, it would be a mistake to use HPS light by itself. The small amount of blue required could be provided by natural sunlight, fluorescents simulating the blue sky, or by halides and HPSs in a checkerboard pattern.

Ultra-Violet B can be supplied as supplemental lighting during the last two or three weeks of budding. I recommend the UV-B six-foot fluorescent, about one tube for every 1,000 watts of plant light. This would simulate conditions at high altitudes which increase flavinoid production. There is much evidence to suggest a causal relationship between the higher UV levels found at high altitudes and high THC content in pot.

The use of UV safety goggles is recommended. The UV light should only be used for 2.4 hours a day in the middle of the light-on cycle.

First printed in Vol. 5, No. 1, page 19.

Light Saving Tips

For those using a rotational, mother/clone bud setup, here's a money saving tip. Instead of using halides in the mother room, switch to a fluorescent system. This will save electricity.

Another tip is reduce the number of hours of light in the mother room. To do this the gardener must test the limits of his strain(s) and determine how many hours of light will keep them from flowering.

Remember when you were new at gardening and you couldn't make that first plant flower? Before *Sinse Tips*, kinda' in the '60s and '70s? Well, use this fact to your advantage and you can save money and electricity by fine tuning your mother room to your strains.

Some strains will not flower if even a small amount of light is shed on the plants during their dark period. This means you can run the mother room on 12 hours of fluorescent light, with two or so brief periods of light (there are many timers available with multiple on/off and even half-hour capabilities).

Another possibility is to divide the day into four periods alternating the lights on and off. This may prevent the plants from accumulating enough "short-day" hormone to start flowering.

Personal and private consumption is definitely the watchword for our times, as well as political involvement, joining NORML, and writing to politicians and registering to vote.

Get a straight job, report your minimal income and get a two bedroom apartment with a "farm" as your roommate. Never engage in a sale of herb— use a proxy. You will thus avoid most paranoia. Just enjoy growing your own personal stash.

Even if some of it does help you survive financially, keep the operation small enough that the Man won't notice you or bust too hard. May the Herb heal and protect you.

First printed in Vol. 6, No. 3.

chapter

6

hydroponics

"Thou shalt be like a watered garden, and like a spring of water, whose waters fail not." —Solomon

Hydroponic Systems

A Look at Different Types

Most hydroponic systems attempt to keep the roots of the plant slightly moist with the nutrient solution, but not overly wet. The nutrient solution is made up of all the mineral elements needed by the plants in water soluble form and in the right amounts, dissolved in just the right amount of water. The hydroponic system also must provide the necessary oxygen to the plant roots. The most popular and successful types of hydroponic systems are:

• **Gravity-flow:** The nutrient solution is pumped up, flooding the growing container. The container drains by gravity.

• **Sub-aeration:** The air pump supplies oxygen to the roots of the plant.

• **Wick System:** A porous wick draws nutrients up to the roots.

• **Drip System:** A slow trickle of nutrients and water keeps the growing medium moist.

• **Spray system:** A fine mist keeps the roots and growing medium moist.

  All of these systems can either be large or small, and can be made inexpensively.

  Most plants need a slightly acid nutrient solution, between pH 5.5 and 7. The pH scale varies from one (very acid) to 14 (very alkaline or basic), with 7 being neutral. Most plants also require a temperature of between 60 and 90 degrees for good growth. A temperature controlled greenhouse or grow room provides the fastest growing environment. Soil heating cables warm plant roots, aid in germination and growth. These cables also work well with hydroponic systems.

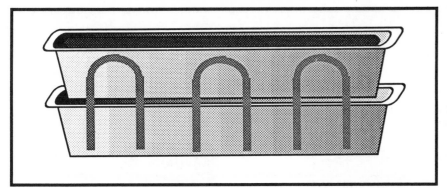

Wick Systems

Special nylon wicks draw nutrients up to the roots. Use one part vermiculite to one part perlite as a growing medium. A good system for leaf crops, starting plants and experments

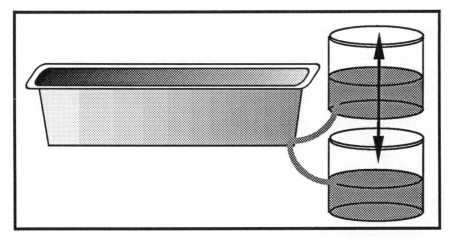

Gravity-flow Systems

Nutrient container is raised to flood gravel growing medium, then lowered to drain.

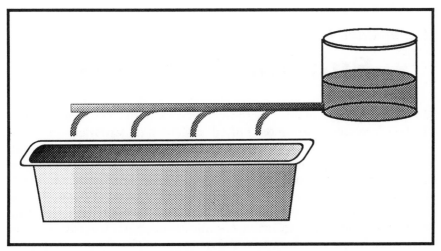

Drip Systems

Small feeder tubes supply constant moisture and nutrients to the plants. Growing media might include vermiculite, sand, perlite, peat moss and alder saw dust.

Nutrient-flow Systems

The pump supplies a constant flow of nutrients across an absorbant layer of material. A one to four inch slope assures proper drainage.

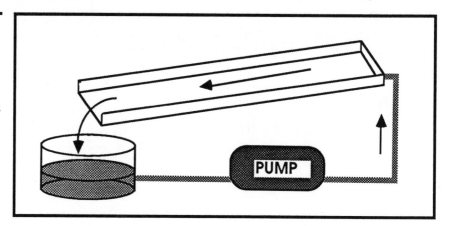

Sub-aerated Systems

An air pump delivers air through the gravel to the roots using an air wand or air stones. The system must be flushed and drained with a syphon tube.

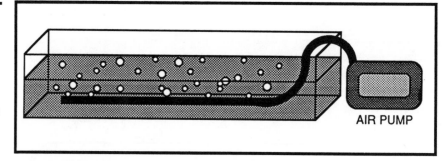

Excerpted from "Hydropnics," Vol. 2, No. 4, page 12. Reprinted from information provided by Eco-Enterprises, Seattle, Wash.

Home Made Hydroponics

Building Your Own

Of the many types of hydroponic systems available, two, gravity-flow and wick systems, are most suited to the small gardener.

For wick systems, two nested trays supported by wood, metal blocks, or inverted three or four inch plastic flower pots are used. The growing medium must be absorbent, sterile and loose for good aeration. A combination of vermiculite, perlite, sand or peat moss is normally used. Nylon wicks are threaded through holes in the bottom of the upper growing container so that they can absorb nutrients in the lower container. The nylon wicks should be looped up through the growing medium every three to six inches and come within one inch of the top surface for even moisture distribution.

The system should be flushed with fresh water and the nutrient solution changed every two to three weeks. Seeds can be started in a wick system using one-half strength nutrient solution. With larger plants, some top watering and feeding may be necessary.

Gravity-flow hydroponic systems using pea gravel or other suitable sterile growing medium are the most popular. Automated with a pump and timer, they usually out perform other types of systems. Most commercial growers use this type of system because of the ease of operation and superior results. The advantages of the gravity-flow systems are good control of nutrient type and amount and easy pH correction. It also offers quick sterilization and flushing/nutrient replenishment, and good aeration of the roots.

After the system is flooded (two to three times daily), atmospheric oxygen is pulled down to the plant's roots as the nutrient drains out of the system. This 100 percent aeration contributes to faster growth. This kind of aeration rarely occurs in soil or potted plants.

To construct a gravity-flow system, the area should first be selected and analyzed. A greenhouse, spare room, basement or attic are all candidates. Water and power should be available. Natural or artificial light should be selected so adequate illumination, between 200 and 1,000 foot candles, is assured. If metal halide or sodium vapor lighting are selected, power requirements should be considered. Floor loading in attics and upper floors should also be considered — gravel is heavy, averaging about 50 pounds per square foot for larger systems. Growing trays and holding tanks can be made from plastic, fiberglass, vinyl-lined wood frame construction, or Epoxy-coated concrete. To determine the amount of gravel needed, water volume of holding tank, nutrient requirements, pump size and total weight of the system, the following example is given for two beds, 10 feet long, three feet wide and nine inches deep:

requirements

Amount of gravel

Multiplying the length times the width times the height of one bed gives a volume of 22.5 cubic feet, or 45 cubic feet for both beds. At 104 pounds per cubic foot of gravel, it will take 4,680 pounds (2.34 tons) to fill both beds.

Water volume

Gravel takes up to 60 percent of the volume of the growing beds, nutrient solution (water) takes up the other 40 percent. We have 45 cubic feet of gravel, so 40 percent of 45 equals 18 cubic feet of nutrient solution. There are 7.48 gallons in one cubic foot of water. By multiplying that amount by 18, we get 134.64 gallons of water or nutrient solution. If we use overflow drains to make the timing cycle less critical, we should have a holding tank volume of approximately 150 gallons.

Nutrient requirements

If two teaspoons of nutrient per gallon are required, we would need approximately 300 teaspoons (two times 150) of nutrient every two weeks. It takes about 100 teaspoons to make a pound of nutrient, so we would need approximately three pounds for every two-week feeding cycle.

Pump size

We want to raise the nutrient level no faster than one inch per minute so the roots will not be disturbed for a distance of three feet from the bottom of the holding tank to the top of the growing tray. Thus, we have to pump 150 gallons in 30 minutes or more. The Little Giant model 1-A pump will pump 168 gallons to the required elevation considering a 50 percent reduction due to friction.

Total system weight

To figure the total weight, simply add the estimated weight of the tanks and equipment; the weight of the gravel; and the weight of the nutrient/water solution, calculated at 8.4 pounds per gallon or 63 pounds per cubic foot.

First printed in Vol. 4, No. 2, page 23. Copyright 1982 by Eco-Enterprises, Seattle, Wash.

Low Cost Equipment:
Junkyard Hydroponics

by Professor T. H. Custer
Of The Homegrowers of Connecticut

When most people speak of "high tech" agricultural methods, an image usually comes to mind of antiseptic laboratories, lab-coated scientists and expensive equipment.

To some degree, this image continues to be enhanced by slick ads portraying expensive, albeit efficient, hydroponic equipment. The fact is, most of this equipment is hybridized; it is a collection of devices and hardware originally manufactured for other purposes.

There are thousands of manufacturers of pumps, hoses, fittings, and molded plastics, which accounts for the variety of designs we see advertised as hydro systems.

Actually, with a little imagination, excellent hydro systems can be constructed from virtually anything handy. Even good growing media can be scrounged, made or obtained very cheaply. I used to work near a Firestone tire recapping plant, and one of their by-products was shredded rubber—tons of it. This stuff is the perfect consistency for a medium, although I haven't tested it for pH, chemical leaching, or stability. But it feels and acts like an artificial peat.

My own choice currently for a medium is crushed brick. After having been in touch with several commercial hydro companies, it seems that either their media is "special and secret," hard to get, usually expensive, and each is always "the best." These companies are not rip-offs, just businesses promoting sales. I applaud their own research, I just don't like paying through the nose for it.

Basically, an ideal medium is heavy enough not to float, shouldn't be organic (should be stable and not decompose), should have sharp or uneven edges to form air pockets, and should be porous enough to soak up nutrients and hold them for awhile.

One hydro company sold volcanic pumice lava, which was excellent but expensive. It is amazing how crushed brick is so close to lava as a medium. Most brick companies toss it out or sell it very cheaply. Mine costs me $4 for 100 pounds. And like all other good media, it is reusable. Other hydro companies are now selling crushed porcelain, which may also be another industrial by-product. I don't think it holds nutrients as well as brick or lava, and like gravel, micro-roots of plants don't grab it as well.

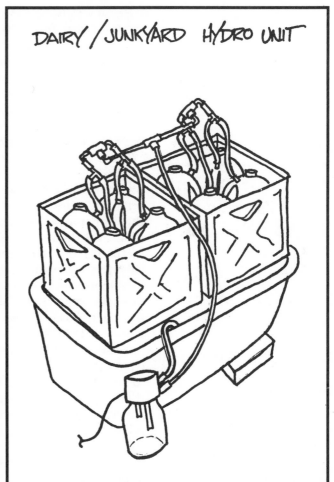

DAIRY / JUNKYARD HYDRO UNIT

When you buy pre-designed hydro units, you are usually "locked-in" to that particular design, and any inherent problems it may have. One problem I ran into was a reluctance on my part to leave male root systems in a community tank, or pull up roots of sick or male plants, thus risking root damage to the remaining plants. The logical answer is a modular system, with one plant per container, each being easy to move around for growth, or remove entirely, if desired.

Being a tight Yankee, it also had to be cheap. Thus was born my "Dairy Hydro" (page 109), using gallon dairy jugs and dairy cartons. In this case, an old baby's plastic bathtub is just the right size drain tank for two cartons, or eight plants. The whole thing only occupies a little more than three square feet of floor space. I'm using a few cinderblocks to help hold up the cartons. The gallon jugs each have a 12-inch tube fitting, and I used my soldering iron to make neat drains. The jugs are filled to the top with brick, and in the top of the jug hole, I stuff enough peat mixture for germination.

There has been much discussion of flush times, and logically, knowing Cannabis' tendency to expire rather quickly when over watered, I don't understand why many growers let their systems flush for hours. Since oxygen prevents wilted or rotted roots, it seems that only moistening the growing medium, then allowing it to drain well, and doing it in the shortest time possible, is the optimum method. I use a combination of two timers on my pump (an old salvaged aquarium diatom filter by the way), a 24-hour timer (in hour increments) and a seconds timer (second increments). My system flushes every three hours for 30 seconds, which is enough to thoroughly wet the medium. A seconds timer isn't that hard to find, with a little looking.

A similar device which does the same job and is easier to find is called a "timing relay." Choose the "delay on operate" type. The "delay on release" type will hold its contacts closed until your hours timer clicks off, then it goes through its delay afterward. This means you would need an interposing relay, which would "pulse" the timing relay to reset it. Since the momentary pulse turns off immediately, the seconds timer kicks in right away, as desired. Using two timers together enables me to set my flushes as far apart as 20 seconds once a day, to 200 seconds once per hour.

Unless you are a chemist, about the only commercial hydro item that must be purchased is your nutrient. Personally, I favor going as organic as possible whenever possible, but at any rate I think experts are needed to properly formulate chemically balanced synthetic nutrients. If they are ever really complete, anyway.

That is the real leading edge in hydros— an organic fertilizer which is complete and yet is as stable as the chemical ones. Organics always seem to give the grower more leeway for error, which is usually sorely needed in amateur operations. It also works well at producing a superior smoke.

First printed in Vol. 5, No. 1, page 6.

Professor Custer's Yankee Ingenuities, No. 1

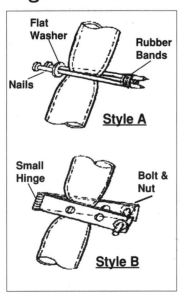

Cheap hydroponic hose clamps to regulate nutrient flow to individual tanks. The tubing used is PVC hydro hose.

Nutrients and Nutrient Management

Doctor Hydro

The sizes and types of hydroponic systems are limitless but they all have one thing in common: the need for a complete and balanced nutrient formula. To be effective for all aspects of plant growth, your nutrient must contain all of the following: nitrogen (N), phosphorus (P), potassium (K), calcium, magnesium, sulfur, iron, copper, manganese, boron, zinc, molybdenum, and cobalt.

Because of federal and state regulations, the nutrients are sold and labeled according to the standard "NPK" three-number designation, such as 8-6-12. To the science of hydroponics these numbers have less of a significance than you might think. What really makes a nutrient formula correct is the balance or ratio, of the different elements to each other, and the solubility of the compounds.

One important ratio is that of potassium to nitrogen which should be at least 1.5 to 1. In other words, if your nutrient contains eight percent nitrogen, it should contain at least one and a half times, or 12 percent, more potassium.

An imbalance in your nutrient solution may cause other types of problems for your plants. The *"Western Fertilizer Handbook,"* Sixth Edition says "a heavy application of phosphorus may induce a zinc deficiency" and "excess iron may induce a manganese deficiency."

Due to the complicated nature of chemical handling and the involved mathematics, I suggest leaving the nutrient mixing to the experts.

After the choice of a quality commercial nutrient is made, the next consideration will be controlling the solution. Always use the nutrients according to the manufacturer's suggested dosage, usually one or two teaspoons per gallon. The freshly mixed solution should contain between 1,300 and 1,500 parts per million (ppm) of total dissolved solids (DS). These are the scientifically correct terms for the measurement of the actual strength of your nutrient and you should become familiar with them.

Most suppliers of home hydroponic systems recommend that you maintain the solution level in your system by adding tap water. Then every two or three weeks they tell you to change the entire solution. Although this method is easy, it is not correct.

The nutrient capacity of most home systems is too small to be

nutrient monitoring

replenished with only tap water. Every time your system feeds the plants, roots are removing the elements needed to support growth. As the plants grow and mature, they can deplete your nutrient in a matter of days.

I am sure many gardeners have found it necessary to change nutrient every three or four days to sustain budding; some have probably even tried changing formulas. Both of these methods have been widely used with varying degrees of success and failure. If, however, you are serious about hydroponics, and really do want to enjoy twice the yield as soil growers, you must take one more simple step ahead in technology. You should purchase any one of a number of nutrient testing devices and start monitoring your nutrient solution.

This equipment will allow you to maintain the strength of your solution at the recommended 1,300 to 1,600 ppm. All serious hydroponic suppliers are using this type of equipment and should have it available for resale. These devices range in price from $1,000 for a complete portable testing laboratory, to $300 for a dissolved solids meter that instantly reads in ppm, all the way down to a simple phosphorus tester that sells for around $50. Any of this test equipment will enable you to accurately maintain the strength of your solution by adding small amounts of nutrient along with tap water every day or two.

You will still need to change the entire solution every two or three weeks to remove any excess plant wastes and allow you to keep your storage tank clean. It is also a good idea to rinse your growing medium thoroughly every time you change nutrient. This one simple step ahead in the science of growing will assure better results in every size and type of hydroponic system. If your current supplier of hydroponics can't help you find this equipment, locate one who will.

Always use hydroponic nutrient at a pH of 6 to 6.4 and the solution temperature at feeding time must be between 70 and 80 degrees.

ask doctor hydro

Dear Dr. Hydro:
I plan to build my own hydroponic garden and would like to know how much nutrient storage I should have for 25 plants.
    L.F.

Dear L.F.
In a home hydroponic system, regardless of size or type, you should have a minimum of two gallons of nutrient storage for each plant. The bigger the storage tank, the easier the pH and parts per million (ppm) of dissolved solids will be to control. I might also suggest you read the

book *"Home Hydroponics and How To Do It"* by Lem Jones before you start your project. Mr. Jones has many designs and tips on building your own system.

Dear Dr. Hydro:

I have heard that you can use baking soda or vinegar for adjusting the pH of the nutrient solution. Are these OK or should I use the special products available for pH control?

Richard

Dear Richard

Baking soda is great for cookies and cakes, and vinegar when mixed with a little salt is perfect for cleaning copper kettles. In the interest of purity, however, only diluted solutions of nitric or phosphoric acid should be used to lower the pH of hydroponic nutrient.

Potassium hydroxide is the standard of the industry for raising the pH. The reason these are used is because they only add nutrient elements back into the solution. Nitric acid adds calcium nitrate and CO_2. Potassium hydroxide adds potassium, oxygen and hydrogen.

First printed in Vol. 5, No. 3, Summer 1985, page 42.

The High Tech Revolution in Hydroponics

by Doctor Hydro

There is little doubt that hydroponic gardening, especially in controlled environments, indoors or in greenhouses, has the ability to provide much larger yields and better quality than soil-grown crops.

A well designed and properly maintained hydroponic system will provide the grower with years of low-cost high performance gardening. The sizes and types of these systems are numerous and most are readily available. Many suppliers can also provide you with pumps, timers, tubing, fittings, etc. to build your own garden.

So when it comes time to start or improve your indoor or outdoor gardening project the question is not "do I use dirt or hydroponics?"; it is "do I build or buy my hydroponic system?" The following is a

buying a system

discussion of the advantages and disadvantages of both.

The Advantages

• Most systems are sold complete with the possible exception of the growing medium, although some systems even come with medium.

• The system has already been tested and the manufacturer should have all the problems worked out.

• They are provided with set-up instructions and usually have some tips on gardening.

• Most suppliers can furnish you with the commercial type nutrients and pH controls.

• Most quality constructed systems should last for many years.

• The manufacturer will provide you with technical support and replacement parts if necessary.

• The odds of crop failure due to system related problems are reduced.

The Disadvantage

• Cost! Depending on the size of the system, they can be fairly expensive.

Building your own hydroponic system should not be attempted until some research is done. I highly recommend reading one of the books listed at the conclusion of this article.

building your own

The Advantages

• Cost. Depending on your ability to buy or acquire materials the cost of hydroponics may be reduced.

• Your system can be designed to make the most of the growing area you have.

• Different types of systems or growing media can be used to see which suits your application the best.

The Disadvantages

• You may have to go to several different suppliers to find all the material you need.

• Much trial and error will be required to get the system running smoothly.

• The odds of crop failure due to a system related problem are increased.

• Your design may overlook some of the standards that have been established.

some basic tips

The following are some basic tips for successful hydroponic gardening:

• Provide a complete plant food manufactured for use specifically in hydroponics. Organic mixes and water soluble soil fertilizers are not acceptable.

• Make sure your nutrient solution is at 70 to 80 degrees when your

plants are fed.
• Make sure your nutrient solution is at a pH of 5.8 to 6.5 when your plants are fed.
• Change your entire nutrient solution every two weeks.
• Flush your plants thoroughly with tap water at every nutrient change.
• Don't use any metal in the construction of your system. It should be 100 percent plastic.
• Don't use a screen over your drain outlets in your growing trays. A handful of 3/4-inch rocks over the outlet should keep it from clogging. The best idea is to keep the entire drain and fittings exposed for easy cleaning.
• Don't make your system too complicated. The more timers, pumps, hoses, fittings, etc. that you use the more chances of leaks and failures.
• Don't try to grow in too small of a container. Most mature large plants will need approximately 3/4 of a cubic foot of growing medium. This is the equivalent of a five-gallon bucket for each plant.

For the do it yourselfer:
Home Hydroponics and How To Do It, By Lem Jones
Beginners Guide To Hydroponics, By James Douglas.
For the more advanced gardener:
Hydroponic Food Production, By Dr. Howard Resh.

First printed in Vol. 6, No. 1, page 47.

recommended reading

Primary Plant Nutrients

by Doctor Hydro
Nitrogen is a key element affecting plant growth and crop yields. It is absorbed by plants primarily in the nitrate form (NO_3) and is used by plants to synthesize amino acids and form proteins. It is also required by plants for other vital compounds such as chlorophyll and enzymes. Too much nitrogen will produce lush plants with dark green foliage with few blossoms and poor fruit set. Nitrogen is a mobile element in plants which means any deficiency symptoms will appear first on the older leaves.

Nitrogen deficiency symptoms include:
• Slow growth and stunted plants.

• Foliage becomes yellow (chlorotic)
• "Firing" of tips and margins of leaves

phosphorous

Phosphorous stimulates early growth and root formation and is absorbed by plants as PO_4. It is used by plants to form nucleic acids, DNA and RNA, and is very important to the plant's energy transport system. It can hasten maturity and promote seed production. Phosphorous is also a mobile element and is greatly affected by temperature. Too much phosphorous will interfere with the normal function of other elements such as iron, manganese, and zinc.

Phosphorous deficiency symptoms include:
• Slow growth with thin stems and small leaves
• Purplish coloration of foliage on some plants
• Dark green coloring with the tips of the leaves dying
• Delayed maturity with poor fruit production

potassium

Potassium is taken up by plants in the form of potassium ions (K+) and tends to remain in ionic form within the cells and tissue. It is essential for translocation of sugars and for starch formation. High potassium levels are required for protein synthesis and fruit production. It will increase the size and quality of the harvest and helps make plants more resistant to disease. Potassium is another mobile element in plants. Too much of it can induce a calcium or magnesium deficiency.

Potassium deficiency symptoms include:
• Older leaves develop marginal burning
• Weak stalks
• Slow growth
• Forward curling of leaves

secondary plant nutrients

Calcium

Calcium is absorbed by plants as the calcium ion (Ca++). It is essential for the formation and structure of cells. Calcium is nonmobile in plants which means that any signs of deficiency occur first in the newer leaves.

Calcium deficiency symptoms include:
• Shoot tips yellow and die back
• Abnormal dark green foliage
• New leaves distorted
• Premature shedding of blossoms and buds
• Root tips die and acquire black spots

Magnesium

Magnesium is used by plants in the form of the magnesium ion

(Mg++). It is contained in the chlorophyll molecule which means it is essential for photosynthesis. It is also required for activation of many enzymes involved in the growth process.

Magnesium deficiency symptoms include:
• Yellowing of older leaves
• Withering of leaves
• Upward curling of leaves along margins

Sulphur

Sulphur is used by plants as the sulfate ion (SO_4). It may also be absorbed from the air. Sulphur is a constituent of amino acids which means it is essential for protein synthesis. It is also present in the oil compounds that are responsible for the characteristic odor of plants. The deficiencies appear similar to nitrogen except that the symptoms appear in the new leaves.

Sulphur deficiency symptoms include:
• New leaves appear light green to yellowish
• Yellowing of older leaves
• Small spindly plants
• Retarded growth and delayed maturity

micronutrients

Iron

Iron is required by plants for chlorophyll synthesis. It activates biochemical processes such as respiration, photosynthesis and nitrogen fixing. Iron can easily combine with other elements and should be provided in a chelated form for hydroponic nutrient solutions.

Iron deficiency symptoms include:
• Yellowing between the veins of newer leaves
• In severe cases, death of entire limbs may occur

Manganese

Manganese serves as an activator for enzymes and aids iron in forming chlorophyll. It also helps produce oxygen from water during photosynthesis.

Manganese deficiency symptoms include:
• Yellowing between the veins of leaves near the tip of the plant
• leaves may turn brown and drop off

Boron

Boron is used to regulate the metabolism of carbohydrates in plants. It is a non-mobile element and a small but continuous supply is required at all growing points of the plant.

Boron deficiency symptoms include:
• Dieback of shoots and root tips
• Young leaves appear thick and curled

• Reduced flowering

Molybdenum

Molybdenum is required by plants for the utilization of nitrogen. Plants cannot transform nitrate nitrogen into amino acids without it.

Molybdenum deficiency symptoms include:

• Yellowing of older leaves moving into newer leaves
• Stunted plants
• Some cupping or rolling of leaves

Copper

Copper is an activator of several enzymes and also plays a role in vitamin A production. A deficiency interferes with protein production.

Copper deficiency symptoms include:

• Stunted growth
• Poor pigmentation
• Wilting and eventual death of leaf tips

other factors

The hobby gardener must remember that these symptoms were discovered under ideal conditions. There are many other simpler factors which affect plant growth. These other factors include:

• **Ventilation** is probably the most ovelooked problem in controlled environment growing. Plants absorb nutrients when the water in which the nutrients are dissolved is respirated (evaporated) from the leaves. The better the ventilation, the higher the respiration rate is and therefore the rate of nutrient uptake is also higher.

Remember that ventilation means changing the air, not just blowing it around the grow room. You need to have an equal amount of fresh air blowing in as you have used air blowing out. The average commercial greenhouse can completely change the total volume of air every minute. This may or may not be possible in an indoor grow room.

• **Nutrient solution pH** should be maintained in the range of 5.8 to 6.5. Too high or too low of a pH value in the solution (or in soil for that matter) can restrict nutrient uptake.

• **Temperature** of nutrient solution should be in the range of 70 to 80 degrees at feeding time. Many nutrient elements, most notably nitrogen and phosphorous, are greatly affected by temperature and may not be available at all if the nutrient is too cold.

• **Light** — the higher the light level, the bigger the harvest.

what to do

This brings us to the final question. What do I do if I notice a problem with my plants?

If you are fortunate enough to already be growing in hydroponics, the answer is quite simple. Drain all the nutrient from your system and rinse the growing medium thoroughly with tap water at the correct pH. Mix a new batch of nutrient (be sure the nutrient you are using contains all the elements which were discussed above), correct the pH and restart the system.

Always use a high quality, proven hydroponic nutrient formula.

If you are still growing in soil, you are on your own!

First printed in Vol. 6, No. 2, page 73.

Rockwool
The Medium of the Future

Rockwool is an inorganic, stable and water absorbing growing substrate. Rockwool consists of various types or rocks, primarily diabes, melted at a temperature of 2,500 degrees. The high temperature of the manufacturing process results in a growing substrate which is sterile, free of organic matter such as weed seeds, hidden diseases and other harmful components.

Rockwool has generally the same chemical composition as most of the soil minerals. But these are combined in a form which is not available to plants. This means the growing substrate is inactive, which is the main advantage of rockwool. All fertilizers must be added to the irrigation water enabling an exact control of the culture. This ensures equal conditions for the plants, thus opening up possibilities of higher and earlier yields, in addition to better quality, labor savings and lower energy costs.

Rockwool is available in two forms:
• The propagation block
• The growing slab

In both types, there are all kinds of dimensions and sizes available, specially designed for each type of crop.

The form most frequently used in marijuana cultivation is a three-inch-square block. It can be used to plant pre-germinated seeds and to make clone cuttings. Germinate the seeds between wet paper towels or tissue.

Wet the rockwool blocks by putting them under water where they will get soaked automatically. Do not add nutrient to the water. Make

the propagation block

a hole in the block of such size so the germinated seed fits in it exactly. After a couple of days, a small plantlet should appear.

Water the blocks with a very weak (13 to 12 strength) fertilizer solution. Using a very weak fertilizer solution after germination is important. The newly germinated seed cannot endure a full-strength fertilizer solution. The roots and the whole plantlet which have grown after germination are very weak for the first couple of weeks of its existence.

After two weeks of growth, the nutrient solution can be raised to 23 strength. After three weeks the fertilizer can be applied at the recommended full strength.

The rockwool block should remain saturated during the entire propagation period. Regular checking, especially during the second and third weeks is necessary. Never let the block dry out. Water from above until a considerable amount of water runs from the bottom of the block. The bottom of the blocks should never be sitting in a pool of nutrient solution. The roots receive insufficient oxygen, becoming brown and die off within a few days. A sloping surface tightly covered with plastic and some perlite granules placed underneath each block prevents trouble.

After the second week, a number of roots will be visible under the block. The more white the roots are, the better their quality. Be careful with the blocks, do not pick them up time and again, but leave them standing quietly.

After three weeks, the propagation period is over. You can then continue growing in soil, rockwool or your own hydroponic system.

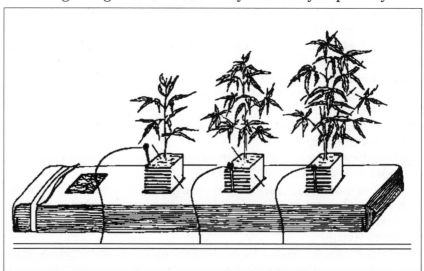

In water environments where light can penetrate, the growth of algae can be expected. It can occur during propagation where the blocks become covered with a greasy, dark-green substance. Do not panic, this is algae. Just like plants, algae contain chlorophyll granules. By day, oxygen is produced during photosynthesis, so this poses no problem.

It is a different case when, for whatever reason, wholesale dying off of algae occurs. This destruction consumes a lot of oxygen, creating adverse consequences for the plantlet in the rockwool block. Growth of algae can be prevented by covering the block with a piece of black plastic which is impervious to light. Cut a hole in it to make room for the stem. If you continue growing on rockwool and the plants become so big that they inhibit almost any light falling on the block, the piece of plastic can be removed.

After the propagation period, the plant has become so big that it is ready to be transplanted. In rockwool this is extemely simple and there is absolutely no transplant shock. Place the propagation block on a bigger, water soaked piece of rockwool, the so called "rockwool slab." The roots grow from the propagation block into the slab. Attach the propagation block to the slab with a little wooden stick. If you don't do this, the plants can become top-heavy and topple over.

The slab is used in all kinds of special dimensions for a diverse selection of crops. For the marijuana crop, the dimensions are not very important. It just depends on what system you want to use— from a few to many plants per square foot. With many plants per square foot, hence smaller sized plants, a slab with a volume of one gallon (231 cubic inches) suffices. With bigger plants, a bigger slab is recommended. From a physiological point of view, it does not make any difference whether a big or a small slab is used. Since rockwool has an excellent oxygen/water ratio the possibilities for first-rate care of the roots is no problem.

The smaller the slab, the greater risk of damage by mistakes. If the irrigation fails for only one day, you can run into serious trouble. It is therefore wise to choose a slab with a volume of at least one gallon.

Before the propagation block can be placed on the slab, the slab has to be filled with a nutrient solution. The slabs are pre-wrapped in a white plastic bag. The bag is folded in such a way so that it is a

algae growth

Rockwool slab with drip emitters installed.

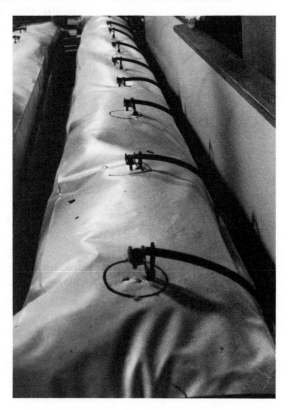

water tight jacket with the rockwool slab in it. These are available at most indoor grow shops. It is very important that the bag is watertight. If this is not the case, you would not be able to fill the bag entirely to the top with nutrient solution. The slab would then remain dry in some places.

Every spot which remains dry does not count for the volume of the slab. If the slab remains half dry when you fill it, the volume in which the roots can grow is then also immediately halved. From the top of the packet (bag plus slab), a square piece of plastic precisely the size of the bottom of the block is cut away exactly in the middle. Now from the top, the slab can be filled with nutrient solution. Pour the nutrient solution into the slab so that it almost brims over and there are no more dry spots in it. Place the block with the plant on it, fixing it in place with a wooden spike.

The roots begin to grow from the block into the slab. After three or four days, the plantlets stand fixed on the slab. During the first few days no nutrient solution needs to be added. After the fifth day you may carefully irrigate a bit. After eight days, the time has come to drain the slab. In each corner of the slab, about 1/4 inch above the bottom, a small cut is made. Now the bag has drainage holes in each of the corners. When nutrient solution is poured into the slab, after a few moments excess nutrient solution drains from the corners, depending on the degree of saturation of the slab. Drainage is extremely important.

leaching

The essence of growing on rockwool is that every time irrigation is done, it should be done to such a degree that the slab becomes filled to overflowing with the excess nutrient solution draining out the four small holes in the corner of the bag. This drainage is called leaching.

The beautiful thing about growing in rockwool is that every plant has its own container. It is a cheap container: a piece of rockwool in a plastic bag. Up until the end of the cropping period, the slabs remain transportable. You can shift and remove as much as you like. The slabs are light and easy to lift.

A disadvantage of many other hydroponic systems is that often more than one plant is placed in one container. The plants are then no longer transportable and must remain where they are. Cultivation with seeds may cause a problem, because 50 percent of the plants turn out to be male. Using only female clones is recommended.

Another possibility is to place more than one plant on one slab. You can do this when you work with cuttings. You know beforehand that the plants with which you start are the same sex as those with which you will finish. So you can give all plants a place to grow and don't have to shift them around anymore. You can then take, for example, a slab of 3 1/2 feet, wrap it in a bag, make four holes at regular distances on top of the bag and place four plants on it. Four little cuts in the corners and you have a container for four plants. Never use a slab that is longer than 3 1/2 feet.

Growing on rockwool can be divided into two main types:
• Drainage system
• Recirculation system

In brief it comes down to the following: the nutrient solution is brought into the slab by means of a pump and a trickle irrigation system or simply by hand.

Every time you irrigate you introduce so much nutrient solution into the slab so that 30 percent of the volume runs off as waste through the small drainage holes. This is especially used in large grow rooms. Slightly sloping plastic gutters are located throughout the entire greenhouse or grow room.

These gutters are of disposable quality. The slabs are placed in the gutter. Beside the gutter or in the gutter beside the slab there is a trickle irrigation spaghetti tube branching to every slab. Four times per day the nutrient solution is trickled into the slabs from a reservoir via the trickle irrigation system. Trickling takes place so that 30 percent is drained as waste, via the gutter along the slabs, to the ditch or the outlet.

The drainage system is not the most efficient system to use in a grow room.

The nutrient solution is introduced into the slabs by means of a pump and a trickle irrigation system four times per day. If done by hand, it is done twice a day. An overdosage of 30 percent is again applied. However, the excess nutrient solution does not run out as waste into a ditch or outlet, but runs back to the reservoir from which it was pumped.

The recirculation system is best suited for the grow room.

The recirculation system can be applied in many different ways. The two most important methods are:
• Gutters
• Ready-made systems

We have used a system with gutters for years with great success. The gutters are slightly sloping to facilitate the drain water running back to the nutrient reservoir.

The slope of the gutters should not be greater than two percent because the liquid level in the slab will have the same slope which will result in dry spots in the slabs.

The nutrient reservoir should be as tight as possible. This will prevent the evaporation of water from the nutrient solution and

the drainage system

the recirculation system

gutters

hence fluctuations in the nutrient concentration level.

This system does not necessarily involve the use of a pump and trickle irrigation system. If you do use a trickle irrigation system, place the nozzle onto the block. After eight days, place the nozzle beside the block in the slab.

It is important to arrange the drip nozzle so that the nutrient solution goes directly into the block. This way the upper side of the block remains dry, preventing the formation of fungi or algae. It is possible to scoop the nutrient solution from the reservoir manually with the aid of a watering can, and pour it into the slab. You should do this twice a day. If the plantlets' size is not yet of any significance, irrigating once a day may suffice.

Using a measuring jug, pour at least a half a gallon of nutrient solution onto the rockwool slab. Pull the elastic away from the cube. Pour the nutrient solution through the opening in the slab. Continue pouring the solution onto the rockwool until a fair amount of the liquid returns via the cuts in the slab and the holes in the upper tray, draining into the lower tray. At this point you can now leach. An ideal leaching percentage is 30 percent.

Judge the amount for yourself.

The logical continuation is to automate the irrigtion system. Most existing American grow room hydroculture systems can achieve good results with some modifications.

Instead of systems filled with loose hydroculture media, a system could be used with fixed compartments in which a certain size rockwool slab fits exactly.

Here in Holland, we are both waiting and looking forward with great excitement for a company to be the first to put a ready-made rockwool system on the market.

Rockwool has a great future, you can be assured of that fact. Within a few years, rockwool will be an established part of the assortment of products in all the good, progressive indoor grow shops.

If you want to develop a system for yourself that is suitable for use with rockwool, make sure the whole system is manufactured solely from high grade plastic. Any small item made of copper, or any other metal for that matter, will start to corrode when it comes in contact with the nutrient solution. This corroded metal/nutrient solution will be taken up by the plants during feeding and will poison them.

This corrosion occurs because the nutrient solution contains acids. All metals have an inherent tendency to dissolve in acids. If you use a pump which you will place in the nutrient solution reservoir, make sure all parts on the pump are made out of a plastic material. A single metal screw or rivet makes a pump unsuitable for use in a nutrient reservoir.

The above article was reprinted with the permission of The Super Sativa Seed Club, Amsterdam, Holland. It was first printed in Vol. 6, No. 2, page 57.

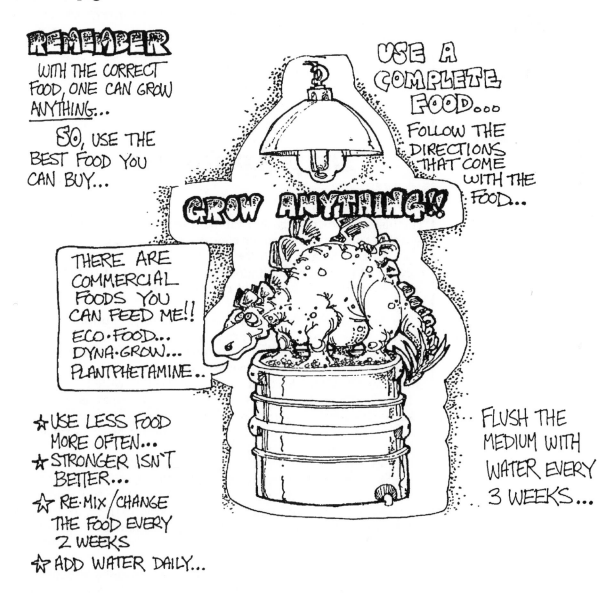

chapter

7

irrigation

Drip Applications

by Tom Alexander

The history of drip irrigation can be traced back to the early Roman aqueduct period when broken clay pipe distributed water along plant rows. But it was not until the formation of modern Israel that the concept of placing a small amount of water only at the root zones, when needed, and at an exact rate began to be developed commercially.

The Israelis were faced with inadequate water supply, often of a saline nature, and a lack of prime, agricultural land. They laid out lines of perforated polyethylene tubing. These early systems reveled a number of problems. Plants close to the water source received too much water, while plants at the end of the line wilted.

Despite the early problems, hundreds of thousands of acres of money-producing crops are now being irrigated exclusively by drip. Many commercial ornamental and greenhouse growers raise their plants with drip/trickle systems.

The experience gained through agricultural use now makes it possible to better irrigate trees, shrubs, flower and vegetable beds, ground cover, potted and hanging plants. Drip is found in an increasing number of homes, highway median strips, and freeway landscaping. The use of drip systems has dramatically increased as the public has been faced with increased scarcity and rising water costs.

The objective of drip irrigation is to continually provide even moisture to just the plant's root zone. Overhead sprinklers saturate entire areas followed by a drying out period. They are designed for lawns that need only shallow watering. Slow applications over long periods are required to get the deep water penetration required for deep-rooted vegetation.

Drip irrigation promotes growth and increases crop yields. It also improves water penetration without run off or puddling. Water will spread laterally, too. Normally, a pear shaped area is moistened three feet at the surface of the soil widening to six feet and to a depth of four or more feet, in average soils.

Valuable water is saved because of reduced evaporation and coverage of root zones only. Energy is saved because less water is pumped. Labor savings results from less weed maintenance, elimination of hand watering and simple installation.

A fertilizer injector can be added to the system which adds the proper diluted form of liquid fertilizers right in the root zone.

Drip irrigation promotes better growth on slopes. Water sprayed from overhead sprinklers usually runs off faster than it can penetrate the soil.

A drip system can be buried or left on the surface. When buried, it prevents vandalism and is not conspicuous in the woods. It is suited for potted plants not normally covered by sprinkler systems.

Using a drip system reduces mildew on flowers because it does not wet foliage.

It is simple to automate a system using soil potentiometers, automatic valves or new moisture sensing emitters. There are over 50 different emitters on the market made by both domestic and foreign manufacturers. They can be divided into four types: fancy, protected holes in the line; the pressure-loss type; pressure compensating; and automatic moisture sensing.

emitter types

The first usually provides some guard to discourage bugs from causing clogging. They require careful attention to tube sizing, restrictors or flow control valves to make them emit equal amounts of water for the full length of the run. The pressure-loss type directs water through a maze that causes the water to lose its pressure and emit as drops. Both of these classes are more subject to clogging due to their fixed orifice size and inability to automatically flush. Elevation and pressure variances cause different flow rates. While generally lower in price, maintenance can be expensive with these systems.

Pressure compensating emitters, act like a tiny valve. They emit a constant drip of water that varies little with changes of pressure between 15 and 45 pounds per square inch (PSI). These emitters can maintain low, even pressure for the entire length of the tubing even while dripping. This simplifies hydraulic engineering problems of tube sizing, pressure losses and elevation differences under 50 feet.

The emitter closest to the water source has approximately the same flow rate as one 500 feet down the line. It automatically flushes through a variable sized orifice every time the system is turned on or off. It can be manually flushed at any time or taken apart and cleaned. The standard emitter can be buried because it will not siphon dirt back into the line. A shrub nut adapter is available to fit one-half IPS risers.

tubing

Drip systems have very low gallonage and pressure requirements, thus permitting the use of lower priced tubing. The use of plyethylene and, in some cases, polybutelyne, offers many advantages, emitters can snap-in, saving the cost of tees and risers. The tubing is flexible enough to make a turn with a radius of 30 inches without special tools, fittings or solvent weld cement.

A word of caution. Use only virgin, specially formulated tubing for drip use. One-half-inch diameter pipe (.580 inside diameter by .704 outside diameter) works best.

PVC pipe is usually used for supply lines. One-half-inch PVC pipe should not flow more than seven gallons per minute (GPM); 3/4-inch at 12 GPM; and 1-inch at 30 GPM. Many small installations can operate directly from 1/2-inch poly tubing that flows at five GPM. Because of pressure loss, a safe rule is to use no more than 200 gallons per hour (GPH) on a 500-foot run of 1/2-inch tubing, or 300

typical configuration

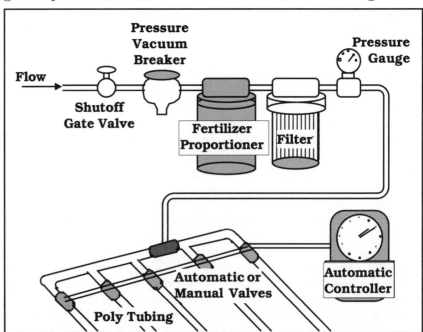

GPH on 750-foot runs of 3/4-inch tubing. If your total system requires more GPH than can be run through 1/2-inch or 3/4-inch poly tubing, then divide your system by using multiple valves off of the PVC supply line.

Use a gate valve to be able to shut off the entire system. Local codes may require a backflow prevention device. With a pressure vacuum breaker you can have separate valves downstream. If you use atmospheric vacuum breakers they will have to be after each line valve. Either of these has to be 12 inches higher than all piping downstream. Otherwise, you will have to use a reduced pressure backflow preventer.

Each line should have a manual or automatic valve. Seriously consider automating the system because good drip practices require daily, or at least every other day, watering to achieve even soil moisture.

You will have to select a sprinkler controller with dual programming, one that will give you the time variances for running some valves for minutes only on different days for turf and for hours every day for drip. If you don't use such a controller, you will need a separate controller for the drip system. I recommend a single station (valve) controller that offers a wide variety of hours and days of operation. If more stations are required, there are other models for up to 22 stations.

Drip systems offer the most efficient method of fertilizing. By installing a proportioner in the line, nutrients can be injected into the root zone. Fertilizer will be mixed proportionately with the water.

This can be a simple hose washer screen inserted into a garden hose swivel for single runs of up to 500 feet when using potable water as a source. For areas up to an acre or when using non-potable water, use the larger cartridge type with disposable filters or permanent stainless steel screens. Larger installations with a potable water supply should use filters that are sized from 3/4 to 6 inches to handle one to 500 GPM. Larger installations using non-potable water should use sand and screen filters.

Drip systems operate under low pressures of 15 to 45 PSI. Preset regulators are available that reduce 175 PSI or lower pressures down to 20 or 30 PSI plus or minus 10 percent for flows of two to 16 GPM. A low-flow regulator is for flows of .10 to eight GPM. A combined valve and adjustable pressure regulator can simplify installation. This will allow exact pressures desired. It is equipped with a test valve for mounting a test gauge.

Adapters are available to tie into hose thread, IPS thread, and PVC slip sockets while the other end accepts a compression fitting that

fertilization

slips over 1/2-inch or 3/4-inch poly tubing. Polybutylene tubing requires special fittings. Each end of the line should have an end plug with either an unscrewing cap or an automatic drain plug so that lines can be flushed.

Run flexible poly tubing within drip line of each plant. Plants 10 feet or higher should be looped by tubing to more evenly spaced emitters. Spaghetti tubing may be inserted into the 1/2-inch or 3/4-inch poly lines for laterals not to exceed 10 feet. An emitter is then pushed into the end of it.

operation

After assembling the system on the soil surface, open all end caps. Set pressure regulator to "off" if it is adjustable. Turn on water. Gradually increase water to operating pressure and thoroughly flush all lines. Turn off and secure end caps. Repressurize and examine every emitter to be sure none are clogged from dirt in the line. Manually flush emitters if necessary.

Operate your system at the lowest pressure (15 to 30 PSI) that your elevation differences will allow. It takes 43 pounds to raise water 100 feet in elevation. If you have a 30-PSI preset regulator, you can push water about 70 feet in elevation. To irrigate at the top of a 70-foot hill, you will need an additional 12 PSI for a total of 42 PSI. When drip lines go down hills, they pick up pressure. Set the pressure low when feeding from the top of a hill. Running drip lines level on the sides of hills avoids the need for pressure adjustments.

The drip lines may be left on the surface or buried. When buried, it is best to place the emitter about three inches under the surface. The visible wet spot insures that the emitter is operating. Standard emitters can have spaghetti tubing added to the one side that ports. This can then be raised to three inches above the surface and be sealed with a drain cap to prevent bugs or dirt from entering and staked to maintain its postion.

First printed in Vol. 2, No. 2, page 25.

Water Conservation

by Ed Rosenthal

Growers east of the Mississippi rarely need to water their plants once they are established. The reason is twofold; the ground water table is much higher in the East and plants do not have to search far before they hit moisture. In addition, there is usually no drought during the summer. Farmers in the East expect their gardens to be irrigated naturally.

The situation in most parts of the West is different. The ground water level is so much lower that plants can not reach the levels where there is ambient moisture. Many parts of the West experience a drought between late spring and autumn. In these areas grasses and many other plants brown out by June or July as a result of the lack of water. This is a good guide as to whether marijuana will need to be irrigated.

Another way of determining the need to irrigate a marijuana garden is whether corn grown in fields is given any water. If farmers usually irrigate, then the marijuana garden will also need to be watered.

Water delivery is a sexy subject. Pumps, piping and the plumbing associated with them makes good copy. Growers spend their time seeing how they can get enough water to their gardens. Since marijuana gardens are surreptitious affairs, the delivery method must be discrete. Farmers have used their resourcefulness to develop ingenious systems using gas and battery powered pumps, hydraulic ram pumps, siphons, gravity and human power to move water.

Water delivery is only one half of the water equation, though. The other half is water use or water consumption. The less water used, the less that has to be pumped. Rather than just investigating methods of delivering water, the wise farmer also tries to find ways of conserving the precious liquid.

More water is wasted because of inefficient agricultural practices than for any other reason in the United States. The supreme example of this are the giant center-pivot irrigation sprayers agribusiness uses to water fields in the West. Before the water actually hits the plants or the soil, a good percentage of it is lost to the atmosphere, some of the water is delivered between

waterflow control in soil

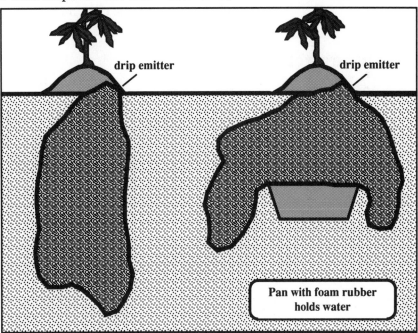

drip emitter

drip emitter

Pan with foam rubber holds water

the rows and to parts of the field which are not supporting any crop, just weeds. The crop plants receive only a small percentage of the water delivered to the field. The plants actually use only a fraction of this water, too. Some of the water is lost to the atmosphere from the ground and another part of it washes down into the soil.

The West is continually in a "water crisis." If sane agricultural water conservation practices were used, water consumption could be reduced by at least a third. Luckily, marijuana farmers are not restricted to using conventional practices and are free to develop practical methods of water conservation.

Growers using planting holes can decrease water use 50 percent by placing an impermeable shield such as a piece of plastic or wood at the bottom of the planting hole. Forcing the water to move laterally increases the amount of time it is in contact with the roots. Growers planting in areas where adobe, pastiche or other impermeable layers are close to the surface may have nature's own version of this.

There are other versions of this simple technique. Instead of placing material only at the bottom of the hole, plastic sheeting is wrapped along the lower sides of the planting hole. An oil drip pan tray or dish pan tray can be used. The space can be filled with perlite, vermiculite sponge rock, foam rubber, or any low-mass material. The space serves as a reservoir. When the hole is irrigated, the tray holds the water until it is drawn up by the soil. One grower covered trays

wick system

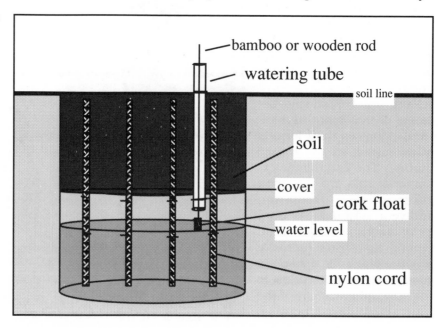

bamboo or wooden rod
watering tube
soil line
soil
cover
cork float
water level
nylon cord

with a wooden plank that allowed water in the sides. She ran nylon cord to the upper regions of the hole so that it acted as a wick.

A few years ago I mentioned that a backyard gardener punched pinholes in a one gallon jug and filled the jug periodically to supply his plants with drip irrigation. Last year a grower adapted this technique. He placed the jugs in a planting hole with a tube placed at the soil surface to refill. The farmer filled the jugs quickly using a hose and funnel connected to a portable water tank inside his van.

Some soils hold water poorly. They drain quickly, wasting water. One grower I know planted in a sandy silt soil near a river. The soil had very little organic matter to hold moisture. He was forced to run a pump 12 hours a day during the hottest part of the season. The plants probably used less than five percent of the water. The rest drained to ground water.

The soil did not have to be prepared or turned, so the farmer added only water soluble nutrients. Had he prepared the soil, he could have added organic matter such as compost and a starch called "Terra Sorb" which holds about 100 times its weight in water ("Agrosoke" is a similar product that is currently available). This material looks something like whole-wheat flour when it is dry. When it comes into contact with water it swells up as it absorbs the liquid. As the surrounding material dries, the particles release the water.

Water applied at the soil surface evaporates at a high rate, especially on sunny days. The reason for this is that the soil has millions of tiny peaks and valleys that create a large total surface area in contact with air. If the area in contact with the air and light remains dry, no moisture will be lost. As much as 10 to 15 percent of the water normally used can be saved by watering the plant below the surface. No elaborate gizmos are needed. Simply place the drip irrigation emitter a few inches below the surface of the soil or cover it with a mulch such as wood chips or bark.

Two years ago, I met a grower from Arizona who claimed that he grew right in the desert. He said that he conserved water with an underground delivery system using drip emitters that he "punched" into the soil using a steel pipe. He covered all lines to avoid infrared detection. He claimed another advantage to this method. Usually the roots are near the surface of the soil. Temperatures vary quite a bit at the soil surface due to the heating of the sun and the 30-degree drop in ambient air temperatures each evening. Further down, the temperatures remain more even and in general the environment is less harsh. Since the roots follow the trail to water, the roots were less exposed to the vagaries of the environment.

In times of drought, or when plants are being transplanted, the

soils

plants' water requirements may be lowered by using "WiltPruf" (for another opinion on this product, see "A Closer Look at Spider Mites," p.84) which is available at many nurseries or wholesale garden supply warehouses. The product comes in both an aerosol can and as a mixed concentrate. When it is sprayed on the leaves, it forms a film as it dries which partially blocks the pores so that the plant transpires less, and loses less water. This may be especially helpful on the sunniest, hottest days if there is a limit to the amount of water that can be delivered to the plant.

how much is too much?

Growers frequently deliver more water than the plants actually need. Before assuming that the plant requires water, test the soil to see if it is moist. If there is moisture two to five inches below the surface, the plant probably does not need irrigation. A moisture meter with a long probe may be helpful. Experienced growers can observe the earliest stages of wilt and water only when the plants start to show symptoms of dryness. This method should be attempted only by experienced growers.

Sometimes plants wilt slightly during the hottest part of the day. The reason for this is that the roots cannot supply water as fast as the leaves are using it. It does not necessarily mean that there is not enough moisture in the medium. If the wilting becomes more severe or the leaves do not recover when the sun's intensity wanes, the medium is too dry and should be watered immediately to prevent permanent damage.

The time of day the plants are watered can affect the amount of water that is required. Water delivered in the morning as the plant's peak water needs begin, is more likely to be utilized than water delivered in the late afternoon or evening. Water delivered just after peak light is more likely to sink out of the range of the

plant's roots than water delivered as the plant needs it.

The best delivery is gradual, perhaps by a drip emitter, so that the plant has a chance to grab it before it journeys downward. A properly timed drip emitter may cut water needs by 50 percent. Plant requirements increase on sunny, hot days and decrease on cloudy, cool days. Water delivery should be adjusted to take the weather into account. The plant's peak water requirements are during mid-summer when it is growing vigorously in the vegetative growth stage. Once it makes the transition to flowering, total growth slows and the plant's water requirements decrease. As fall approaches and the weather cools, the amount of water needed decreases even more.

Probably the most efficient way of conserving water is through hydroponics. Most systems use a reservoir of some sort to conserve water. Virtually all water consumed is used directly by the plant or evaporates from the top. A large plant rarely uses more than a gallon or two of water each day. The unit should be serviced by a reservoir with as large a capacity as can be engineered and is appropriate. Passive units such as wick systems are the easiest for outdoor locations since no energy is required for operation.

If electricity is not a problem, active systems such as flood or recycling drip units can be considered. It is easy to hook up a solar battery unit to a small pump. I know several growers who use a wind-powered water pump. The water is pumped from a lower reservoir into a large upper reservoir about 10 feet above the plants. The water trickles down using drip emitters through five-gallon plant containers and then through flexible pipe to a lower reservoir. Water periods are timed using a battery-powered water meter.

One of the most sophisticated units I have seen was a long plastic tube about four inches in diameter which was connected to several five-gallon containers as it zig zagged down a south-facing hill. The first year, water was delivered to a reservoir at the top of the hill and was automatically delivered to the pipe at a measured rate using a battery operated valve. The end of the pipe was connected to a reservoir several feet above a truck trail. The water was siphoned to a collapsible water tank installed on a pickup truck. New water was added each day to make up for water used by the plants.

The second year, solar batteries were installed at various stations along the hill. Pumps and reservoirs were placed at each location. When the sun came up each day, the devices started their silent work. Water was pumped up the hill from station to station and eventually reached the upper reservoir.

First printed in Vol. 4, No. 4, page 12.

Water Needs

Water is an important factor in the photosynthesis process. Water is needed for the same reason human beings need it, that is for flushing away of wastes and toxins that the plant produces in photosynthesis. The plant depends on a constant supply of water, which is absorbed through the tiny root hairs, up the stem, transpired through the cells in the leaf and discharged into the air as vapor. In the water vapor released, dust and toxic waste are cleansed from the leaf's surface.

Marijuana thrives if watered thoroughly and then left to dry out for a few days. A plant will probably survive underwatering but will most likely stunt or die if overwatered. Overwatering and poor drainage will literally suffocate the plants. The roots need to breathe and too much water prevents this.

In the first four weeks of a young plant's life, proper watering is crucial to the plant's survival. The soil medium should be uniformly moist. Allow the top inch or two to dry out before watering again. When watering, place the growing container in a pan of water so that the moisture will be drawn up from the bottom until saturated. If watering by hand, make sure that the water is penetrating down into the soil. A common problem when watering by hand is that the water does not soak into the soil but rather runs over the surface. Gate valves must be installed to stop and start the water.

Hand pumps are another option if water is nearby. Hand pumps are quiet, making them great for either wilderness or populated areas. They are lightweight and very versatile as a portable pump. Most are self-priming with at least 15 feet suction lift and a 15 feet delivery head. Delivery head is the total distance that a pump can push water vertically. Placing the pump 15 feet above the source of water, it has the capacity to push water another 15 feet straight up, for a combined delivery head of 30 feet. Water can be pumped 1,000 feet as long as it does not have to be raised more than 30 feet.

Whatever method is used to water the plants, be sure to water the soil deeply so that the plant will have roots that grow deep into the soil. The plants will thank you in the fall with large, resinous buds.

First printed in Vol. 1, No. 2, page 6.

"This urge, wrestle, resurrection of dry sticks, cut stems struggling to put down feet, what saint strained so much, rose on such lopped limbs to a new life?"
—Theodore Roethke, *"Cuttings"*

Growing Indoors

by Tom Alexander

Finding a suitable indoor growing room may be difficult if you rent and your landlord drops over to get something out of the basement. Finding a secure growing area is as important indoors as it is outdoors.

Once you do find a room, and before you germinate any seeds, preparations must be made and growing materials gathered. Get together all potting soil mixes, fertilizers, soil additives, growing containers, grow lights, reflective sheeting, and any other odds or ends that you think you might use in your operation. It is better to be prepared in advance than to run around town trying to find a particular item when you need it.

The growing room's walls and ceiling must be covered with some kind of reflecting materials. Some people use aluminum foil. Other growers use reflective Mylar sheeting. Whatever you use, the goal is the same, and that is, to reflect as much light to the plants as possible. Both marijuana plants and the artificial lights should never be visible to anyone outside looking in. This means all doors, windows, cracks, and holes must be sealed so that no light shines out at night. Before you start growing, turn on your lights and go outside, preferably on a dark night. Look carefully for light leaks. If any are found, plug them or find a tighter room.

Light isn't the only kind of leak you need to be concerned with, however. Limit the number of people who know that you are growing. If you do tell someone, make sure that person is trustworthy. Many a grower has been ripped off because too many people knew what was going on. The word gets around fast.

After installing the reflective sheeting, a waterproof tarp must be put on the floor to protect it from moisture. If no protection is given, the cost of repairing the floor may be more than your crop is worth.

Initially, artificial lighting was considered a poor substitute for the stimulation provided by strong, direct sunlight. But improvements in the technology and the development of strains suited to the indoor environment have changed all of that. It is now possible to produce a crop as good— some say better— with high intensity discharge (HID) lamps indoors.

If you are purchasing fluorescent tubes and fixtures, some good ones on the market are those labelled "VHO" for very high output. Make sure you obtain VHO tubes and fixtures. The best lights on the market today are the high intensity discharge metal halide lamps. Although list prices are close to $500, most grow shops sell HID systems for under $200. Some growers say that both the flavor and the high are improved with these lights.

A problem that is encountered with insufficient lighting is long, spindly plants that fall over without support. Fluorescent tubes should be about three or four inches above the tops of the plants. As the plants get bigger, side lighting may be needed.

First printed in Vol. 1 No. 1, Spring 1980, page 13.

Common Sense for Indoor Gardening

by Cactus Pete
The attractions of indoor marijuana growing are fairly obvious: indoor gardens are difficult to detect, and crops can be grown year round. It can be a satisfying and rewarding experience. However, that doesn't mean that indoor gardening is for everyone. It seems to be working nicely for me after a lot of reading, planning and work. If you are thinking of indoor gardening, you should think hard about it and decide if it can work for you.

no sure thing

It takes considerable work to set up a grow room properly. And the growing itself requires a good deal of time and attention. It's not as trouble free as some would have you believe. Also keep in mind that any kind of agriculture is not a "sure thing" and crops can be lost for any number of reasons. If the power goes out in the middle of winter it could ruin your crop and break your heart. Or if a fungus or some other problem develops, you may not be able to save your plants. Remember, just going out and buying some equipment will not guarantee results.

Even though I've done a lot of gardening and pot growing over the years, I'm a newcomer to indoor growing. In fact, I'm working on my first crop right now, and while it's really looking good, I don't consider myself an expert on the subject. Still, I have noticed a few troublesome notions among people who are thinking of growing indoors.

First, many people seem to feel that indoor growing is easy, a "sure thing," and by spending a few hundered dollars to set up a little equipment, they will be in business. Secondly, there is a certain fascination among indoor growers— or at least those who sell the equipment— with the latest gadgets and "state of the art" technology to the point of relying too much on it.

I've found that it takes a much greater investment in time, effort, planning and money to set up a grow room than many people assume. Also there is a lot more equipment and gadgets available to indoor growers than there is information and common sense.

I visited a store in the Bay Area that specializes in grow lights and hydroponics systems. Two young guys, about 19 years old, arrived just before me and since there was only one salesperson available, we were all kind of talking together.

These guys had no experience at growing plants, but were planning to set up a grow room in the closet in one of their parent's garage. From their questions, I could tell that they hadn't thought it through too carefully and were relying on the salesperson to give them reliable information. However, this particular salesperson was a fast talker and could just as easily have been selling used cars or life insurance.

He told them how easy indoor growing was and that all they needed was the latest equipment including his super hydroponics system which was completely trouble free, automatic, and almost never needed attention! I asked these two if they had ever considered how they were going to vent the room, what they were going to do about the odor, whether the hum of the ballast would be a problem, how they were going to explain the higher electircal bills, etc. They admitted that they hadn't thought very much about any of those matters.

The salesperson's response was to try and sell them an exhaust fan and air cleaner, glossing over the other concerns. When he went to answer a phone call, I suggested that maybe they need to walk out of there and clear their heads, do some reading, get some information, and think it through before they bought anything.

People have heard that growing martijuana indoors is easy and are ready and willing to spend money before thay have good information and consider carefully what they are about to do.

When I first started looking into it, I figured it would be a pretty simple affair. I'd fix up a little space, go out and buy a light along with some other equipment and get some plants going. I talked with several people who were considering the same plan and thought the whole thing could be set up for a few hundred dollars. In fact, there was a recent article in a San Francisco newspaper in which Kayo wrote that "a grower can buy the whole farm (including hydroponics) for about $600."

The implication was that with a modest cash investment, you're on your way with everything you need. This is misleading. Unless you have your grow room already set up— with your tools and other supplies purchased— you could be in for a considerably greater expense.

Yes, one light, a CO_2 system and hydroponic set up— if that's the way you choose to go— will run about $600, but what about the cost of setting up the room, buying garden tools and supplies, soil, fans, containers, etc.?

Fortunately, before I proceeded too far, I read books on the subject of indoor growing. I began to discover that I needed more equipment than I had counted on.

know what you need

Not only did I need a halide light, but maybe I needed a sodium light, a CO_2 system, exhaust fan, pH and nutrient test kits, moisture meter, or hygrometer. In addition, I had to think about soils, containers, and a watering system.

I visited several stores around the Bay Area and was told that I should buy a light balancer, mylar for the walls, a negative ion generator, and hydroponic system. I wrote away for catalogs and information from various suppliers and read about several other products they wanted me to consider— everything from super bat guano, to plant hormones that would guarantee female plants, to a ready-made vortex chamber grow room. There are a lot more tools and equipment that you might want for your grow room than you might think, and it all costs money.

know the jargon

One reason to do some reading on the subject is to familiarize yourself with the jargon of the trade. Like any hobby, occupation or trade, indoor growing has its own vocabulary and if you are going to make wise choices, you need to know the language.

There is one thing all beginners need to consider before spending any money: Will the space selected work as a grow room? Some spaces just don't work. None of the literature I saw deals with the subject in any detail.

Like my two young friends I met at the local gardening store, some people may be inclined to rush out and buy equipment before making certain that the room is going to work for growing plants.

Keep in mind with whatever space you choose, it will need to be light tight, ventilated, and may need to be heated in the winter. Where will you vent the air? Will noise from the exhaust fan or ballast be a problem? I have a friend who lives in an apartment where you can hear the neighbors breathing through the walls and even a quiet ballast would give him away. What about odor? Are you willing to pay $60 to $120 for an air cleaner if that's what's needed? Because soil and water are involved, you need a way to keep things clean. How are you going to do that if you're growing in a closet or a spare bedroom?

You need to make sure that you have an adequate electrical supply. Be aware that one 1,000 watt light draws 9.2 amps and that you can only operate one lamp for each 15/20 amp circuit safely. You may want two rooms, one with a halide light for vegatative growth and one with a sodium light for flowering. In that case you will need more space, more planning, more electricity and more of an investment.

All of these things, and more, are worthy of consideration. And while it is true that just about any room may work out, it is also true that many rooms won't work for one reason or another. Think it through before you go out and spend your money. You will save yourself trouble and headaches later on.

First printed in Vol.6, No. 1, page 55.

Indoor Cultivation

by Tom Alexander

Many of the factors important in outdoor cultivation are also important indoors. Fertile soil, ample spacing between plants, and an adequate water supply are all necessary for a good crop.

Once a grow room is set up, selecting containers and soil are the next step. Select any large growing container. Anything will do, except galvanized tubs, buckets or pails. A five-gallon bucket is the minimum size container that you should consider. Outdoors, the plant's root system has unlimited space to grow. Marijuana's root system will sometimes grow as much as 12 feet deep and five feet across. So, the larger the indoor container, the better.

You can buy a commercial potting mix but sometimes the manu-

containers

potting soil

facturer puts fungicides or herbicides in the soil to prolong shelf life. Try to get all the information from the manufacturer before purchasing. Or, better yet, make your own.

A good potting soil can be made using a mixture of 10 to 25 percent sand, 30 to 50 percent humus material (compost), 20 to 30 percent rich loam, and 10 to 20 percent vermiculite. The potting mix must be sterilized to kill any fungus and other organisms that could be harmful to emerging seedlings. Place the potting mix in an oven with the temperature at 350 degrees. Bake for one to one and a half hours. After sterilizing, add a cup or two of lime, granular seaweed, steamed bone meal, greensand, blood meal and any other organic fertilizer per 50 to 75 pounds of potting soil.

The chlorine, fluorides and chemicals present in city water are not good for growing plants. Use either distilled water or let the tap water sit in an open container for 24 to 36 hours to allow the chemicals to evaporate. Pot grown indoors will need water more often than pot grown outdoors. Check the soil often with your finger and if it is dry the length of your finger, it is time to water. Remember that too much water is worse than too little, so water thoroughly and let the plant use it up before watering again. Put gravel in the bottom of the container to allow good drainage.

By controlling the length of light hours, it is possible to produce buds at any time of the year. Usually after three to four months of long-light days (12-16 hours), growers start to decrease the number of light hours to between eight and 12 hours, but this can be done after one month or six months. The decision is up to the grower.

The advantage of indoor cultivation over outdoor is that three and sometimes four crops can be grown in the same space over one year while outdoor growers usually reap only one crop; although a strain of seed has been developed in California that flowers as soon as the sun starts to decrease in daylight hours, June 22. Still the indoor grower can harvest much more in the same space over the course of one year.

cloning

Using a healthy, vigorous female plant, many new but genetically identical plants may be started. Take a sharp scissor or knife and cut four to six inches below the tip of a lateral branch. Dip the cut end into some dry Rootone (promotes rooting and prevents fungus disease). Plant the stem in moist vermiculite, making sure that it is not too wet or that it dries completely out. Once rooted, place in a proper sized container and treat like any other seedling.

The advantages of cloned plants are a high potency crop can be produced year after year and you do not depend on seeds for each crop. Outdoor growers who are growing an indoor crop through the winter months, can use cuttings from a choice female from the past outdoor season.

Many times the rooted plant will take on a dwarf appearance for a month or more. Increased light lengths often help the plant to start normal growth patterns.

Some growers start seedlings in small jiffy peat pots and then transplant into larger containers. Other growers like to transplant as few times as possible, so they start the seedlings into a large container from the beginning.

container size

If you are using a fluorescent lighting fixture, the minimum size container for healthy plants is a three-gallon bucket. Growers using high intensity discharge lights (metal halide or high pressure sodium) should use a minimum five-gallon container. Whatever the size of container you use, be sure to put gravel for drainage in the bottom of it.

reflective material

New Mylar reflects about 97 percent of incidental light, while a white surface will reflect about 85 to 93 percent. If using HID lights with a Mylar reflecting material, remember that it does reflect the ultraviolet light wave lengths which cause spot burning of the eyes and protective goggles are recommended.

water

Most city water supplies add chlorine and fluoride which is not good for your plants' growth or general health. City water may contain heavy metals, toxic chemicals and other pollutants. Use distilled water or water from a pure country source.

Water that has been used to soak or rinse alfalfa, mung or other sprouting seeds is a great help in producing healthy, strong marijuana. The water contains enzymes, amino acids, sugars, starches, minerals and other nutrients that the plant will use quickly. Lush growth should be observed soon after using sprout water.

best bud mix

4 parts worm castings	1/4 part lime
2 parts vermiculite	1/2 part peat moss
1 part granular dried seaweed	1/2 humic acid soil
1 part sand	conditioner
2 parts compost	1/2 part rock phosphate
2 parts sterilized soil	1/2 part pure wood ash

Mix all ingredients well and moisten with a little water. You are now ready to plant.

First printed in Vol. 1, No. 3, page 21, and Vol. 1, No. 4, page 31.

Part one

Indoor Growing for Beginners

Beginning indoor growers always have more enthusiasm than ability. The temptation to run out and buy some hi-tech equipment hoping the advertised promises will replace inexperience leads to all sorts of expensive disappointments including a mediocre crop.

Clearly, beginners give far too little consideration to the basic requirements of setting up a grow room. And, when faced with the three basic growing medium options, can't tell in advance which is likely to be the easiest to learn while doing.

the grow room

While setting up a grow room for a friend new to the business, I made careful note of the various steps my experience dictated and relate them below. I am indebted to her for allowing me to include photographs of her final set up.

Picking the right site is essential. Security requires a door you can lock, walls thick enough to block noise, and it needs to be lightproof. The plants require temperature and humidity regulation independ-

The grow room is nearly done. Note exhaust fan mounted high on left wall.

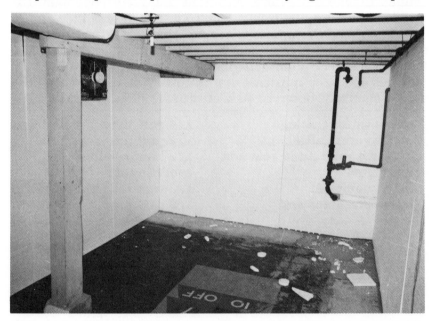

ent of the rest of the dwelling, a way to introduce fresh air and a way to exhaust spent air while minimizing unintentional air exchanges to trap CO_2 gas you introduce. Keep in mind that water, dirt and plant matter will wind up on the floor.

An area in the basement is the very best choice. An upstairs bedroom is a poor second and a spare room in an apartment isn't worth the trouble. Whatever you choose, your first job is to clean it 'til it's spotless, including the ceiling, which should be at least seven feet tall.

After a thorough cleaning, buy a small container of general purpose fungicide (Captan or Maneb), a quart spray bottle and some liquid bleach. Mix separate quart solutions, 1/4 cup bleach and one quart of water, and one tablespoon fungicide and one quart water. Spray the entire area down with one, then the other and leave for 12 hours. This kills the bugs and spores likely to attack the plants as seedlings.

Next, you need to maximize light reflection. Mylar is a bit expensive. Painting the walls flat white is fairly easy but to enclose an area in the basement, the best choice is four by eight sheets of styrofoam one-inch thick. It's flat white, has insulating properties to aid in temperature control and is easily cut to shape with an electric knife. You can frame in the area with two-inch square strips of furring wood.

Note that the black plastic was put over every basement window to prevent sight seeing, and a black plastic sheet was hung to block light on the exposed side. Joints in the styrofoam were sealed with three-inch clear tape.

The size of the room is dependent on the number of plants you want to grow. If you grow from seed as most first-timers do, figure that 50 percent will be male and all but one or two (saved for breeding) will be culled. So your space requirements are likely to change during the growing cycle.

The first time, I think, coping with 10 to 15 females grown four to five months from seeds will be plenty to deal with. This means you start with 20 to 30 plants. This will fit in a 10-by 12-foot area using one phosphor coated 1,000 watt metal halide HID. During flowering you add a second high pressure sodium 1,000 watt bulb, which requires its own firing system (ballast, socket, etc.). A rough measure is seven flowering plants, four or five feet tall, from soil line per bulb and that's the max.

If you're already thinking ahead to yield, throw out your fantasy. A good first crop would produce one to two ounces of manicured bud per plant on average if you use an Indica dominant strain. Through breeding and experienced gardening technique, four to six ounces

preparation

per plant can be achieved, sometimes. While this is not a seed selection article, I strongly urge you to use Indica strains if you can. Sativa needs more light, more root space, is too sensitive to high root moisture and atmospheric humidity, and has a narrower range of fertilizer tolerance than a beginner can handle.

ventilation

An exhaust fan sucks out humid, spent air, drawing in fresh air. The fan in the photo was more than needed. The fan you buy will come with a CFM (cubic feet per minute) rating. Buy one that is rated at one-fifth the volume of your grow room. A 10-by 12-foot room, seven feet high is 840 cubic feet. It needs a CFM rating of approximately 175 CFM. This allows the fan to run about five minutes for one complete air exchange, all you need each exhaust cycle.

Mount the fan close to the ceiling, no more than two feet down, maximum. The exhausted air has to go someplace. Likely you'll have bought a "squirrel cage" or "rams horn" style fan and the outlet is easily mated to a four-inch diameter clothes dryer exhaust hose kit. If you go out a nearby window, camouflage the exit port, but be conscious of close neighbors who may hear noise or smell flowering Cannabis. A better choice is the ash door at the base of the furnace chimney. Be sure to tap in below the furnace smoke exhaust tap or the grow room will fill with smoke.

HID ballast is placed on scrap wood in a plastic tub to keep spilled water from electrocuting the grower

To hang the HID bulb fixture, use pulleys and parachute cord. You'll raise and lower it a lot. A reflector is necessary in my opinion—

four feet wide, a shallow cone. In the basement a 30-amp, 220-volt dryer outlet may be available. If it's not, strongly consider paying an electrician $100 to install one before starting on the project. Keeping HID ballast amp demand within circuit load capacity is crucial. On a 30-amp, 220-volt dryer circuit the ballast draws 4.5 amps. There's room to spare using three 1,000 watt HIDs wired for 220 volts. On a 110-volt circuit, the ballast draws nine amps and the majority of household circuits for 110 volts are 15 to 20 amp capacity, which means one HID per circuit. The ballast needs 50 percent above its base operating amp draw for start up. HID ballasts are wired for 220 or 110, buy the right one.

The HID is regulated by a timer. Get one equal to the amp rating of your circuit. I recommend the 18-hour vegetative cycle run from 3 p.m. to 8 a.m. when you are likely to be home. Wire everything up working backwards from socket to plug; wipe the bulb with alcohol after screwing it in, then fire it up.

As the bulb fires up, get your air circulation fan, bought beforehand. It should be eight inches or larger in diameter and have a sweep of 90 degrees or better. Set it on something or aim it upward so it's moving air in the three to five foot layer. Turn it on and then bring in a note pad, mercury thermometer with at least a six-inch reading tube and a hygrometer (it measures humidity), also purchased beforehand. Put both instruments about four or five inches off the floor and take readings every four to six hours for a full 18-hour light cycle. This phase is crucial! The temperature range during light cycle must be between 66 and 80 degrees and the humidity can go no higher than 60 percent.

Grow buckets with drip outlets installed.

If the temperature is over 80 degrees, move the ballast out of the grow room; if not, leave it in, the dry heat lowers humidity. If the temperature approaches 80 degrees only at the tail end of the 18-hour light cycle, it's okay. If it's over 80 degrees earlier in the light cycle, run the exhaust fan for one five-minute cycle, then see how far the temperature drops and for how long.

Basically, you're identifying specific times to run the exhaust fan to keep temperature within tolerable ranges. Record the necessary exhaust cycle intervals. Humidity in basements could be a problem. If it is over 60 percent with no plants in the grow room, it will certainly go higher with them in and mold and fungus can become a problem. The answer is a dehumidifier or a vigilant eye for mold.

After the light cycle ends, the temperature will drop, down to 56 degrees is okay. Humidity will rise. After the plants are in, adding exhaust cycles to lower humidity during the dark period will work as the basement will be relatively drier outside the grow area.

If the humidity and temperature ranges are okay then the timer you buy to control the exhaust fan only need cycle it two times per day, 12 hours apart, to introduce enough fresh air for steady growth.

CO$_2$ injection

840 X .0014 = 1.176

After you are an experienced grower, a thermostat/ humidistat can be used to control the exhaust fan. But in my own grow house, I've found that coordinating them with CO$_2$ injection is a real handful. Also, in my experience, the best pot I've grown has been in conditions of a low "night" temperature of around 60 degrees with a "day" maximum temperature of 80 degrees and humidity about 40 percent. The buds seem to have a higher resin content.

The subject of CO$_2$ injection can be confusing. I'm going to skip a lot of detail and give you a quick formula. First, the air circulation fan stays on 24 hours per day. Rent a five-pound CO$_2$ tank, aluminum ones are much easier to lift if you have a choice. You'll also need a pressure regulator to step the tank pressure down to safe levels for the flow meter and a short- interval electric timer, one that has on/ off settings in one-minute intervals, plus a solenoid regulator for the timer to activate on the tank. Regardless of what regulator/flow meter you buy, make absolutely sure you know how it works and can regulate the final discharge flow to 20 cubic feet per hour. This isn't what you inject! Read on.

Calculate the cubic-foot volume of your room. The one I set up was 840 cubic feet. Multiply your volume in cubic feet by .0014, as in the example at left.

The result here, 1.176, is the cubic feet of CO$_2$ you release per injection. If your flow meter is set at 20 cubic feet per hour, that's .333 cubic feet per minute. Divide your CO$_2$ cubic feet objective, here 1.176, by .333. The result here is 3.52 or the equivalent of four minutes. So every injection cycle, regulated by the short-term timer, should be four minutes. Then set the timer to inject four minutes of CO$_2$ every 2 1/2 hours after the beginning of the light cycle, to the end. Don't add CO$_2$ during the dark cycle, there is no need for it. Make sure each CO$_2$ timer cycle happens just after any exhaust cycle and synchronize timers or you'll waste CO$_2$. Run the CO$_2$ outlet tube to the center of the ceiling to allow the gas to drift down over the plants and get mixed by the air circulating fan which runs 24 hours a day.

All of this may sound complicated, and frankly, a good grow room is harder to do than most think. But if you do it right the first time it is like riding a bike, you never forget, and the plants will thrive.

selecting a growing medium

The lure of hi-tech hydroponic units and its promise of a bigger, better crop is hard to resist. But you're a beginner, resist it. The truth is that some of the simplest approaches work as well as any and are much easier to learn while doing.

Hydro set ups are tricky to regulate. The nutrient solution has a critical pH range to maintain at all times. Full recovery systems require close nutrient combinations monitoring. And trace mineral problems— too much or too little— can give even the pros fits. All in all, they are not that bad once you've had some experience, but not the first time out.

Organic soil mixes in containers are expensive. Correct supplement fertilization ratios require continual adjustment as plants exhaust the container's original contents and trace mineral problems are difficult to deal with. They are also less forgiving of over watering or over fertilizing.

Of all the approaches a soilless mix is best. It is porous enough to drain easily (beginners tend to overwater), can be leached of excess fertilizers with a heavy clean water rinse (beginners tend to over fertilize), and is light weight. Rather than grow bags, I recommend the five-gallon plastic buckets used to ship food products. You need a five-gallon size for a four-to five-month old flowered plant to avoid root constriction and stunting. Plants in too small a container tend to flower prematurely.

Drill six 1/4-inch holes in the bottom for drainage. A five-gallon bucket is close to one cubic foot. A good mix is 50 percent perlite, 25 percent vermiculite, 12.5 percent peat moss (no more) and 12.5 percent clean, course sand. Add one cup of finely ground dolomite lime to each bucket's mix. Buy the amount you need of each for the number of buckets you have and mix the ingredients thoroughly.

soil or soilless growing?

Jane's crop at three to four weeks already displays the oversize fan leaves of Indica dominant Cannabis.

application

This is an awful job, wear a mask and be glad you do it once a crop. Fill the buckets to the rim and put them in the grow room.

The next concern is water and fertilizer application. Hand watering is best for the first few weeks of seedling life when plant needs vary a lot and they are most sensitive to more or less than optimum levels. After that, you knock the plants around too much making a path. By the time the plants are three months old, there won't be room to move around in the grow room much anyway.

Regular delivery of water and fertilizer is best done through a drip system. Correctly set up, a drip system is similar to a non-recovery hydroponic unit and you get many of the same benefits. A good drip system allows irrigation at a slow steady rate avoiding soil compaction or unintentional leaching. You've got the adjustment just right when only a small trickle, 1/2 cup or less, emerges from the drain holes after a water cycle. As the plants grow, you will have to add more watering cycles as the plants consume more. It is preferable to add short watering cycles rather than having a longer one. A wand style water meter is inexpensive and by probing the mix at varying levels in a few spots you can tell if the plants are getting enough water. Test three pots for every 10 in the room to get a representative sample. The meter reads higher or lower relative root moisture. I've never seen one that came with guidelines for correct Cannabis root moisture, but after using a few, the high one to low two reading level seems the objective to maintain.

A mixer proportioner (MP) can inject a dilute fertilizer into the drip system each time you water. The emphasis is on dilute. I think Peters' brand products are the best to learn with, are easily available and dissolve completely even in the highly concentrated solution you load the MP with. Somewhere between 1/3 and 2/3 of the recommended outdoor application levels is right. Read the instructions that come with the MP and the Peters to figure out how to load the MP correctly. It is always better to slightly under fertilize than risk burning the plants' roots. They do not recover from the latter very well.

Peters sells a number of mixes but the following applies to nearly all commercially available mixes. In the first few weeks of seedling life, hand water with a root stimulating substance like Ortho Upstart. At three weeks, switch to a balanced NPK combination like Peters 20-20-20. This is a transition fertilizer. At six weeks switch to Peters Pete Lite 20-10-20. The higher relative N level promotes leaf/branch growth. The lower P level slows root growth and prevents premature flowering. At three to four months when you flower, switch to Peter's Blossom Booster 10-30-10 to aid floral (bud) formation.

timers

As a convenience I like a self-contained programmable timer

controlling the watering cycles. The Rainmatic models advertised in *Tips* are reliable and easy to program. You can get by without them but they never forget or have to go out of town for a few days. And when correctly adjusted, do it exactly right every time.

Linking the drip system, MP and water timer together requires a bit of experimentation. Remember two things: a little trickle out the bottom of the bucket is your objective, and the faucet pressure is the real key. When puzzled about how to regulate the system, think faucet pressure— more, faster drip rate, less, slower drip rate.

You've gotten this far and I still haven't even mentioned germinating a seed. When you see how much work is involved in set up you might wonder why the hell home grown appealed to you in the first place. But take heart, the hard part is over. The rest, the actual growing, is easy if your grow room is set up right in the beginning.

First printed in Vol. 6, No. 2, page 34.

Part two Indoor Growing for Beginners

Each time you grow a crop, you'll go through some close variation of the techniques described here. Follow them rather closely your first time so you can develop basic plant skills needed to improve quality and quantity in subsequent harvests.

The critical plant skill is the ability to tell at a glance whether a plant is healthy and growing at close to the optimum rate, and if not, what's likely to be wrong with it. This skill is learned through careful, regular observation of the plants and the intentional variation of fertilizer and water quantity application to a few test buckets— more on this below.

When growing from seed, as you probably will the first time, the emphasis will be on yield per plant. But as you grow your first crop, you'll learn to clone, and with clones the emphasis shifts to yield per growing area. This is the production basis for commercial growing operations.

As it happens most of the photos accompanying this installment were taken at a commercial specialty seed breeding operation. Consequently there is a much larger variety of plant phenotypes and start dates than you will experience. Unless you intentionally grow a variety of strains your crop plants will be of relatively similar size and appearance up to the point you induce flowering

step I

Start with a larger number of seeds than your mature plant objective— about 100 seeds for 25 adults. Beginners with no local access to quality seeds are strongly encouraged to order from one of the two Dutch mail order companies that advertise in *Tips*. Both are reliable and provide the strains as advertised. Soak the seed in room-temperature water for one hour to soften the hull and begin germination.

Peat root cubes are the preferred germination environment. Purchased compressed and dry, they swell to full size when soaked in water for a half hour. After soaking, slit the covering mesh to ease later removal and place one seed in each cube 1/8 to 1/4 inch below the cube surface.

Note the texture and color of the moist cubes. It's essential to maintain this until the cubes are planted in the larger grow buckets. Initially, place all the seeded cubes in a waterproof lined box 2 1/2 feet below the bottom edge of the HID (1,000 watt, clear or phosphor-coated). Begin the 18-hour timer-controlled light cycles that characterize the vegetative cycle now. If you can control grow room temperature, push it up to 80 to 85 degrees and keep it at that level for the first seven days. If the room is cooler, raise the cube container a foot or two off the floor (adjust the HID above that) where it will be warmer.

Start a grow room diary the day you seed the cubes. Record regularly key measures, such as air temperature, humidity, root moisture, growth rate and general comments about your activities and observations in the grow room. A good diary will be more useful than you can imagine.

Ordinarily, I'm strongly opposed to any fungicide/pesticide application on the plants. The one exception I make regards damp off prevention. The micro-organisms that cause this are everywhere in the environment, plague even the cleanest grow rooms and can quickly kill young seedlings. Apply a dilute Captan (or Maneb) fungicide spray after you seed the cubes, again in three days, and again three days later. A light mist is better than a heavy drench. Rinse the plants with a room temperature plain water spray one day after each application.

step II

At 80 to 85 degrees, seeds sprout in two or three days. First to emerge will be opposing, single, paddle-shaped leaves called cotyledon leaves. Keep track of the first to sprout, colored toothpicks in the cube margin help.

After sprouts show give them a dilute (33 percent of the recom-

Thai seedling at three weeks. Note the Sativa type thinner leaves and lack of blade overlap.

Two week old seedling, Afghani pure strain.

Two week old seedling,
Pacific Northwest bred
Indica.

Two-week old South
African pure strain,
Durban Killer.

mended strength) Ortho Upstart root stimulator solution each watering. To water, pour some of this mix in the cube container, let them soak it up and remove the excess in a few minutes. Don't let them stand in water, they'll die.

You'll want to select the most vigorous starts to transplant into the grow buckets. Keep in mind that the most robust seedlings make the most vigorous plants. Desirable sprouts are those that emerge first, have the thickest stems and have their first true leaves emerge one to two inches above the cube surface. This last point assumes a 1,000 watt HID 2 1/2 feet above the cubes. If your seedlings' first true leaves (true leaves have serrated edges and look like a Cannabis leaf) emerge above three inches, the light intensity is too low or the grow room humidity is very high. Leggy seedlings do not make very good plants.

You may be surprised at the variation in seedling appearance in a sample as small as 100 seeds but the more vigorous starts are usually easy to spot. Good experience can be gained by germinating seeds from commercial junk pot and noting the changes they go through in a week.

Grow room supply shelf, CO$_2$ set up and HID wiring.

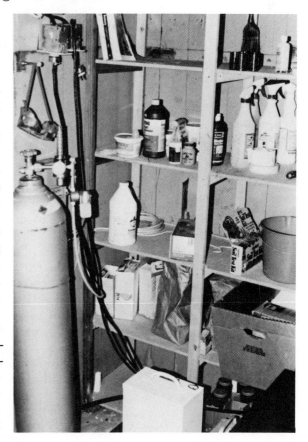

Transplant selected starts into the grow buckets three days after they emerge. Any longer often results in roots penetrating the cube's containing mesh. These roots will be broken off when removing the net as you transplant and this will shock and slow down the plants.

Just before transplanting, soak the soilless mix in the grow buckets. I try to bring it up to No. 7 on a Sudbury moisture meter. Scoop out two holes near the container center, *carefully* remove the mesh keeping the exposed cube intact and place it in a hole with the cube top even with the soilless level. Fill in around them and pat down to insure contact. Place the drip system emitter between them. Repeat this process until all 25 buckets have two starts in them.

Left over, lower quality starts should go into several extra buckets;"more fertilizer," "less fertilizer," "more water," and "less water." The relative level of water and fertilizer applied to these buckets will teach you a lot about plant tolerances. Only the crop plants are on the drip system. You must hand apply variables to the test

Mixer/proportioner for
fertilizer, drip system
timer and tangle of drip
system hoses.

buckets. Carefully watch and record the effects. Test plants are more
or less damaged by the extremes. Plant tolerances are, by the way,
relatively narrow. I give "more" buckets twice as much and "less"
buckets half as much as the crop plants. Any more variation than
that would not provide useful information.

Huddle the grow buckets under the HID. A five-gallon bucket is one
foot across, and 30 fill a five-by six-foot area. Keep the HID 2 1/2 feet
above the seedlings. The seedlings on the outside suffer a bit from
lower light intensity. Compensate by using four by eight sheets of
styrofoam to create temporary walls around the grow buckets'
perimeter.

As soon as plants sprout they begin making chlorophyll (the green
in the leaves) and can benefit from the CO_2 supplementation
schedule described in the preceding article (Indoor Growing, Part
One). The exhaust fan timer should also be activated at this time.

For the first seven days most growth is below the soil line. The root
structure rapidly expands (it will nearly fill a five-gallon bucket in
four weeks) to support later vegetative growth. At 10 days, survey the
buckets and remove the second best start in each by clipping at the
soil line. Do not pull it up as you'll damage the remaining plant's root
structure.

You now have 25 buckets with one plant each as your main crop
plants and four test buckets with two or three plants in them. Test

buckets do not need to be thinned to one plant. Two or three are okay.

During the first two to three weeks, aim for a water meter indicated root moisture of 2 to 2 1/2. To achieve this, apply 15 to 25 ounces of water/fertilizer Monday, Wednesday, and Friday, one hour after lights on. This is applied to the crop buckets using the timer-controlled drip system with an in-line fertilizer mixer/proportioner. On Sundays, override the timer control and add an additional amount of water depending on the root moisture reading, growth rate and plant appearance. The test buckets receive their water and fertilizer by hand.

You read a lot about pH and plant health. Soilless mixes have a buffering effect, moderating water which is too alkaline or acid closer to the desirable range of 6.6 to 7.1. In rare cases the tap water feeding your drip system can be so acid or base it results in a pH measure in the buckets above or below this range. If that happens, pH up or pH down concentrates can be bought from sources that supply the hydroponic gardener who's much more concerned about pH regulation. These pH adjusters are added to the mixer proportioner along with the fertilizer concentrate until the drip solution has an acceptable pH.

As the plants grow, you must adjust the drip control timer. Aim to maintain a slightly lower root moisture meter reading of one to two. Obviously the meter readings will fluctuate. Just after the drip cycle it will be higher and on the off days, drier. A good general perspective on watering is to note that in nature, plants start in the wetter months of spring and grow and mature under the drier environmental conditions of summer.

Fertilizer application takes place with each watering using the drip system described. The first five days apply a dilute (33 percent) Ortho Upstart Solution. Then switch to Peter's 20-20-20 applied at the rate of 1/2 teaspoon per gallon for two weeks. After that, switch to Peter's Pete Lite 20-10-20 for the balance of the vegetative cycle.

The most reliable measure of water/fertilizer application effectiveness is growth rate. At four weeks from start date, expect plants to average nine inches tall, and all to be over six inches. *Indica* plants may be a bit shorter but they will be very wide. *Sativa* will be taller and narrower. Around the fourth week the plants will take off and average 1/2 to 1 inch minimum growth per day. Measure them every four days and chart all plants. Growth should be steady throughout the vegetative period. A sudden spurt or lag can foreshadow a problem, refer to diary notes taken three to five days before to see if anything changed. Changes in fertilizer and water application do not show immediate effects although continually underwatered plants

pH and plant health

fertilizer application

Plant pruned at apical
meristem for clone. Note
Tree Seal-Stump.

Sixth generation Indica.

often shoot up overnight after a good soak.

An even, green color should predominate. The plants in the "more" fertilizer buckets may be a very dark green and show leaf burn at the edges. The plants in the "less" fertilizer bucket will grow slowly before they yellow, but you can slowly back off on fertilizer and watch the effect to gain experience. "Less" water plants usually look okay, but are smaller. Interestingly "more" water, if it's severe enough, will drown the roots and the growing tips of the plant will yellow mimicking a nutrient deficiency. A classic beginner disaster is to over water until the plants yellow, mistake it for a nutrient deficiency and apply a big shot of fertilizer and burn the daylights out of the plants. Lest you think anybody is a born expert, note that I speak from experience on this last point.

Light intensity is increased by getting the HID bulb closer to the plants. Leave it at 2 1/2 feet above the soilless mix surface for the first four weeks, letting plants grow toward it. At four weeks, lower it to 12 inches from the closest plant. A week later adjust it to six inches above the closest plant. After this you'll be raising the light as the plants grow to keep it six inches above the plants.

Spread the plants out as they grow to avoid extreme plant leaf overlap. At four to six weeks the buckets will spread over about one-half a 10-by 12-foot grow room. At eight to 10 weeks, they'll fill it.

The vegetative period lasts, most economically and practically, until plants average 30 to 36 inches tall from the soil line. A room with higher (80 to 85 degrees) light cycle temperatures, CO_2 supplementation and plants carefully tended with correct fertilizer/water application will be ready in eight weeks. Cooler rooms, with no CO_2 and erratic plant care procedures could require four to six weeks more. The next installment will cover exactly what happens when you shift from the end of the vegetative to the flowering cycle.

Cloning is the key to increasing yields without increasing electrical consumption. It allows you to raise only female plants if you choose and the best ones at that.

step III

Cloning is somewhat mystified in the literature. It's actually fairly simple. Here is a "foolproof" method. Plants should be two months old and two feet tall. Pour a gallon of plain water through the bucket once a day for three to four days. Wait two days and do not apply any water or fertilizer during this time. Select lower, if not the lowest, branches. They should be at least as big as a farmer's match in diameter. Cut off a length approximately six inches from the tip and midway between sets of leaves.

Snip off one set of leaves above the cut line leaving two 1/8 inch nubs. Dip the stem in a root stimulator like Rootone to a point 1/4 inch above the nubs and stick it in a quart container of soilless mix. The soilless mix should be presoaked. Make a guide hole with a tool larger than the stem so you don't scrape off rooting powder during insertion. Insert the stem to a point equal with the rooting powder level and tamp the soilless mix into contact with it.

Keep the soilless mix evenly moist, watering with a 50 percent Upstart solution as needed. Cover the clones under a clear plastic sheet with an open air passage to raise humidity while allowing air exchange. Put the clones in boxes two feet off of the floor where the temperature is likely to be higher. For the first week, keep them in a corner away from the HID until the clone root structure starts up and can supply the plant nutrients and moisture more intense light will require. Mist the clones lightly each day. At the end of one week move them closer to the HID and remove the tent. They may wilt a bit along the way but they will perk up seven days after cutting if they are going to make it.

The clones will outgrow the quart container in two to three weeks. Transplant them into larger containers before they get root bound. A plant grown from seed needs a container equal to one gallon per month of plant life. A five-gallon bucket sustains a plant for five months before it becomes root bound and sickens. I put clones in three-gallon containers anticipating 30 days of vegetative growth after placement in the bucket and then a maximum eight-week flowering cycle (More on this in Part Three)

When you clone, carefully record the parent plant for each. To establish a perpetual clone crop with these starts you'll need a second, smaller grow room. Follow carefully, the clones can stay in the main grow room while the 18-hour light cycle is maintained. But soon after cloning you drop to 12 hours for flowering. To avoid flowering the clones they go into the second grow room which stays on an 18-hour light cycle. As the crop plants flower, the males will be easy to identify. If you kept track of the clone's source, toss the clones taken from them leaving only females. To insure a full grow room with your clone crop, take two cuttings from each parent plant (More on this in Part Three).

Bringing your first crop to this point will be an enormous education. If you've read Jorge Cervantes' *"Indoor Marijuana Horticulture,"* a true classic, take the next step and read Robert Connell Clarke's *"Marijuana Botany."* These books are the best I've read and are written by experienced growers, not inexperienced, but widely read students of the subject.

relax

One last point. Cannabis thrives in the correct mental as well as physical climate. Relax around the plants. Beginners are forever meddling with their plants. Don't. They often do a little better with less attention than too much. And, sister marijuana knows if you have a positive mental attitude. Growers driven by greed and other shallow, irresponsible motives don't do very well, and they shouldn't.

First printed in Vol. 6, No. 3, page 34.

Part three

Indoor Growing for Beginners

Even though I've watched over many a crop, I still find flowering and harvest utterly fascinating. In just a few short weeks the appearance and character of the plants changes dramatically. Experiencing it gives truth to all the hype you read and hear about the psychological rewards of home growing.

Causing the plants to flower is essentially a matter of reducing the timer-controlled light cycle from 18 to 12 hours by taking six hours off the front or back end of the original schedule. The new 12-hour cycle is maintained until the plants are harvested. When you flower is your choice, but certain practical considerations will generally determine the timing.

timing

Plants from seed should not be flowered before they are four to six weeks old. Prior to that, the ratio between bud and shake will be low and sex reversal problems can crop up. Further, the younger a seed-grown plant, the longer it takes for it to react to photoperiod reduction and begin vigorous floral formation. The best rule of thumb is to flower seed-started plants when they are three feet tall from soil line to growing tip or three months old, whichever comes first. If you do everything right with light, water and fertilizer, plus add CO_2, they will be ready in eight to nine weeks. Before or after this time, the yield ratio of bud to plant size is less favorable for most strains.

When you set back the light cycle you must make other modifications:

• Reduce the CO_2 injection period by six hours because of the reduced light cycle. Plants do not require significant amounts during the "night" period.

• Carefully monitor the hygrometer's humidity reading at "lights on" the first 10 days and add exhaust cycles during the "night" to keep

Male flowers on an Indica plant. The closed flowers are the size of a pencil eraser and shaped like a cantaloupe or football. As they mature, they look like a star shaped umbrella with yellowish pollen sacs dangling below.

it below 60 percent as necessary. The longer dark period results in a lower bottom temperature which will raise humidity. To prevent this from sponsoring a mold attack on the buds, add exhaust cycles.

• Check for any light leaks, particularly at the top and bottom of the grow room door. The grow room must be absolutely dark during the "night" period. No "midnight" inspections with flashlight in hand, either.

• Change the fertilizer from the growth formula (20-10-20) to a bloom booster with a higher proportion of phosphorus or P (10-30-10). After the first three to four weeks of flowering, discontinue fertilizing and use plain water. Do not alter the fertilizer application concentration or frequency, just the NPK mix.

Also, do not withhold water to promote resin formation. Instead, you will reduce harvest. A number of growers I know use a home brew the last couple of weeks before harvest. Usually it's a dilute fruit juice mixture like orange juice, apple or pineapple. They feel it sweetens the bud. I think it gunks up the drip system and acidifies the soil. I've not been able to taste the difference myself but plants harvested with no let up in fertilizer application do taste a bit bitter.

• Lastly, no sprays of any kind can be used in the grow room from now on. They can cause bud mold, and smoking the plant transfers all spray residues to your lungs. Never, ever use any type of poison on a crop you smoke or sell.

Adding a second light now will increase light intensity and, consequently, bud formation. The preferred choice is a 1,000 watt high pressure sodium (HPS) bulb. The yellow/orange cast of the light discharged indicates the particular segment of the light spectrum emphasized. The combination of HPS and MH light approximates the harvest sun spectral mix that occurs in nature during the fall months and encourages floral growth. The bulbs and reflectors should be offset, equidistant from the ceiling center to insure even light distribution. A circular light balancer is beneficial but not necessary. Rail type light balancers, in my opinion, travel the circuit too slowly. I do not recommend them.

Plan to check your garden every day for at least a half hour the first two weeks of flowering unless you want an early male to spread pollen and fertilize every female in the room. After your first crop, you'll probably be able to distinguish males from females when they are only four to six weeks old.

Specifically, you look for the single immature sex organs (flowers) they display at the branch crotches on the upper third of the plant. A 10-power magnifier helps to spot them. The photo on the facing page shows a mature male plant. Male plants produce pollen sacs that look like tiny cantaloupes when closed and umbrellas with dangling bags of pollen when about to release. One flower even though it's the size of a pencil eraser, can pollinate an unbelievable number of female calyxes, ruining your sinsemilla crop. Female flowers look like two hairs emerging from a small pod. The hairs are anywhere from 1/8 to 1/2 inch long and can be white (most common), green, reddish purple to a beautiful lavender in certain strains of Indica from Afghanistan.

Watch your plants' development closely. As they mature and males are identified, remove them before their flowers open. If you started with 30 plants, expect about 12 to 15 to be male (there are slightly more females in any seed sample). Most growers immediately harvest all identified males except for one or two saved for breeding. The saved males go into a different room with a sunny window. Except during the summer months, the males will mature enough flowers to be a pollen source for breeding.

If your plant strain is relatively potent, the males will be smokable/saleable, although harsher and not nearly as potent as the females.

maturity

While total yield from the grow room is a combination of good gardening and genetic potential, the potency is solely determined by the genetic makeup of the plants and a sufficient flower period to mature the bud. How long it takes your particular plants to mature will vary. Rather than tell you to wait four, six or eight weeks, then cut and dry, it's better to learn to recognize a mature bud. The following is open to debate but here's what I teach others and use myself.

In the first 10 to 14 days, the plants will elongate the upper one-third of each branch anywhere from eight to 14 inches. After that nearly all vegetative growth will stop; no more multibladed leaves will form. Lower fan leaves will begin to yellow partially due to the lower nitrogen level in the fertilizer. The plants also find it convenient to cannibalize lower fan leaves for assimilated nutrients, thus conserving energy to reproduce.

The plants, if healthy, will rapidly form calyxes one atop another into bud formations of varying length with the biggest forming on the main stem. During the first 10 days, use your 10-power magnifier to

A date tag recording the pollen donor and the mother plant plus the fertilization date is attached to each pollinated branch.

watch the resin glands pop out on the buds. There are a few types of glands but check for those which look like a mushroom, a small clear globule on a clear stalk. The first few weeks of flowering, the buds will usually smell faintly sweet, the hairs protruding from the calyxes will retain their original color and the resin glands will be clear.

After that point, the odor will become coarser. Some strains are quite acrid smelling, like gasoline, skunks or anything else that comes to mind. Odor and resin gland formation are linked and a sign of increasing potency. The calyx hairs will begin to wither and turn brown toward the base of the bud and this will progress toward the top. If a male flower releases pollen and fertilizes the calyx the hairs will turn brown immediately. Grossly pollinated plants will immediately slow new calyx production and begin to emphasize seed production. Lightly pollinated plants will keep going.

The key indicator of maturity is the resin heads. As the majority on the central bud cloud to a milk white or turn a reddish color, that bud is ripe and the rest of the plant is close behind. If you've regularly observed the plants with your 10-power magnifier you won't miss this.

Generally, all females from the same strain will mature at the same time. You'll have to watch yours to know, but when a few are ready, most will be.

The fan leaves will yellow and drop rapidly as the plants ready for harvest. Some of them, as well as small leaves subtending the bud, may turn shades of purple or rust. This isn't a sign of higher relative potency as many believe. It's genetically linked but essentially expresses declining vigor much as trees outdoors turn assorted colors and lose their leaves in autumn.

In the final days before harvest, the plant may produce tiny unserrated leaves near the bud tips. These leaves will look like the first cotyledon leaves that emerged on the seedling. When all of these circumstances have occurred you have reached peak floral development and harvest is called for.

Most growers attempt improvements in their particular strains by selectively breeding for certain traits. The subject of selective breeding is beyond the scope of this article but the practical techniques are not.

Once you've isolated one or two selected male plants as pollen donors, place them in a sunny room before their flowers mature and release pollen. A pollen trap can be made from a small brown paper bag. Cut a three-inch square hole in one side and tape down saran wrap to cover it. The bag will breathe enough to avoid harming the plant. Slip it over the top stalk of the plant and secure at the base with

A pure strain Afghani from the Chitral (Afghanistan) area. It sported beautiful lavernder calyx hairs. Bred for hashish production, its calyx to leaf ratio is low.
Note the string tiedown bending the upper stem horizontally to allow lower buds more light. This plant is half way done.

a garbage bag twistie. Keep the bag closed but don't pinch off the flow in the plant stalk. In about 10 days, you'll see a number of male flowers open up and shed pollen.

To capture the pollen, give the bag a healthy shake to part pollen from plant. Cut the stalk off a couple inches below the bag neck. Invert the bag, loosen the seal and carefully draw out the top of the stalk while gently shaking to toss pollen off into the bag. Next, lay a 12-inch square sheet of wax paper, creased in the middle, on a flat surface in a draft free room. Turn the paper bag upside down a few inches above it and pollen and flowers will cascade onto the wax paper. Then collect the pollen in the crease by holding the wax paper Taco style and chase it with a brush into a dry 35mm film canister. Label the canister with the source. Wash the brush between collections from different donors and use fresh sheets of wax paper each time to avoid unintended mixing.

There are two common ways to pollinate females you select. A small amount of pollen can be put in a baggie which is then placed over a lower branch bud on a plant with fresh, ripe pistils (calyx hairs). Use a twistie to seal the baggie neck and shake the branch to insure pistil/pollen contact. Leave it on a day or two, any longer and the inside of the bag will be soaked. Putting the bag on and taking it off risks spreading pollen to other plants.

Consequently, I prefer to apply pollen directly from the 35mm container using a small paint brush. Lightly touch the end of the brush in the pollen and then touch it directly to the fresh pistils. You can easily create 20 or 30 viable seeds this way in just a minute. I find it much easier to control the pollen this way. Turn off the grow room fan when you're doing this.

If a shitload of seeds from a great male and female is your goal, there is only one way to go. Wait until the female is heavily flowered but the pistils are still fresh. Then place her right next to the male in the sunny room for a couple of days. Periodically shake the male to liberally distribute pollen over the female. Then return the female to the grow room but first take a small fan or blower and "dust" the female of loose pollen or it'll blow around in the main grow room pollinating the rest of the plants.

Seed must fully mature to be viable. Pollinated lower branches need to be left unharvested and attached to the lower third of the plant stalk. As the seeds develop they'll split the containing calyx and turn dark brown. Spread newspapers under the plant to catch seeds which fall early. Seeds must be dark brown and "rattle in the pod" or drop easily to be reliably ripe. It takes three to six weeks from fertilization for seeds to form and ripen. When harvesting a plant with some lower branches intentionally seeded, cut off all the rest of the bud and branch ends leaving one-third of the main stalk with seeded branches attached. The plant will still be able to ripen the seeds. If there are only a few seeded plants, concentrate them under the HID and turn off the HPS after the main harvest. The seeds will turn out fine.

Always change clothes and wash your hands between visits to the male room and the female room or you'll carry in unwanted pollen.

After each intentional pollination, record the info in your grow room diary and tag the seeded branches with relevant information so you won't lose track of what you've done. Again, let the seeded plants/branches go on under the HID as long as necessary after the bud harvest. The seeds cannot be planted right away. You should store them after they are completely dry in a film canister with a dash of Captan fungicide to prevent mold. They'll need three to four months in storage in a cool place to stabilize before they will germinate vigorously and produce healthy plants.

harvest

The harvest process needs the same patient attention you gave to growing. It's best to cut one branch at a time and do a wet manicure. Remove the fan leaves for "Grade B" shake. They dry fine in a paper bag. Toss the bag contents occasionally to prevent compression rot. Then trim back the small leaves in the buds leaving a small amount protruding, 1/4 to 1/2 inch. I think it's best to suspend the buds upside down during drying. The trimmed small leaf is separated into "Grade A" shake. The stubs left will curl down over the bud and dry to a shield protecting the resin covered calyxes. The smallest buds can dry on screens but all bigger ones benefit from a rack. A fan in the drying room helps air circulation and discourages mold. A room temperature of 72 degrees is a good minimum.

Take it easy when manicuring and drying. Rough handling will cause the resin glands to break off the bud carrying away THC. Afghani pure strains bred for Hashish manufacture need very tender care.

The buds are dry when the central stems snap when bent and the calyx/leaf portion feels slightly flexible and moist. The buds should then be packaged for market. Zip-lock bags are the "plain brown wrapper" of the industry and do not adequately protect the harvest. If you're serious about your business, buy a Seal-a-Meal plastic bag closer. These bags are airtight so the buds better be dry or they will mold on the way to market.

It will take you about 10 to 12 hours to manicure a pound of bud and allow one or two weeks to slow dry the crop unless you use a hurry up method, like a room dehumidifier or forced, heated air circulation. Unless you wear rubber gloves, your hands will be coated with resin. Periodically rub your hands together and save the little resin balls. Dip the scissors in alcohol to wash off accumulating resins and keep them sharp. The phrase "snip 'til you flip" is accurate. If you have surplus pollen, take a dab of alcohol and mix it with the collected resins, then dry. This delicate and rare smoke is quite satisfying.

Going back a couple of stages, if you cloned per the guidelines in Part Two, this is the basis for your second crop. If you did two for every plant and carefully recorded the mother source, you'll know which are males to toss and females to keep.

'sea of green'

The clones must be moved to a second grow room with a 1,000 watt HID when you flower the main grow room. After harvest and seed collection are finished, clean the main room thoroughly and move in the clones. I recommend that you grow two or three clone crops this way before going on to another technique.

Eventually I'd recommend you evolve to what is commonly called the "Sea of Green" method if you want to maximize your production capacity and make it your main income source. It is not a complicated technique and reduces your dependence on yield per plant to yield per area by raising a very large number of short clones. The main skill is to be able to start a lot of clones simultaneously, keep them all healthy and put them into the flower phase just as they root.

The result is a grow room that looks like the floor is carpeted with green spikes 12 to 18 inches tall in one-gallon pots.

If you've come this far you've learned a lot. But there is more to know. Selective breeding can do much to custom produce your own super plant, producing a yield, appearance and high closely matching your own tastes. Robert Connel Clarke's *"Marijuana Botany"* stands far above any other book on breeding and along with Jorge's bible, *"Indoor Marijuana Horticulture,"* is a must read.

First printed in Vol. 6, No. 4, page 69.

Carbon Dioxide Enrichment Methods

by Roger H. Thayer

Carbon dioxide is an odorless gas and a minor constituent of the air we breathe. It comprises only .03 percent (300 parts per million, or ppm) of the atmosphere. But, it is vitally important to all life on this planet.

Plants are made up of about 80 to 90 percent carbon and water, with other elements like nitrogen, calcium, magnesium, potassium, phosphorous and trace elements making up only a small percentage. Almost all of the carbon in plants comes from the 300 ppm of carbon dioxide in the air.

Plants take in CO_2 through pores, called stomata, in their leaves during daylight hours. They give off oxygen at the same time, the results of a process called photosynthesis. The oxygen they give off is used by humans and all animal and marine life on this planet. Without it, animal and human life would not be possible.

Oxygen comprises almost 20 percent of the earth's atmosphere. Most of it was generated by plant life. The process of photosynthesis combines CO_2 and water to form sugars and free oxygen. Simple sugars like $C_6H_{12}O_6$ provide plants with energy and are formed into the more complex plant parts such as carbohydrates, amino acids, protein, cellulose, leaves, roots, branches and flowers.

People and animals breathe in oxygen generated by plants and breathe out the CO_2 that the plants need— a truly symbiotic relationship. In ancient times, millions of years ago, when there was only plant life on the earth and no animal life, the atmosphere was quite

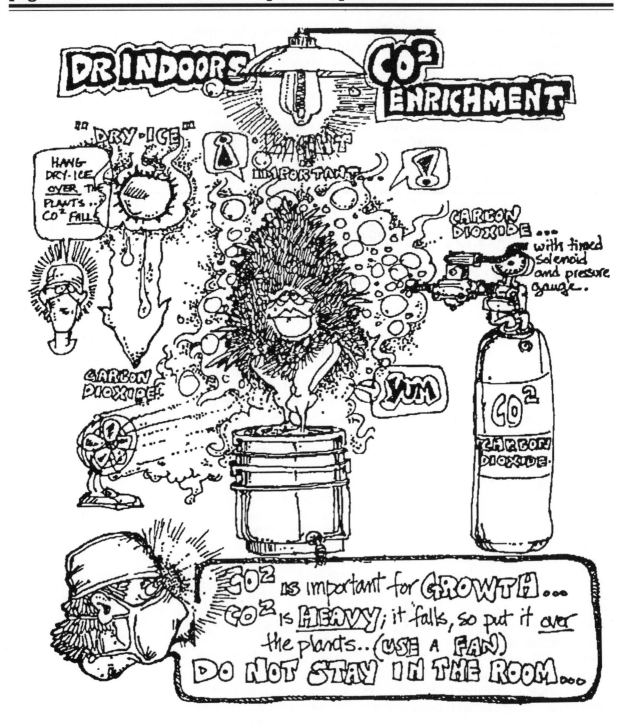

different. There was much more volcanic activity, one of nature's sources of CO_2, and the air contained three to four times as much of it as it does now. Plants thrived. Giant deposits were created by them during that long-ago time.

Plants would benefit from more CO_2 in the air today. Plants are actually benefiting from humans burning more fuels, with one by-product being carbon dioxide. CO_2 in the air has increased from 270 ppm to over 300 ppm, more than an 11 percent increase, in just the last 40 years! This has also worried many scientists because of what is called the "greenhouse effect." The more CO_2 there is in the atmosphere, the higher the planet's temperature will go. Too much warming of the planet can melt ice caps, flood coastal cities, spread deserts and famine and drastically change the climate. This effect is somewhat self-regulating, however. The oceans absorb a great deal of CO_2, giving 90 percent of the plant matter on earth, algae and plankton, more CO_2 to grow on. Plant matter on land also makes use of the CO_2. This decreases the amount of CO_2 in the atmosphere, thereby regulating it. Scientists are just now learning to understand the self-regulating systems that stabilize most factors in our environment.

Biologists and plant physiologists have long recognized the benefits of higher CO_2 content in the air for plant growth. Horticulturists and greenhouse growers have used CO_2 generators to enhance growth rates on plants for many years with good results.

With the advent of home greenhouses and indoor growing under artificial lights, along with the developments in hydroponics in recent years, the need for CO_2 generation has drastically increased. Plants growing in a sealed greenhouse or indoor grow room will often deplete the available CO_2 and stop growing.

Below 200 ppm, plants do not have enough CO_2 to carry on the photosynthesis process and essentially stop growing. Because 300 ppm is the atmospheric CO_2 content, this amount is chosen as the 100 percent growth point. Increased CO_2 can double the growth rate on most plants. Above 2,000 ppm, CO_2 starts to become toxic to plants and above 4,000 ppm it becomes toxic to people.

With the advent of ideal growing conditions provided by metal halides and other high-intensity discharge (HID) lighting systems, hydroponics, environmental controls such as temperature, humidity, etc. and complete, balanced plant nutrients, the limiting factor on plant growth rate, quality, size and time to maturity becomes the amount of carbon dioxide available to the plants.

There are five common methods of generating extra amounts of CO_2:

CO_2 enrichment

common methods

- Burning hydrocarbon fuels
- Compressed, bottled CO_2
- Dry Ice
- Fermentation
- Decomposition of organic matter

We will discuss these five methods briefly. In order to make an effective comparison of CO_2 generation, benefits and drawbacks A standard eight foot square (512 cubic feet) growing area will be used.

burning hydrocarbon fuels

Burning hydrocarbon fuels has been the most common method of CO_2 enrichment for many years. A number of commercial growers and greenhouses use it in their larger structures. The most common fuels are propane, butane, alcohol and natural gas. Any of these fuels that burn with a blue, white or colorless flame will produce carbon dioxide, which is beneficial. If a red, orange or yellow flame is present, carbon monoxide is being generated due to incomplete combustion. Carbon monoxide is deadly to both plants and humans in any but the smallest quantities. Fuels containing sulfur or sulfur compounds should not be used, as they produce by-products which are also harmful.

Most commercial CO_2 generators that burn these fuels are too large for small greenhouse or indoor grow room applications. Some small ones are available or a Coleman lantern, bunsen burner or small gas stove can be used. All of these generators produce heat as a by-product of CO_2 generation, which is rarely needed in a controlled environment grow room but may prove beneficial in winter growing and cool area greenhouses.

The rate of CO_2 production is controlled by the rate at which fuel is being burned. In a gas burning CO_2 generator using propane, butane or natural gas, one pound of fuel produces approximately three pounds of carbon dioxide gas and about 1.5 pounds of water vapor. Approximately 22,000 BTUs of heat is also added. These figures can vary if other fuels are used.

To relate this to our standard example, if you used ethyl or methyl alcohol in a gas lamp or burner at the rate of 1.3 ounces per day, we would enhance the atmospheric concentration of CO_2 to 1,300 ppm if the room was completely sealed.

requirements

An enrichment standard of 1,300 ppm was chosen as it is assumed that 1,500 ppm is ideal, and that the plants will deplete the available CO_2 supply by 100 ppm per hour. Remember, the normal atmosphere contains 300 ppm of CO_2. A 100 percent air exchange (leakage) every two hours is assumed to be the average air exchange rate in most grow rooms and tight greenhouses. If many cracks and leaks are present, this exchange rate will increase significantly, but added

CO_2 (above 300 ppm) will also be lost. If a vent fan is in use, disregard CO_2 enrichment, as it will be blown out as fast as it is generated.

A circulation fan is beneficial, as it moves the air about in the greenhouse or growroom. If the air is still, it can cause a "depletion layer effect." This effect causes the CO_2 right next to the plant leaf to be quickly depleted. If fresh air carrying additional CO_2 is not brought to this surface, photosynthesis and growth will diminish and eventually cease.

There are a number of factors involved in keeping the CO_2 content at the desired concentration level: If the greenhouse or grow room is not tightly sealed, add up to 50 percent to the CO_2 generator production volume. If temperature is increased from 70 degrees to 90 degrees, add 20 percent to the volume generated, and vice-versa. If the grow area contains large or tightly spaced plants, add 20 to 30 percent to the CO_2 volume generated.

If more light is used, more CO_2 can be utilized and should be produced proportionately up to the practical limit of 5,000 ft. candles per square yard and 1,500 ppm CO_2 atmospheric content. When more CO_2 is generated, more water and plant nutrients should be used, again to a practical limit of two times normal. If your plants are going to grow faster because of CO_2 enrichment, they will need more nutrients and water.

The last factor to consider in maintaining a set CO_2 level is the size of your growing area. This is determined for gas burning and the following methods by setting up a mathematical ratio. In our "standard" room, we have 512 cubic feet. If, for example, your growing area contains 2,000 cubic feet of volume, you will need to recalculate. If you want to use the ethyl alcohol/gas lamp enrichment method, set up the ratio using 1.3 ounces of alcohol (by weight) per day, giving the following equation:

512 cubic feet = 1.3 ounces per day
2,000 cubic feet = X ounces per day

Then cross multiply: $512 X = 1.3 \times 2,000$. Dividing both sides by 512 gives you $X = (1.3 \times 2,000)512$. Now solve for X:

X = 5.07 ounces

You need 5.07 ounces of ethyl alcohol per day for a room with a volume of 2,000 square feet (10 foot by 20 foot with a 10 foot ceiling) to generate the same amount (1,300 ppm) of CO_2 as in a 512 cubic foot room.

To generate 1,500 ppm above the available CO_2 (200 ppm) in the same size area, set up the ratio as follows:

1,300 ppm = 5 ounces
1,500 ppm = X ounces

$$X = (5 \times 1500)1300 = 5.77 \text{ ounces}$$

(NOTE: One pound of CO_2 is equivalent to approximately 8.7 cubic feet of gas at standard temperature and pressure.)

If different hydrocarbon fuels are used, the heat content in terms of BTU should be taken into account. If the BTU per hour rate is half that of ethyl alcohol, twice as much must be burned to generate the same approximate amount of CO_2 desired. The amount of CO_2 generated depends on the carbon content of the fuel being used. The BTU per hour heat content can be obtained from literature or suppliers.

compressed, bottled CO_2

Bottled CO_2 is the second most popular method of CO_2 enrichment and provides fairly accurate, controlled results. Compressed CO_2 comes in metal containers under high pressure. Small cylinders contain 20 pounds of compressed CO_2 and large tanks hold 50 pounds. Pressure ranges from 1,600 pounds per square inch to 2,200 PSI.

To enrich available CO_2 with compressed gas, the following equipment is needed:
• Tank of compressed CO_2
• Pressure regulator
• Flow meter
• Solenoid valve, (plastic or metal)
• Short-interval 24-hour timer capable of having an "on-time" variable from one to 20 minutes.
• Connecting tubing, fittings and adapters.

This method allows for the injection of a controlled amount of CO_2 into the growing area at a given interval of time. The pressure regulator reduces the compressed gas pressure from 2,200 PSI to a more controlled amount (100 to 200 PSI), which the flow meter can handle. The flow meter will deliver so many cubic feet per minute of CO_2 to the plants for the duration of time that the solenoid valve is opened. The timer controls the time of day and length of time that the solenoid valve is open.

To operate this CO_2 enrichment system in our standard grow room area, we will want to add enough CO_2 to increase the near depleted level of 200 ppm to 1,500 ppm. We must then add 1,300 ppm of CO_2 to a volume of 512 cubic feet. We would like to do this in intervals of time relative to the natural air exchange rate (leakage rate) to keep the CO_2 level near the 1,500 ppm range.

Let's select an injection time interval (CO_2 enrichment time) of every two hours. First, we must determine how many cubic feet of CO_2 must be added to 512 cubic feet of volume to increase our 200 ppm to 1,500 ppm. To do this, multiply the room volume of 512 cubic feet by 0.0013 (1,300 ppm) to obtain .66 cubic feet of CO_2 that is needed. Set the regulator at 100 psi and the flow meter at 20 CFH (cubic feet per hour) or 0.33 cubic feet per minute. If we set our timer to stay on for two minutes every two hours, we will get the 0.66 cubic feet of additional CO_2 we need to bring the CO_2 level to the 1,500 ppm optimum level needed.

Each pound of CO_2 compressed gas contains approximately 8.7 cubic feet of CO_2 gas at atmospheric pressure. Compressed CO_2 costs around 50 cents/pound at most supply houses. At a rate of 0.66 cubic feet every two hours for 18 hours per day, this method will cost around 30 cents per day to operate. The timer would be set to deliver CO_2 during the "on" time (daylight time) for which the lights are set. This is the only time the plants can use the CO_2; they do not use it when it's dark.

The compressed gas method of CO_2 enrichment has the advantages of fairly precise control, readily available equipment with a $150 to $300 average cost for an installation and it does not add extra heat to the growing area. It also works well for small growing spaces and after initial equipment costs, is not expensive to operate.

Dry ice works well for small areas, especially if some cooling effect is desired. Dry ice, solid carbon dioxide, is very cold—about 109 degrees below zero—so we suggest you handle it with gloves to prevent burning your skin. Dry ice is available through freezer and meat packing outlets and is relatively inexpensive. In our standard room, you would need about .8 pounds dry ice per day to raise the atmospheric CO_2 content to 1,300 ppm. If the growing area is quite warm, .8 pounds can melt much faster than 18 hours. Two methods can be used to regulate this. One is to cut just small pieces, about .1 pounds, and add a new piece every two hours to the growing area. The second method is to put the required amount in an insulated styrofoam box with a few small holes cut in it. This will slow the rate of melting considerably but must be "tuned in" to get it just right so .8 pounds melts in the 18 hours of light "on" time. Extra dry ice must be kept in a freezer to prevent loss due to evaporation.

Since CO_2 is heavier than air, one good method of distributing it to the plants is to attach the container of dry ice to the light relfectors, which are normally placed over the plants. The CO_2 will then flow down through or over the lights and evenly bathe the plants. If a circulation fan is used, the dry ice or its container should be placed directly in front or behind it for even distribution. Common to all CO_2 enrichment methods, try to seal up the room or greenhouse as best you can especially around the bottom of doors and walls.

The dry-ice method will cost around 60 cents per day for our

dry ice method

standard sized, 512 cubic foot room. A possible benefit of using dry ice is the cooling effect it produces.

Sugar is converted into ethyl alcohol and CO_2 when it ferments due to the action of yeast. To use fermentation to produce CO_2 in the grow room, the following ingredients and equipment are needed:
- Suitably sized container, plastic or glass
- Sugar, common or invert
- Yeast, brewers or bourgelais wine yeast
- Yeast nutrient
- Sealant, cellophane, tape or lid
- 1/4" plastic tubing
- 1/4" shutoff valve
- Balloon
- Starter jar or bottle

A pound of sugar will ferment into approximately half a pound of ethyl alcohol (C_2H_5OH) and half a pound of CO_2. One pound of CO_2 makes 8.7 cubic feet of CO_2 gas at normal atmospheric conditions. In our standard grow room, you will need to generate 512 cubic feet times 0.0013 (1,300 ppm CO_2) = 0.66 cubic feet of CO_2 every four hours. It takes time for the yeast to ferment sugar, so the size of container you should use is determined by dividing the cubic feet of growing area (512 cubic feet) by 32 = 16 gallons.

A convenient container to use here would be a plastic kitchen garbage can. These are inexpensive and easily obtained.

To determine how much sugar we need for six weeks of operation or until fermentation ceases, the following calculations are necessary: From the above paragraph, we need 0.66 cubic feet of CO_2 every four hours. If one pound of sugar makes 8.7 cubic feet of CO_2, we will need 0.08 pounds of sugar, but because every one pound of sugar only makes 1/2 pound of CO_2, we must double the amount of sugar needed, i.e. 0.08 times two equals 0.16 every four hours. Since there are six four-hour periods in a 24 hour day, the amount of sugar we need is 0.16 times six, or 0.96 pounds of sugar per day.

If we round this off to one pound of sugar per day, we will need 42 pounds of sugar in six weeks. We must consider that only 80 to 90 percent of the sugar will be completely converted in this length of time, therefore, we should actually use about 48 pounds of sugar in six weeks.

The sugar solution to start with is 2.5 to 3 pounds per gallon. You can use hot water to start with, as sugar dissolves faster in it than in cold water. You must let it cool to 80 to 90 degrees before adding yeast to it or the yeast will be killed. Start with the fermenting container only half-full as you will be adding an extra gallon per week

fermentation method

for six weeks. Begin with eight gallons per week and 24 pounds of sugar.

To start the solution fermenting, you will want to make a "starter batch" of sugar water, yeast and yeast nutrient. To do this, use a coke or beer bottle (approximately one pint), dissolve 1/4 pounds of sugar in 10 ounces of warm water (approximately 3/4 full), add a pinch of yeast and two pinches of yeast nutrient to this sugar mixture. Place a balloon on the bottle and set in a warm location, 80 to 90 degrees, for one to two days or until the balloon expands and small bubbles are visible in the solution.

After the starter solution has begun fermenting vigorously, it is added to the main fermentation tank at the same temperature already mentioned. After a day or so, to see that the system is working properly and that CO_2 is being generated, close the valve to the supply tank and, if the unit is sealed properly, the balloon should expand in a short period of time. To regulate the amount of CO_2 being delivered to the plants, open the valve until the balloon is only half the size of full expansion.

The CO_2 supply tube with in-line valve should have a two-inch loop in it half full of water to serve as an air-lock. This loop can be held in place with tape on the side of the fermentation tank. The open end of this tube can either be positioned in front of a circulating fan or run through "T" fittings to make additional tubes, the ends of which can be positioned above your plants. Remember, CO_2 is heavier than air and it will flow downwards.

Once per week, undo a corner of the saran wrap and add an extra gallon of sugar solution and yeast nutrient, then reseal the top with tape. Use three pounds of sugar and one teaspoon of nutrient per gallon.

After the last gallon is added, after six weeks of operation, let fermentation continue until the balloon goes down and no bubbles are visible in the "U" tube. When this point has been reached, taste the solution. If it is sweet, fermentation is not complete and a new starter batch should be made and added to the tank. More yeast nutrient should also be used. If the solution is dry (not sweet) like wine, fermentation has stopped and the alcohol content has killed the yeast. At this point, it's time to clean your tank and start a new batch.

The fermentation process is quite good for generating CO_2 and relatively inexpensive. Regular or invert (corn) sugar is inexpensive and available. You may have to purchase invert sugar at a wine supply store. This method of generating CO_2 will cost approximately 50 to 60 cents per day.

To save money on extra yeast, you can either take out approximately a gallon of fermenting liquid and save for the next batch, or start a second system identical to the first and alternate them — clean and replenish one, then three weeks later, clean and replenish the second.

decomposition process

When organic matter decomposes due to bacterial action, carbon dioxide is generated. Plants grow lush and vigorously on a tropical jungle floor as a result of this natural decay of dead plant and animal matter. This can increase the available CO_2 content from the normal 300 ppm amount to over 1,000 parts per million. This can also be done indoors, for little cost, but is odorous and unsanitary. For these and other reasons, it is not highly recommended. The sterile conditions of a well-set-up hydroponic grow room or greenhouse could be disrupted and adverse bacteria, bugs and disease could have detrimental effects on your plants.

In conclusion, all these methods will work if done properly. CO_2 enrichment is a very beneficial addition to your greenhouse or grow room systems. Some are more practical than others, some less expensive and some require more time and attention. All chemical reactions are temperature dependent, and photosynthesis is no exception. With CO_2 enrichment, a higher temperature, up to 100 degrees, can be used and more light may be needed as it is required for the photosynthetic reaction to take place. More water and nutrients will also be required, and a machete may be necessary to control the added, sometimes startling extra growth rates possible on most plants by using CO_2 enrichment!

First printed in Vol. 6, No. 1, page 41.

CO_2 Enrichment and Brewing

by Robert Gurney
While a problem of no account for outdoor growers, carbon dioxide deficiency greatly reduces plant production for indoor growers. Carbon dioxide is essential for plant photosynthesis. Its deficiency is one of the reasons that plants grown indoors do not have the lush, green vitality shown by their outdoor cousins.

For years growers of house plants have known that scattering pieces of dry ice (i.e., carbon dioxide in its solid state) around dense concentrations of plants greatly improves plant health. This is as true of Cannabis, as of African violets. A more enjoyable way in which to accomplish this, however, is to ferment beer and/or wine in one's growing area.

Unlike most plants, yeasts are producers rather than consumers of carbon dioxide. In breadmaking, it is their production of carbon dioxide gas that causes the bread to fill with small bubbles of the gas and thereby expand or "rise." The alcohol produced by the yeast is evaporated when the bread is cooked. This evaporating alcohol is a major component of the distinctive aroma of bread baking.

In beer and wine fermentation, one's objective is opposite to the objective in breadmaking. Here, one tries to retain the alcohol while letting the carbon dioxide escape into the air. For most brewers and vintners, the carbon dioxide is merely waste. For resourceful, indoor horticulturists, however, this carbon dioxide can be employed more beneficially as a gift (even a high, perhaps) for their plants.

Given the noticeable effects it will have on plant health and vigor, it is an easy and inexpensive matter to put a jug of fermenting wine into a room filled with plants. Even as little as one gallon of fermenting wine will produce over a pound of carbon dioxide during its month of fermentation. More precisely, if the liquid to be fermented contains two and a half pounds of sugar (this being about average for winemaking), a standard, all-purpose winemaking yeast will convert this sugar to 1.2 pounds of carbon dioxide and 1.3 pounds of alcohol. This is plenty of carbon dioxide for a small room full of plants. A five-gallon batch of beer would produce almost twice this much.

Equipment and expertise-wise, the horticultural vintner would greatly benefit by (a) finding a good store for beer and wine supplies, and (b) reading a few of the really excellent books available for amateur beer and wine makers.

I have lived in several small towns, as well as in large cities. Yet, I have never had difficulty finding, tucked away in some little shopping center, a store selling supplies for beer and wine production. Anyone not having similar success in their own locale will have to rely on mail-order houses of which there are many. Some of these advertise in the magazine *Zymurgy*, published by the American Homebrewers' Association (Box 287, Boulder, Colorado, 80306-0287).

It is easy to produce a fermentation that will supply plants with carbon dioxide. A package of baker's yeast mixed into a gallon of water in which two pounds of sugar has been dissolved will do it. But anyone wishing to maximize carbon dioxide production, as well as have a liquid result fit to drink, will greatly benefit from a moderate investment (about $30) in equipment. For beermaking, the minimal equipment is a single-stage fermentor with an attached fermentation lock (cost: about $10), a siphon hose (less than $5), and a bottle capper (about $15). For winemaking, minimal equipment is a one-gallon glass jug, such as cider comes in (cost: nothing), a two-gallon plastic bucket (about $2), a siphon hose (less than $5), a fermentation lock and a stopper for the gallon jug (about $1.50), a winemaker's hydrometer (about $4), and a bottle corker ($15 or less).

Most books written for amateur brewers and vintners are reasonably good and useful introductions. As specific recommendations, it would be hard to improve on Kathleen Howard and Norman Gibat's, *"Making Wine Beer and Merry"* (Popular Topics Press, 1978) and the two Hawthorn Books publications by Stanley F. Anderson with Raymond Hull, *"The Art of Making Beer"* (1971) and *"The Art of Making Wine"* (1970). A great book of deliciously foolproof wine recipes is Raymond Massaccesi's *"Winemaker's Recipe Handbook"* (published by the author, 1976). All four are available and inexpensive paperbacks.

For more about the beneficial effects on indoor plants of an atmosphere enriched with carbon dioxide, there is a good chapter on the topic in Frederick H. and Jaqueline L. Krantz's book, *"Gardening Indoors Under Lights"* (The Viking Press, 1971).

First printed in Vol 6, No. 3, page 60.

*"Weed—a plant whose virtues have not yet been
discovered."* —Ralph Waldo Emerson

Harvesting and Drying

by Tom Alexander

The fall is usually a time of great excitement and more than a little paranoia for most growers. The female flowers are at their peak bloom and ready to harvest— a fact known as well to law enforcement agencies as to growers.

No growing operation is complete until the buds are dried properly and packaged in an airtight container (and sold in the case of the commercial grower).

The female plant matures in stages. The flowers on the top third to half of the plant mature first, with the other flowers on the remaining portion taking another week or two.

The marijuana flower is like any other flower; the petals on a rose or daisy are fresh and beautiful looking for only a short time. The object is to pick the flower when most of its "V-shaped" hairs are in full bloom. After the start of flowering, the hairs will appear white or light green in color. As the bud reaches full bloom, there are a massive amount of hairs on each bud. These hairs are responsible for much of the taste and potency of the product. If the flowers are allowed to become over mature, the resins and hairs start to disintegrate and the bud will swell— like a gigantic pine cone.

When the buds reach this stage, they will weigh a little more, but flavor, aroma and high are compromised. Maturity is the point when the optimum number of hairs are turning to a red, gold or purple color. If a grower waits too long to harvest, the hairs will start to turn from red, gold or purple to a dead looking brown color. The dead brown hairs then turn to dust and are blown away by the wind.

A warm, dry day is best for harvesting. Marijuana's resin is at

weather

optimum quality when the temperature has hit its highest point of the day. Do not harvest when it is cool, damp and overcast unless your intuition tells you of a bust, rip-off or other catastrophe. A less than optimum harvest is 100 percent better than no harvest at all.

Wind and rain can damage a crop. Provide some kind of support for the plants if the weather turns bad. Always let the buds dry completely before harvesting. Damp buds can cause mold which can disintegrate a beautiful bud in 12 hours.

Remove all medium to big leaves from the plant a few days before the expected harvest. This will save some time cleaning later. Also, check for any signs of mold on the buds because this can spread to other plants or get more severe during drying. If mold is found, remove it completely.

When harvesting, find the point where the buds are at peak maturity and leave all buds below this point on the plant for another one to two weeks. Cut the plant with a very sharp knife or other cutting instrument. Sometimes only a few buds will mature at the same time on a plant.

In areas that have a long, sunny fall (or indoors), multiple harvests can be done two or three times, extending the flower stage much longer. Attempting multiple harvest in early frost areas is not possible. If only the mature flowering tops are removed, the plant will keep sending up new flowers to take the place of the cut ones. After a while, the plant will stop trying to reproduce and will eventually die. So, after a few cuttings, harvest the whole plant.

drying

The drying temperature for the flower tops is critical. Too much heat will turn the tops into dust. On the other hand, drying at too low a temperature, especially with poor air circulation, creates a perfect home for mold spores to grow.

It is a myth that drying the plants upside down draws more resin to the tips of the buds. The resin is produced inside the bud and the stem contains only water and various nutrients and starches necessary for the plant's photosynthesis process The nutrients and starches are processed into the psychoactive resin in the sex organs inside the bud.

Removal of as much main stem when drying helps the bud dry faster. The stems take longer to dry than the buds. Cut out the main stem between the nodes and hang on a line. Even more stem can be cut off if drying is done on racks or in a commercial dryer. The best method for drying is open air with a controlled temperature with as little light as possible.

The best temperature for drying is between 80 and 100 degrees, with 85 degrees as the optimum. Electric heaters are best, but propane heaters with a thermostat are also good. Installing a dehumidifier speeds the drying process a day or so, but only operate it every other day for six to eight hours.

Good air circulation is necessary for the prevention of mold. Hang all plants with enough air space between them and place a fan in the room to help carry away the moisture that is escaping and evaporating from the drying plant tissue. Don't have the fan blowing and swaying the plants as that could bruise the valuable buds. Set it at a speed that gently circulates the air. Depending on all the above factors, marijuana buds will dry to a packagable product in about five to 10 days.

When the buds have reached a point where they are dry enough to smoke but not so dry that they crumble to dust, take each branch and cut off each individual bud that has no stem showing. Depending on the length of the bud, they are graded in three categories.

Manicuring the buds is necessary if you plan to market your product to the connoisseur consumer. Using sharp, small scissors, remove any leaves that stick out from the bud and any bare stem that is showing. Once each bud is manicured, place it in piles according to grade A, B, C, or shake.

When enough graded buds have accumulated to fill a large Ziplock plastic bag, fill the bag and seal it up and store in a dark place for 12 to 18 hours. During this time the stem which has a little more moisture left in it than the bud, transfers moisture to the bud. After the bud has absorbed the moisture, spread the buds on a piece of newspaper and allow to air dry for 10 to 12 hours in a dark, dry place. The buds are now ready for final packaging.

After spending most of a year on producing a potent crop, it only makes sense to package your puct properly once it is dry. Ziplock bags or plastic twist tie bags are both improper containers to store sinsemilla buds. Seal-a-Meal, by Dazey Products, Inc., is usually used to seal food for freezing. Pot growers are also using it to seal pot. It is the best sealer on the market. All sealers use a heating element to fuse the ends of the bag together. Machines with a wide heating ban are generally better than those using a narrow wire.

Cellophane bags are available in different sizes or can be purchased in a continuous roll that can be cut to different sizes. The roll allows you to make whatever size bag that you need for different size buds. Once all the buds are sealed, store in a cool, dry and dark place. When buying Dazey's Seal-a-Meal make sure that it is Model #1 which has a wider and better sealing band than Model #2.

First printed in Vol. 1, No. 3, page 8.

air circulation

trimming and storage

heat sealed bags

Alternative Methods of Harvesting

Ultimately, the decision of when to harvest a crop is up to the individual grower. Try to harvest when you think the flowers just couldn't possibly smell or look any better. If you are growing outdoors there are many variables, such as past, present and future weather conditions. There are also security considerations and timing considerations. Only you can weigh all the factors. After you've picked, it's the patient care you give your buds that will reward you with a perfect stash.

There is no easier time to manicure a bud than when it is at its peak of freshness. Ideally, a bud should be manicured immediately after it is picked. This is fine for indoor growers and backyard gardeners who can clip fresh buds off their plants as needed, but outdoor growers who have harvested a large number of plants face a real challenge trying to manicure every plant before it becomes limp. Wilted buds are aggravating to work with and dried ones are prone to damage.

keeping buds in water

So, like your local florist, you can keep cut flowers fresh by arranging each plant in its own floral bouquet. Having a large stockpile of five-gallon plastic buckets will help. If you field strip all the large fan leaves before harvest, your bouquet will stay fresh longer. There won't be the added demand on the plant's water needs by the larger leaves.

To prepare a plant for your bouquet, take off the lower branches at the main stalk with a sharp hand pruner. Remove all branches to within three or four feet of the top or tops of the plant. Trim all buds and leaves from the bottom seven or eight inches of the branches or top colas so that you have a clean stem to put into the water. A professor of horticulture, from a large state university, suggested snipping off the bottom one-half inch or so of the stem while it's under water. This helps facilitate the flow of water back up into the plant. Using a large bowl of water lets you cut off the bottoms of more than one branch at a time with your hand pruner. A drop of water will stay on the bottom of the branch, keeping the new cut protected during the transfer to the bucket of water. Any smaller branches can be kept in a mason jar in this same manner. Make sure there is water in the bottom of the buckets at all times, but be careful none of the buds are in water. Plants can be kept for a week in this manner. Even wilted plants can be brought back to life using this method.

The professor also suggested pouring 7-Up or Sprite in the water to help the buds keep longer. While it's a good idea for most flowers, this is probably not necessary for your particular crop. Throw out the old water after a few days, especially if leaves have fouled it. Be sure that all the stem tips are covered by the fresh water you add. Putting your floral arrangements in a cool location will help them through the long haul. Even the buds that you clip off the bottom of the branches can be kept fresh for a day or two in your refrigerator without the aid of water. If the temperature is cool enough, whole plants will keep out of water overnight.

While the task of manicuring is made simpler by using fresh buds, there are other considerations that can help speed the work process as well. Having a well-lighted work area is the first priority in preparing your workplace. Suspend a bank of fluorescent lights directly over the table. Use comfortable chairs that will keep you up to the table. The table itself should be large enough so that you are not cramped for space. Music will help pass the time, but if you're interested in speed, television can be distracting.

labor saving tips

Your choice of scissors is very important. An oriental style pair is recommended. These scissors have large flexible handles which allow comfortable, easy cutting for right or left handers. The handles won't dig into your skin, cause cramps, or fatigue, even after long hours at the table. They're designed for powerful leverage which helps their sharp blades get through tough stems. The blades have finely honed cutting edges just right for a quick haircut on the smaller leaves that stick out from within the bud. The tapered point of the scissors makes it easy to get to the base of a leaf in a tight space.

scissors

Fingers and scissors gum up quickly when working with sticky resinous material. This slows you down and makes handling the bud difficult. You can cause severe irritation to your eyes by rubbing them with resin-coated fingers. The protection of a very light coating of mineral oil on your fingers and scissor blades will cut down the resin build-up dramatically. Always clean your scissors after each use. Apply a little more mineral oil to them so that they're ready for your next clipping session.

When manicuring, the goal is to produce a clean, beautiful bud. There is more than one technique to arrive at this end. Many people feel more comfortable working on a whole branch at once. They cut off all the large leaves at the base of their stems, and then go from bud to bud on the branch, giving a haircut to the smaller leaves that stick out from within the flowers. They are careful to give as close a cut to the bud as possible without damaging the individual flowers or hairs.

manicuring

The buds are then cut from the branch. Most people are careful to trim buds from the branch so that each flower top is totally covered with buds and excess stem is removed.

Many prefer the method of clipping, at once, all the buds from a few branches into a pile on the table. Take care not to leave a gap of stem between buds. Then work on each individual bud by first taking off the large leaves and then giving the small ones a haircut. Using this method most people find they have better control and can manipulate the bud for a better trim in the same amount of time when compared with the other method.

Regardless of what technique you use, it's always a good idea to take a break when you start to become fatigued. After many hours at the table you can become careless and make mistakes. If you are working on a plant that's difficult to manicure, you'll tire quickly. Try and follow up the difficult plant with one that is easy. A hard plant to manicure is generally enough reason to eliminate it from your breeding or cuttings work. There are many easy clipping strains that have a pleasant stone, excellent appearance, heavenly fragrance and satisfying taste, so that it makes no sense to keep one around that is a real chore to work on.

Keeping your table clean of trimmed leaves and manicured buds will insure that you don't accidently lose a bud in among the leaves. It's helpful to work over paper plates. When a plate is full of leaves, remove them. When a bud plate is full, spread the buds out on a tray. As soon as each tray is completely covered with a single layer of buds, label the tray with the name of the plant and put it into some kind of rack. Metal baker's racks that hold a dozen trays work well. If you use bread trays it's advisable to line them with brown wrapping paper so that no buds fall through the holes. Always keep the buds of one plant separate from those of another so that you have a pure representation of each particular plant. This is especially important if you have a breeding or cuttings program and want to determine which plants to continue working with. When you have a crop of several cuttings from one plant, treat them

as one and mix their buds.

Drying herb is a delicate art that shouldn't be rushed. Try to maintain a mild temperature and moderate humidity in the drying area. In a very damp area you may need to use a dehumidifier to keep the humidity level down. For air circulation, which is important for mold prevention, keep an oscillating fan set on low. After a couple of days on the tray, turn all the buds over. You can do this by placing another sheet of wrapping paper on top of them and an inverted tray on top of that. By flipping the two trays completely over, you will reverse all the buds onto the other tray. Herb shrinks as it dries, so to conserve space and slow down the drying process, add identical material from other trays that have been clipped at the same time. If no other tray exists, gently gather the flowers of one type into a loose, shallow pile at one end of the tray.

Test for dryness daily by gently squeezing a few buds with your fingers to see just how much moisture they still contain. When they reach a stage where they feel smokable and the stems of the buds are just barely pliable—almost to the snapping point—it is time to package. The meat of the bud will regain a little moisture from the stems when packaged. The best smoking material has enough moisture in it for improved smoothness, but is dry enough so that there is no problem lighting and keeping it lit.

storage

The best methods for packaging and storage are debatable. You may find that a Seal-A-Meal is preferred for airtight protection of stash. Now there is a vacuum-type model that is an improvement over the old Seal-A-Meal II. Both come with a 10-inch wide roll of plastic pouch material that enables you to package a tube of buds any length you want, up to 20 feet long. If you enjoy smoking a large variety of types, make up small packets of two or three grams each. Regardless of what size package you make, place it directly into your deep freeze until you are ready to smoke it.

Freshness can be maintained for many years and seeds can be stored frozen indefinitely. If you choose not to use a freezer, check your herb periodically for mold, especially if you keep the moisture level high. When enough moisture is present, a certain amount of favorable curing can take place over a week or two in an unfrozen sealed bag. There is a fine line between a desirable cure and potential mold damage, so you should be cautious.

Harvest time is your reward, so try and treat your crop to the best care possible.

First printed in Vol. 6, No. 4, page 39.

Storage Diseases and Pests

by The Bush Doctor

Growers harvesting a healthy cornucopia of Cannabis must maintain vigilance over their cut crops. Entire harvests have been lost to molds and insects while curing, drying or in storage. Marijuana is an unusual crop considering the product may reach consumers up to a year after harvest. This leaves wide berth for microscopic "consumers" to contaminate and destroy the product first. In nature, these bacteria, fungi, mites and insects play important roles in the recycling process. If not for them, "renewable natural resources" would not exist.

Anything that dies is broken down by these organisms except for chemically treated mummies, arctic-frozen mastodons, and cryoprotected Walt Disney. Avoiding these storage molds and insects is impossible; they are ubiquitous. Manipulating the environment to maintain suboptimal conditions. Discouraging these storage diseases and pests is the key to their control.

Marijuana plants are exposed to contamination by fungi and bacteria from the moment seeds germinate until the product is pyrolyzed by the smoker. While alive, the plant's natural defenses protect against most infections. Organisms successfully breeching these defenses cause plant disease. Some parasites, such as powdery mildews and rust, can only grow on living plant tissues. When plants are uprooted, these parasites die with them.

Organisms attacking harvested marijuana are classified into two groups: Those infecting plants in the field and continuing their damage after harvest are designated as "field organisms." True "storage organisms" only invade the plants after harvest.

Cannabis provides several products after harvest. Storage diseases of the product marijuana have not been investigated by the scientific community as closely as those of harvested Cannabis seeds (for seed oil) and hemp stems (for rope— the "hemp retting organisms"). I will review the information available:

fungi

Fungi are the most common cause of storage diseases in marijuana. "Field fungi" carrying over as storage molds include *Sclerotinia fuckeliana* (*Botrytis cinerea*), *S. sclerotiorum*, and *Alternaria tenuis*. In living plants these cause gray mold, hemp cancer, and brown blight (respectively). Other field fungi causing minor storage

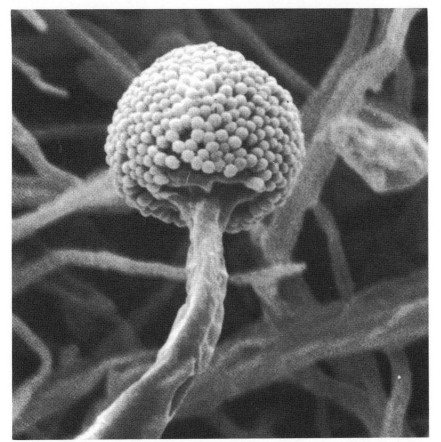

Young conidial head of *Aspergillus niger* seen at 600 times actual size through a scanning electron microscope.

mold problems are *Cladosporium herbarum, Epicoccum nigrum, Cephalosporium cannabis, Stachybotrys lobulata, Stemphylium cannabinum, Pooist sebastianum,* and several *Fusarium* and *Mucor* species.

Field insects continuing their damage during drying, curing and storage of marijuana include *Cydia delineana* (hemp gall moth), and *Heliothis arbigera* (budworms). No field bacteria are reported to cause storage disease. This area is in need of investigation.

Field bacteria, as well as plant enzymes, contribute to the curing process of freshly harvested Cannabis. The unpleasant green "home-grown" taste of fresh marijuana is eliminated during this curing process, in which chlorophyll and complex plant starches are broken down. Any organisms involved have not been elucidated. If damp marijuana is stored in airtight containers, anaerobic bacteria will arise.

insects and bacteria

These include several *Clostridium* species which are discussed under hemp-stem retting. Three species of actinomycetes have been isolated from marijuana cigarettes, *Thermoactinormyces candidus*, *T. vulgaris* and *Micropolyspora faeni*. Viruses, nematodes, rickettsia, MLOs and other fastidious obligate parasites attacking live plants will not cause storage diseases.

True "storage organisms" cause more damage then field organisms in harvested material. Fungi again are the primary cause of storage rots in Cannabis. Dead marijuana leaves and flowers have no natural defenses. If moisture and temperature conditions are favorable for fungal spore germination, the hyphae quickly penetrate and grow in plant tissue.

"Storage" fungi predominate in storage because they have evolved as such. Technically, they are not parasites, but saprophytes. Moldy marijuana is seldom contaminated by only one organism. Competition occurs between fungi. *Antagonistic bacteria* and *actinomycete* species produce antifungal compounds. Under these conditions fungi adapted to the lower moisture and oxygen levels of stored marijuana will predominate. *Aspergillus*, *Penicillium Rhizopus* and *Mucor* species are the most damaging storage fungi, they are discussed in depth below.

Bacteria colonizing marijuana during curing, drying and in storage are basically unknown. Only those also causing disease in people have been identified (e.g.,*Salmonella muenchen*, *Klebsiella pneumoniae*, *Enterobacter cloacae*, group D strep). True "storage" insects are rarely encountered in marijuana. Mites, including *Tyrophagus* and *Aculops* species, cause some damage in storage. Spider mites, nemesis of greenhouse growers, die soon after plants are harvested. A sigh of relief.

signs and symptoms

Detecting storage diseases and pests of marijuana is relatively simple. Irregular patches of white or gray fungal hyphae are often visible. In earlier stages the mold may only be seen along midribs of leaves and cloistered flower clusters. Velvety masses of spores and conidia develop black, green, brown, red or yellow spots on the marijuana.

These spores are easily dislodged by a slight tap or passing breeze, billowing clouds of colored conidia. The product itself often darkens in color, turning black and crumbly. Marijuana having the odor of mold is a give away. Musty, stale or other undesirable odors also accompany fungal rot. Anerobic bacteria produce a particularly offensive odor and turn damp marijuana into brown slime.

Heat is another symptom of fungal and bacterial storage rots. The diseased material will feel warm to the touch, an effect of active

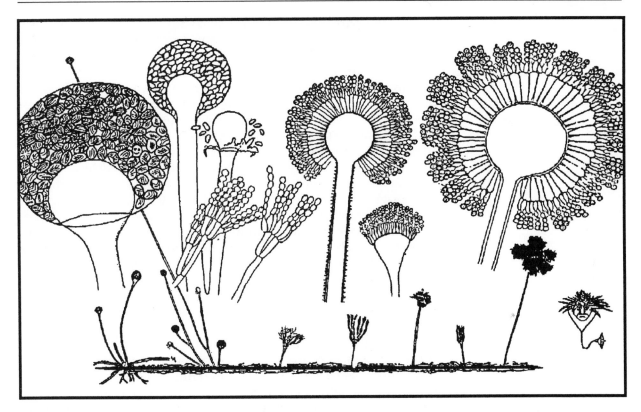

decomposition. At this stage it can be added to the compost heap. To check for storage insects, a No. 10 steel sieve is recommended for screening samples. A No. 30 mesh screens storage mites. Simply shaking samples over a sheet of white paper effectively exposes live insects. A hand lens is helpful for spotting the smaller mites.

Control

The secret to stopping storage diseases is moisture control. Marijuana kept dry after harvest until it reaches the consumer will not mold. Even gray mold disease will be arrested at harvest time if crops are carefully and quickly dried. Flue cured Cannabis develops less storage rot than air or sweat cured crops. Sweat curing is used in Colombia, their product has a tradition of *Aspergillus* contamination.

These different techniques (as well as sun and water curing for small quantities) are described by Frank Rosenthal in *"Marijuana Grower's Guide."* Of the different drying methods, oven drying is safer than slow air drying, but results in a product with a harsher smoke. Slow air drying is successful if plants are suspended upside

storage molds associated with post-harvest marijuana losses

Left to right (below):
Rhiyopus nigrans, Mucor hiemalis, Penicillin, Chrysogenum, P. italic, Aspergillus flavus, A. fumigatus. A. niger.
Top row: sporngia and conidial heads cross-sectioned revealing internal structures, with *H M. Hiemalis* demonstrating spore release.

moisture content

down and apart from each other, allowing air to circulate between them. Drying rooms should be cool and dry, preferably dark. Several storage rot fungi require UV light to sporulate. Thus, darkness insures a reduced inoculum potential.

Living Cannabis plants are about 80 percent water. Properly stored and dried, marijuana contains about 10 percent water or moisture content (MC). MC below 10 percent creates an unpliable product which disintegrates into dust. Loss from storage fungi are negligible below 15 percent MC. Unfortunately, it is advantageous for growers to market their crops at MCs considerably above this level.

Cannabis, like corn flakes, is sold by weight, not by volume; increased moisture weighs more. Tobacco farmers also allow their product to re-absorb moisture before wholesale marketing. They term this risky business, "coming into order." Marijuana purchased for home use should always be re-dried. Storage in refrigerators or freezers will not protect from storage rot (via light green *Penicillium spp.*) if the material is above 15 percent MC. Placing a lemon or orange peel in stored marijuana is also not recommended. It may raise the MC of properly dried pot above the threshold 15 percent level.

Maintaining stored marijuana at optimum 10 percent MC will also prevent most insect and mite problems. Mold will encourage insect infestation. Conversely, insects and mites will spread fungal infections. Occasionally, you will find bugs in your moldy marijuana that feed only on the fungi. Square-nosed fungus beetles and long-haired mites are two such arthropods. All should be eradicated.

Insecticide and miticide sprays have no application on stored marijuana. Their residues pose a danger to the consumer. Also, the water-based sprays may kill the bugs but will trigger a fungal infestation by raising the MC. At best, the pesticide sprays represent a trade-off, at worst, they will kill somebody. Pesticides are useful in disinfecting a drying room after a problem crop has been cleared out.

Fumigants are toxic gases used as pesticides in stored wheat and corn. They will not trigger mold infestations, but do leave gaseous residues in air pockets of fumigated materials. Sinsemilla colas are full of air pockets. Fumigants such as methyl bromide are extremely toxic to humans. They require expensive protective clothing and application equipment. Applicators in many states must have a special license to purchase them. Their advantage lies in the ability to kill fungi and bacteria as well as insects and mites.

Scientists have sterilized marijuana cigarettes with ethylene oxide, reporting no loss of THC from fumigation. These researchers also found high doses of cobalt 60 radiation (15,000-20,000 Gray Units) effectively sterilized marijuana without THC reduction. This method is not recommended for novices. On the other hand, novices are known to treat their marijuana with formaldehyde. This will kill insects and fungi, but is a dangerous practice. The product, known as "Amp," causes psychomotor retardation and anoxia when smoked. Inner-city Amp users I encounter in my southside Chicago hospital, describe their high as "getting stupid."

Manipulating the temperature of stored Cannabis is a simple method of insect and mite control. Low temperatures will freeze an infestation in progress, but not always kill all insects and mites. With rewarming they will continue their destruction.

freezing

Another drawback to freezing involves the aforementioned exacerbation of *Penicillium* mold problems if the MC is above 15 percent. Heating Cannabis in a 150-200 degree oven for 10 minutes will kill most pests. This will also dry out the marijuana, which, again, is the cornerstone of control in all storage problems, Marijuana should not be heated to temperatures above 200 degrees, or longer than 10 minutes, which will increase THC oxidation and loss of potency.

Avoid wounding plant tissue before it completely dries (even while it is still in the ground and growing). Damaged tissues release exudates containing nutrients. These nutrients are used by storage disease fungi. The molds establish a competitive foothold, rapidly invading neighboring tissues when conditions permit. Small amounts of these nutrients are released, even in healthy, intact plants, by leaching and exosmosis. Tobacco researchers say that these leaf exudates are produced in greater quantities by diseased, nutrient deficient and older yellowing leaves, as well as damaged ones. Expect more storage mold problems with these conditions.

The genus *Aspergillus* includes over 500 fungal species. These ubiquitous organisms grow on anything from rocket fuel to tomatoes that taste like cardboard molmpeck. Worldwide in distribution, the genus is millions of years old. While *Homo sapiens* have come and gone, *Aspergillus* will remain. These meek molds, with their sister genus *Penicillium*, shall inherit the earth. Both genera are cosmopolitan, *Aspergillus* being more successful in warmer climates, *Penicillium* in cooler climates.

Aspergillus

As a group, *Aspergillus* species are easily identified. Distinguishing between species within the genus is another matter. Speciation involves expert use of standard in-vitro cultivation on Czapek's agar. Entire tomes are dedicated to this subject. *Aspergillus* speciation is a discipline unto itself; my lack of expertise precludes me from evaluating other's identification of species attacking Cannabis. Hence this account is an uncritical compilation of reports from the literature.

Ten *Aspergillus* species attack Cannabis plants or their harvested products. Several species are dangerous to us as well, producing allergic reactions if inhaled, toxic and/or carcinogenic effects if ingested, can superficially colonize open wounds, eyes, ears or the lungs, and act as opportunistic invaders causing fatal systemic infections. More on this later. All above-ground parts of Cannabis are attacked. Westendorp (1854) was the first to describe an *Aspergillus* species attacking Cannabis leaves, *A. conoideus*. The genus is associated with retting of hemp stems, especially *A. glaucus*. Grebniuk reports *A. versicolor* attacking stems of living plants as well. *A. flavus* and *A. sulfureus* were isolated from moldy seeds by Ceapoiu. Babu et al. also recovered these two species, as well as *A. niger*, *A. repens*, and *A. tamarii* (equals *A. erythrocephalus*) from seeds. Moldy marijuana has been studied by several researchers. As a microcosm of our earth itself, the most frequently encountered organisms are *Aspergillus* or *Penicillium* species. Authors of the popular 1970's manual *"A Child's Garden of Grass "* describe a "black web-like fungus" colonizing damp marijuana, observing the colonized marijuana achieved an increased potency. This fungus is probably an *Aspergillus* or *Mucor/Rhizopus* species. Unfortunately, they did not preserve a voucher specimen.

In my studies, *A. niger* is the most often encountered organism of moldy marijuana stored at room temperature. It does not increase potency. It has been found, however, growing in the sinuses of a marijuana smoker suddenly experiencing severe headaches. Other researchers frequently isolate *A. niger* from marijuana cigarettes, as well as *A. fumigatus* and *A. flavus*. The latter two species are bad actors. Llamas et al. associates smoking moldy marijuana with allergic bronchopulmonary aspergillosis. *A fumigatus* was the causal organism, eliciting a syndrome of asthma with recurrent fever, bronchial

plugs, pulmonary infiltrates on x-ray and eosinophilia. Chusid et al. also cite this organism causing pneumonitis in a 17-year-old with chronic granulomatous disease. They noted the boy had buried his marijuana in the earth for "aging." No doubt he was seeking the "black web-like fungus" and *A. fumigatus* found him instead.

A. flavus is often isolated from Cannabis (Ceapoiu, Babu et al., Kagen, Moody et al.), and is the most dangerous *Aspergillus* on the market. In addition to provoking asthma and causing *aspergilliosis/aspergillomas*, this fungus produces toxic metabolites called aflatoxins. Aflatoxins cause liver disease and jaundice, followed by ataxia, convulsions, and death. Chronic exposure to low-level toxins induces lung cancer, renal cell carinoma and liver hepatomas. Not all strains of *A. flavus* produce these carcinogenic toxins. But Llewellyn and O'Rear report strains of *A. flavus* (and *A. parasiticus*) on marijuana in Virginia. Aflatoxin-producing strains of *A. flavus* can be detected with a Wood's lamp (black light). Contaminated material will fluoresce a green color under the ultraviolet light.

Some ironies present themselves here: Marijuana traditionally serves as a remedy for asthma. Yet herb contaminated with *Aspergillus* will trigger an attack, rather than treat one. Another irony involves the use of marijuana to reduce nausea and vomiting associated with cancer chemotherapy; this immuno-suppressed patient population is extremely susceptible to opportunistic infections. McPartland has noted that inhalation of *Aspergillus* laden marijuana may cause pulmonary aspergilliosis in these debilitated cancer victims. He suggested substituting synthetic THC as an antiemetic agent. Using a water pipe will reduce transmission of fungal spores but not eliminate them. Moody et al. tested glass water pipes with marijuana contaminated with *A. flavus*, *A. fumigatus* and *A. niger*. They report a 15 percent incidence of fungal transmission.

Detection of aspergilli in one's Cannabis is easily accomplished. The product will smell moldy (musty, stale, etc.). Lucas reports *A. flavus* has a particularly offensive odor, and the smell of *A. niger* is "characteristic" (but he did not describe it). White or gray strands of fungal mycelium are visible. They are quickly covered by velvety dark green to black conidia. These send up dark clouds of spores when disturbed. If marijuana is stored under low oxygen tension, the fungus will not sporulate and remains a white mycelial mass.

Space does not permit detailed descriptions of the ten aspergilli associated with Cannabis. Proper identification of most species require use of specialized agar and techniques beyond the range of common reason. Nevertheless, I can describe microscopic features of the easily identified and commonly encountered *A. niger*, as well

detection

as the danger species *A. flavus* and *A. fumigatus* :

A. niger van Tieghem 1867

Conidial heads globose, blackish brown to black, often splitting into several loose but well-defined columns, up to 700 to 800 millimeters in diameter. Conidiophores are upright, straight or curved, up to 33 millimeters long, 15 to 20 millimeters wide, smooth, hyaline or slightly colored at the apex where it swells into a spherical vesicle 40 to 70 millimeters in diameter. The entire surface of the vesicle is covered by closely packed metulae, club-shaped, 20 to 30 millimeters long by 5 to 6 millimeters wide. Phialides arise in groups from metulae, flask-shaped, 7 to 10 by 3 to 3.5 millimeters. The conidia are usually globose, brown, warted, mostly 4 to 5 millimeters in diameter, produced in dry chains. The optimum temperature for growth is 37 degrees C.

A. flavus Link 1809

The conidial heads typically radiate into poorly defined columns, yellow-green, up to 400 to 500 millimeters in diameter. The conidiophores are thick walled, less than 1 millimeter long, and 20 to 30 millimeters wide with a coarsely roughed wall, hyaline, swollen at apex into a spherical vesicle 25 to 45 millimeters in diameter. Almost the entire surface of the vesicle is covered by closely packed metulae, club shaped, 6 to 10 by 4 to 5.5 millimeters. The phialides arise in groups from the metulae, flask shaped, 6.5 to 10 by 3 to 5 millimeters. The conidiais at first elliptical, becoming globose and warted, yellow-green, mostly 3.5 to 4.5 millimeters in diameter and produced in chains. The optimum temperature for growth is 35 degrees C.

A. fumigatus Fresenius 1850

The conidial heads are strictly columnar, compact, often crowded, bluish green. The conidiophores are up to 300 millimeters in length and 5 to 8 millimeters in diameter, smooth, light green to brown near the apex where it swells into a club-shaped vesicle 20 to 30 millimeters wide. Only the upper surface of the vesicle is covered by closely packed phialides (no metulae). They are flask shaped, 6 to 8 by 2.5 to 3.5 millimeters. The condidia are usually globose, light green, warted, 2.5 to 3.0 millimeters in diameter. The optimum temperature for growth is 40 degrees C.

First printed in Vol. 6, No. 3, page 41.

"Force, violence, or compulsion with a view to conformity, are both uncivilized and undemocratic." —Mohandas Gandi

An Overview
Search and Seizure

by Bruce C. Moore

The Fourth Amendment's ban against unreasonable searches and seizures has been the subject of more legal articles and cases than all of the other constitutional amendments combined. What follows is a thumbnail sketch of a legal field replete with exceptions and technical distinctions. With that disclaimer out of the way, I begin with two hypothetical cases:

1. A hunter wanders upon a large marijuana garden in Lane County, Oregon. He relays his find to the authorities. The grower is arrested for unlawful manufacture of a controlled substance.

2. A patrol officer smells marijuana smoke in a vehicle that has been stopped for speeding. He finds marijuana in the ashtray and glove box in a subsequent warrantless search of the vehicle. This time the arrest is for possession of a controlled substance.

If the persons arrested in these cases pleaded not guilty to the charges, one of the first lines of defense would likely be the validity of the search and seizure that produced the marijuana as evidence. If it is determined that the search and seizure was unreasonable, the evidence will likely be suppressed because of the "Fruit of the Poisoned Tree" doctrine, which prevents admission of ill-gotten evidence as a deterrence to improper police conduct.

Many variables are missing from the case facts above, which would bear on the reasonableness of the search and seizure. One is whether the search and seizure was pursuant to a warrant or not as a search can be lawfully undertaken by authorities with or without a search

warrantless searches

fourth amendment requirements

warrant. However, the validity of these two search methods are tested by different standards.

A warrantless search and seizure is much more difficult for a District Attorney to establish as reasonable. The general rule is that warrantless searches are automatically unreasonable, unless they come within an exception to the warrant requirement, such as the following:

• The search of an individual who has been arrested.

• A search and seizure of the evidence that is in plain view of an officer in a place he has a right to be.

• An individual may consent to be searched or have his property searched, even though the search would otherwise be unlawful.

• There is a special exception for the search of vehicles, under which the reasoning that the mobility of the vehicle may make it likely that the evidence in the car will be removed or destroyed.

Even if a warrantless search and seizure is determined to come within an exception to the warrant requirement, it still must pass the test that searches pursuant to warrant must weather. Was there probable cause to believe that the evidence of an instrumentality of crime would be uncovered?

A judicial magistrate will answer the test just stated. His or her decision will be made after reviewing information presented to him or her by either the District Attorney or police. The Fourth Amendment requires that:

• The information in the warrant particularly describes the person and/or place to be searched and the things to be seized.

• That there be probable cause to believe that the things to be seized will be on the person or at the place.

The two earlier hypothetical cases at the beginning of this column are deliberately left general so as to illustrate the interplay of small factual variation and the determination as to whether a search and seizure is valid under the Fourth Amendment.

In the first example, if no warrant was issued by a magistrate for the search, the search would likely be unlawful, as there is no exception to warrant requirement. The "Plain View" exception is not available, as the marijuana was not in "Plain View" of an officer, but of a hunter. Also, the pot field will not likely be removed before a magistrate could be consulted.

If police officers or a District Attorney had sought a warrant prior to the search and seizure, the magistrate would need facts showing that the hunter's allegations are credible. His ability to recognize marijuana and particularly the place where the field is located, are important facts.

In the second case setting, an automobile is involved and, therefore, there is an exception to the requirement of a warrant issued by a magistrate.

Prior to the police officer's search of the vehicle, he or she must have probable cause or sufficient information to have probable cause to believe that he or she would find marijuana. The smell of marijuana smoke may or may not be sufficient, depending on the police officer's experience. The appearance of the driver (the classic is the "red-eyed" allegation), the movements to hide, the passing of a burning object, and many other facts can lead to a determination of probable cause.

This column should leave you with more questions unanswered than answered, as it just scratches the surface of a rich body of law dating back to colonial times.

Bruce C. Moore is an attorney in Eugene, Ore.
First printed in Vol. 3, No. 1, page 27.

Probable Cause and Search Warrants

by Bruce C. Moore

The concept of probable cause has historical roots tracing back more than two centuries. Probable cause is a predetermined standard for both police and citizens in the critical areas of both arrests and searches.

Probable cause finds its way into our criminal justice system via the Fourth and Fourteenth Amendments to the U.S. Constitution. Because of the heavy burden placed on the police to justify a search without a warrant, the determination of whether probable cause exists for a search is invariably left to a neutral judge rather than the police. The courts severely penalize police who fail to abide by the spirit of the Fourth Amendment by declaring evidence gathered without the requisite probable cause inadmissible in criminal proceedings.

Probable cause for the issuance of a search warrant is defined as facts or apparent facts, viewed through the eyes of an experienced police officer, which would lead a person of reasonable precaution to believe that there is something connected with a violation of the law on the premises to be searched.

There is no limit on the kinds of facts that may be used to justify a search. Nonetheless, the Fourth Amendment, absent exigent circumstances (e.g., open fields, hot pursuit, automobile mobility) requires that a judge make the determination as to the existence of probable cause prior to the issuance of a warrant to search.

probable cause

• Informants, identified or unidentified, reporting seeing the plants.
• Open air warrantless surveillance wherein an experienced officer recites positive identification of a growing marijuana crop.
• Observations by police from areas they are permitted to be in.
• Increased electrical usage in rural areas.

Most marijuana cultivation defendants that are successful in their defenses have prevailed at a pre-trial hearing on their motion to suppress evidence seized without probable cause.

hearsay evidence

The ultimate weapon of the police in establishing probable cause is hearsay information. "Hearsay" evidence, while usually not admissible at a criminal trial, is one of the main sources of facts used by police in establishing probable cause for the issuance of a search warrant.

Hearsay information is a communication of facts from a person to the police officer conducting an investigation. The hearsay communicator can be an anonymous hunter walking on property of the suspect, a citizen, a fellow police officer, a judge or anyone. The presence of the hearsay speaker is not necessary at the application for the search warrant before the issuing judge.

The only major constitutional safeguard concerning the use of hearsay, is that the officer submitting an affidavit must swear in good faith that he believes the hearsay facts contained therein are true. Where the applying officer has no firsthand knowledge of the facts relayed to him, the courts insist on knowing as much as can be possibly revealed about the source of the information. If the source is himself a criminal, an unreliable person, or an anonymous person, courts are loath to place reliance on such relayed information. The reliability of the informant is one of the utmost considerations by the judge who is asked to issue a search warrant.

Identification of the source of information being the most important consideration, the next highest concern of the issuing judge is that the facts alleged as hearsay are corroborated by some other source. Corroboration is confirmation.

protections

While the definition of probable cause is extremely elastic, three factors are always working to protect citizens from unreasonable searches and seizures:

Particularity: There must be a particular crime suspect. The police are also required to state exactly what it is they expect to find, where they want to look and why. Fishing expeditions are frowned upon by the courts.

Adequacy: The facts asserted in an affidavit supporting a request for a search warrant must not be mere assertions, conclusions or generalizations. The essential facts must be set forth in detail.

Reliability: Facts, especially hearsay facts, must be trustworthy. There must be a disclosure as to how exactly the informant came to know the information conveyed to the police.

Each case involving a search warrant presents different issues contributing to the determination of whether probable cause actually existed for the issuance of the search warrant.

Attacks against a warrant in the marijuana cultivation defense case invariably are made by a motion to suppress evidence, or a motion to controvert the facts alleged in the affidavit supporting the warrant. Often times, the court's ruling on these motions are determinative of the case. If the defendant prevails, the evidence is suppressed and the state's case is destroyed. If prosecution prevails, the state's case is usually easily proved.

Many times, the trial court judge may make an adverse ruling on the defendant's motion attacks against a search warrant. On appeal, a defendant may get a higher court to reverse the ruling. The added expense of an appeal is sometimes justified, given that the appellate courts, with judges removed from local pressures to punish criminals, are sometimes more sympathetic to technical attacks against search warrants. This is not to say that trial judges are not upholding the Constitution. However, in an area with such broad discretion and interpretation as is involved in probable cause issues, opinions of the law may vary according to the concerns of the decision maker.

appeal

First printed in Vol. 3, No.3, page 22.

Legal Tips

by Ron Sinoway

Except under certain circumstances in the state of Alaska, the cultivation, possession and selling of marijuana is a crime in this country, and under certain circumstances, can result in the forfeiture of land and personal property. As a lawyer, I advise everyone reading this column to not break the law.

The cultivation of even one plant can result in federal charges. U.S. Code Section 841 makes it a crime "to manufacture, distribute,

federal charges

dispense or possess with intent to manufacture, distribute or dispense a controlled substance." If the amount of marijuana is 110 pounds or more (excluding stalks) the maximum penalty is 15 years imprisonment. If the actual weight of the marijuana is less than 110 pounds, the maximum penalty is five years. In either case, the maximum fine is $250,000. Upon conviction, there is a period of parole (up to five years) and a "special parole" which is a minimum of three years. If someone violates a term of parole (including "obey all laws"), the person must then serve the entire amount of the special parole term in federal prison. (Since this article was written federal penalties have increased substantially. As of 1986, possession of more than 220 pounds carried a mandatory minimum sentence of five years and a maximum of 40 years. The maximum fine is now $2 million. The manufacture or possession of 100 plants or more, regardless of weight, now carries a maximum penalty of 20 years.)

Federal prosecution for cultivation charges was rarely or ever done prior to 1984. Except in the case of attempts at marijuana land forfeiture, most cases where the federal government has indicted people, have involved multi-hundreds of plants.

It does not matter whether local, state or federal law enforcement officials have conducted the raid which has led to the charges; it is discretionary with law enforcement whether to bring charges in state or federal court. This can sometimes lead to unfair results.

For instance, in California, someone who cultivates for personal use has a right to be diverted from the criminal charges with all charges eventually being dismissed. There is no such right to diversion in federal court for cultivation, although, there is a similar type of law for possession of small amounts, or for distribution of small amounts of marijuana for no remuneration. The constitutionality of this difference between simple cultivation and simple possession in federal court has not yet been challenged.

land forfeiture

Since October, 1984, for the first time in the history of our republic, the federal government has had the legal authority to forfeit real property used to grow marijuana. This federal authority has led a number of state and local governments to pass land forfeiture laws and ordinances. The constitutionality of many portions of the federal as well as state and local laws is not settled.

One of the foundations of our republic was the prohibition against forfeiture. In England, anyone convicted of any felony would lose his land to his liege lord and his personal property to the king. In America, the founders seemingly prohibited all forfeiture in the constitution except for the crime of treason, and then only for the life of the person committing the treason. That is, the property would then go back to the person's descendants upon his or her death.

The government never attempted a criminal forfeiture of real property until 1970, when racketeering statutes were passed by Congress. These authorized the taking of real property connected to racketeering. The government first tried civil forfeiture of real property in the year 1870 in connection with property used for stills to make alcohol without a license. The ruling in the civil distillery cases for over 100 years has been clear: the government can only get that portion of the property used to commit the felony (that is, the still, the waterline, the electricity line, and a path going in.)

The federal government's position is that if one grows one plant on 5,000 acres, the entire 5,000 acres is subject to forfeiture, either civilly or criminally. Such a harsh result would seem to violate the Fifth, Eighth, and Ninth Amendments to the U.S. Constitution, among other things. In the only published opinion to date, United States v. Anderson, et ux, the federal district court in San Francisco has held that the government can only get that portion of the real property which was used to commit the felony of growing marijuana. Thus, the court has wisely held that the punishment must fit the crime. The federal government has appealed this ruling and the final result on this extremely important issue will not be decided for some time.

The type of forfeiture the government seeks from growers, especially "mom and pop," is forfieture of the land because it was used as an implement of the crime. There is yet to be a clear cut favorable decision for the government, either civilly or criminally.

In the Northern District of California in 1985, where the government's first big thrust occurred, mom and pop were able to pay fines, which averaged around $15,000, with one person pleading to a felony with a recommendation of no imprisonment, and in two cases, to misdemeanors with the same recommendation. We expect the federal government to get tougher in this regard, so we will see more and more of these cases going to trial. Since most Americans have a built-in resistance to harsh results such as taking one's home for a minor drug offense, the last best hope of the people will reside with juries.

The California Campaign Against Marijuana Planting (CAMP) is the model helicopter assault operation for eradicating marijuana in the United States. It uses a number of different federal, state and local agencies and is broken down into "teams" of federal and state narcotics officers, combined with private contractor helicopter personnel and U.S. Forest Service helicopter managers. These teams

operation CAMP litigation

operate with local sheriff's personnel under whose control they supposedly function. The program is allegedly run and its policies set by a steering committee of high state government officials. The federal DEA provides the leadership and majority of the money.

The program started in 1983 and for three years it has been out of control. Through design and/or neglect, there have been warrantless break-ins into homes, the illegal taking of weapons and other personal property, harassment and buzzing by helicopters, spying by U-2s and satellites (supposedly abandoned after 1983), illegal use of roadblocks and detentions of people, as well as other forms of harassment.

In 1984, U.S. District Judge Robert Aguilar prohibited warrantless break-ins and entries into the home and curtilage, and created a 500-foot privacy bubble over persons, vehicles, homes and other structures. In 1985, Judge Aguilar tightened the injunction to require basic police work: daily planning of all raids with an eye toward the constitution and obeying the injunction. He also felt it necessary to appoint a monitor to oversee law enforcement activities during CAMP raids.

This is the first time in the history of the United States that law enforcement has been monitored by a court. The overflight cases decided by the U.S. Supreme Court this year (Ciraolo v. California, and Dow Chemical v. United States) are not likely to change the restrictions (including surveillance by helicopter) to any appreciable degree because of the intrusive nature of helicopters. The lawsuit is a statewide class action. The lawsuit also seeks damage, including $100 million in punitive damages.

Damages issues will be decided far down the road, but there are hundreds of people in California who have had their rights violated in a serious manner by the antics of the CAMP hot rodders and ground forces. The restrictions in the CAMP injunction provide a good definition for reasonableness of law enforcement activity during marijuana raids. In our cultivation cases in state and federal court, we argue that the terms of the CAMP injunction define reasonableness and one's right to privacy under the Fourth Amendment. There are no clear rulings on this argument yet.

fixed-wing aircraft surveillance

This spring, the United States Supreme Court in two five to four votes (Ciraolo v. California and Dow Chemical v. United States), determined that fixed-wing aircraft flying at 1,000 feet or more above ground level in public air space are not "searching" person's backyards when law enforcement fly these routes and look in and take photographs.

The Supreme Court reasoned that since the flights are nonintrusive and a Sunday traveler could look down and make the same observation, no search is involved and there are, therefore, no Fourth Amendment rights of privacy involved. If flights are below 1,000 feet and were otherwise not in public air space, or in some other manner are intrusive, it is possible to argue that Fourth Amendment privacy rights are involved and a warrantless search is illegal. To be successful, this argument would need a clear set of facts.

Ron Sinoway practices law in Phillipsville, Humboldt County, Calif. He handles federal and state cultivation forfeiture and civil rights cases. Ron is the lead attorney in the Operation CAMP litigation in California (NORML v. Mullen, a statewide class action), where the marijuana eradication program is operating under a court-ordered injunction prohibiting civil rights violations and is being checked on by a court-appointed monitor.

First printed in Vol. 6, No. 3, page 50.

What to Say to the Police

by Balance of Douglas County, Oregon
You answer your front door and suddenly face a police officer asking to search your house. What you do or say in the next few minutes may well mean the difference between a bust and trip to jail, or merely a scare. After talking to several lawyers, Balance has assembled these brief suggestions about how to handle the situation.

First of all, if the police are at your door and you have to talk with them, step outside and close the door behind you. If the police can see into your house, they have already gained visual entry; stepping outside demonstrates that you are not afraid of them and forces the officers to take a step backward.

step outside

Ask if they have a search warrant. If they do, tell them they cannot search anyway and call a lawyer. Have the attorney come to your house to be present during the search. Read the search warrant. It must state what the police are looking for and where they intend to look. If there are a number of people present in the house, sit together but do not talk among yourselves. Stay calm.

Say as little as possible. The police will use everything you say against you. As one lawyer put it, "Admit nothing, deny everything, and demand a lawyer." When you do speak, be calm and speak very clearly. The police are experts at intimidation. They know people make mistakes when they are scared or shaken up.

don't believe anything

keep your mouth shut!

Remember that the search is only the beginning of the matter, and it is the ending which is important.

Do not believe anything the police say. If they say that they can get a warrant, tell them to do it. Without exception, all our legal advisors agreed that if the cops could have obtained a search warrant they would already have done so. If they mention to you the name of the person who told them about you, and if that is a person you know, do not believe them. Especially, say nothing about your friend.

When the police start asking questions, tell them that you want a lawyer present before you reply. Lawyers will most likely tell the police their client has nothing to say about the matter. As soon as the police realize that you know what you're doing, they will lighten up and quit wasting their time asking questions which you are not going to answer. Another attorney told us that 99 percent of the people in jail talked themselves into it. So, keep your mouth shut.

If you are driving and are stopped by the police, immediately get out of the car and walk to the space between your vehicle and the squad car. Talk there. This puts you and the officer more at ease and you speak as equals, standing up, face to face. Be respectful when you speak. Never get smart with the police. Humor can be misinterpreted. Talk to the person behind the badge. On the other hand, don't be too friendly. If they ask to look around in your car or search it, you do not have to agree. Tell them no. You are not obligated to say why.

Another important step in defending your legal rights is to register to vote. By doing this, you will be able to vote for candidates who better represent your point of view and you will also be eligible to serve on juries. If you are arrested, no matter how guilty, demand that the police and the District Attorney prove your guilt in front of a jury. This is both difficult and expensive. And, when sympathetic people start appearing on the juries of this country, the authorities are likely to recognize the futility of their efforts. If they want to convict you, make them pay money to do so when money is scarce.

By sticking together, holding our peace, and standing our ground, we can gain far more than if we try to fight as individuals.

First printed in Vol. 6, No. 3, page 61.

Spies in the Skies

Are Aerial Searches Constitutional?

by Bruce C. Moore

The helicopter, with detection equipment, comes over a densely forested hill. At a height of barely 100 feet, the noise becomes deafening as it circles a small box canyon in the Coast Range near the Southern Oregon coast. The startled figure on the ground was tending his 250-plant marijuana patch when the copter swooped down on him. The grower half expected to hear Wagner's "Ride of Valkuries" blaring from the machine as in the film *"Apocalypse Now."*

The copter hovered over the field for ten minutes, obviously recording data. Then it was gone, climbing up into the expansive blue Oregon sky until it disappeared.

Later in the day, as the sole basis of the surveillance of the helicopter, the grower/owner was arrested and charged with manufacturing a controlled substance— marijuana. The copter operator did not have a search warrant. The grower's conviction at trial was upheld in the appellate courts, as he lost his constitutional challenge that the aerial surveillance by the helicopter was a warrantless search of his property which violated his Fourth Amendment right against unreasonable searches by the government.

Sound Orwellian?

The appellate court (courts which review trial court proceedings) cases which deal with aerial surveillance are few and far between, but the outcome of those cases are nearly unanimous in reaching the improper conclusion described above.

Most courts use the following three-step reasoning process to reach the conclusion that warrantless aerial searches are permissible:

1. Warrantless searches are automatically unreasonable and illegal under the Constitution except where the search falls within a particular category of search where warrants aren't required.

2. Two exceptions are applied to warrantless aerial surveillance for marijuana: the "Open Fields" exception, and the "Plain View" exception.

3. Since marijuana patches out in the privately and publicly-owned forests are by definition, an "open field" and/or in "plain view" of anyone who happens to be passing over, no warrant to search from

three-step process

the air is necessary.

The problem with the reasoning process just described is that the "open field" and "plain view" exceptions are old legal concepts which arose prior to the development of ultra-sensitive devices now being used by the government in law enforcement.

The U.S. Supreme Court has recognized that old concepts of search warrant requirements must be occasionally revamped when new search techniques are developed which grossly intrude into people's privacy expectations. This was done in Katz v. United States, 389 U.S. 347 (1967), where the court held that warrantless wire taps, even in public phone booths, were unreasonable, stating: "The Fourth Amendment protects people, not places. What a person knowingly exposes to the public, even in his own home or office, is not subject of Fourth Amendment protection ... But what he seeks to preserve as private, even in an area accessible to the public, may be constitutionally protected."

It is hard to understand why it would be more reasonable to expect that a phone call on a busy street corner is not bugged than to expect that your own privately owned field won't be subjected to surveillance from low flying aircraft. Since the U.S. Supreme Court hasn't ruled on the latter issue, all is not lost, even with poor lower court decisions to the contrary.

Several marijuana growers arrested after warrantless overhead surveillance have succeeded in getting their convictions overturned by appellate courts where the following factors were present:

the curtilage

• Where the marijuana observed from the aircraft was located by or near the dwelling house of the grower, so that the patch is within an imaginary "space" called the "curtilage" of the house, courts have held warrantless air searches unconstitutional because an individual's expectation of privacy is more reasonable and greater in those areas located next to the home. See State v. Verhagen, 272 N.W. 2d 105 (Wisc. App. 1978).

expectations

• Where the grower takes special precautions to hinder views of his plants from the air, he exhibits an expectation that the plants will be concealed from observations in the air. State v. Kender, 588 P2d 447 (Haw. Sup. Ct. 1979). Fencing, plant camouflage, coverings and field placement are all factors which courts have looked at in determining whether the grower was exhibiting an expectation that his fields will not be observed.

Conclusion

The current crop of cases dealing with warrantless open air surveillance techniques are poorly decided, given the lack of emphasis on increasing technical advances in the spying field.

Reasonable people expect that they will not be subjected to concentrated efforts to view from above by government agents. Sometime in the near future the U.S. Supreme Court will be called upon to reverse the improper decisions which have, in effect, granted government law enforcement agencies a license to intrude, without probable cause, into the solitude of individual activities with an all-seeing eye in the sky.

First printed in Vol. 2, No. 3, page 14.

Protecting Your Ass(ets)

by Kurt Priebe

If you have been the victim of a police bust in recent years, you have probably noticed a tendency on the part of police to confiscate both personal property and financial holdings, in addition to drugs and other contraband. This procedure, which is known as forfeiture of assets, comes to us through past history of medieval English kings who instructed their feudal judges to seize the ships of smugglers who attempted to land goods without paying the Crown its duty.

In 1970, this medieval judicial instrument was reborn in the United States in the form of the infamous RICO Act (Racketeer Influenced and Corrupt Organization). Under this legislation, the federal courts were empowered to seize assets and/or property of an individual or organization if that individual or organization had gained those assets directly or indirectly, by criminal activity.

Although the original supporters of RICO had assured Congress that it would extend to all forms of criminal behavior, in fact most RICO prosecutions have been targeted at individuals arrested for drug offenses.

Forfeiture of assets differs from confiscation in that confiscation usually implies seizure of goods that are illegal to begin with or were used in the commission of a crime. For example, the police will confiscate slot machines during a gambling raid or an automobile which was used as the getaway car during a bank robbery.

On the other hand, the courts will order forfeiture of a valuable painting which was purchased with non-drug money or valuables given to a forfeiture victim by a friend. In addition to the federal RICO Act, many states have enacted forfeiture statutes of their own. If you receive any form of your income from illegal sources, then it is your responsibility to learn how to protect your assets from seizure.

methods

Basically, there are three methods which you can employ in order to protect your assets from being seized by the government:
• Putting your property under the control of a trusted friend who is not involved in any criminal activity.
• Storing your assets in a foreign country.
• Hiding your property in such a manner that the police can not locate it no matter how diligently they may search.

No one method of asset protection is right for everybody or every situation; each has its advantages and disadvantages. Still a basic knowledge of all three methods is necessary, especially if you have large sums of money or other valuable assets.

One of the cleaverest ways to protect your assets is to leave them in the custody of a trusted friend or relative. This can be as simple as leaving a bag of gold coins at Uncle Harry's house or as complicated as hiring an army of CPAs to set up a trust account in your friend's name. Of course, the obvious drawback here is trust, if you do not have complete confidence in the person you select to guard your treasures, you will never enjoy a good night's sleep. From a safety point of view, it is probably best to select a person with whom you have a loving relationship, such as a close relative.

By doing this, you will be reducing the chances of having your property ripped off or forfeited to just about zero, unless dear old dad has taken to hauling Colombian in the family semi.

In the case of money, it would be best to keep large sums in your straight friend's savings account and share the interest with him or her. If your friend needs persuading, you can honestly point out the benefits of befriending a rich doper, "Gee, just think how impressed all the gals in your bridge club will be when they see an original Monet hanging in your living room." For total security it would be best to farm out your assets to different people. You are protecting your valuables from possible seizure while at the same time enriching your friendships and family ties.

foreign investments

The idea of depositing one's assets in a foreign land has intrigued crooks and common folks alike for several decades. Like all methods of protecting assets from government seizure, it is not without its disadvantages, the least of which is the high minimums required to open a bank account at most foreign financial institutions.

For example, most Swiss banks insist that their depositors maintain a balance of at least $5,000 (U.S.) although Migros Bank, PO Box 2826, CH-8023, Zurich, has no minimum requirement for Swiss franc savings accounts. Like their American counterparts, Swiss banks tend to smile on customers who maintain large accounts although some like Migros will accept small accounts.

Many folks who have money to hide, hop a plane up north and open an account at a Canadian bank such as The Bank of Nova Scotia or Guardian Trust Company. Although Canadian banks are safer than U.S. banks when it comes to sheltering "dirty" money, the fact that U.S. and Canadian law enforcement authorities cooperate very closely should be taken into consideration by the serious investor especially if he or she is "hot."

Investors should also take heed of the infamous U.S.-Swiss Mutual Assistance Treaty of 1977, which is considered by many international financial experts to be a serious dent in Swiss bank secrecy. Under this treaty the U.S. government may ask the Swiss government to require a bank to turn over a depositor's banking records to the Swiss National Police so that they may be examined by U.S. authorities in order to aid in an on going criminal investigation. Dopers should pay special attention to Article 30 which states that involvement with Cannabis Sativa in any way is cause for U.S. authorities to request access to your Swiss bank account.

Theoretically, if you got busted for smoking a joint in the parking lot of your local supermarket, Uncle Sam could demand access to your Swiss bank account although in reality, the U.S. government is only interested in the foreign banking records of major smugglers, growers and/or dealers.

If you are hot, you should consider depositing your money in a country other than Switzerland. For special circumstances I recommend Andorra and Hungary, as these countries have no financial disclosure treaties with the United States. Andorra is a tiny feudal kingdom nestled high in the Pyrenees Mountains between France and Spain. Unfortunately, Andorran banks require enormous sums of money for foreign residents to open an account; if you have the bucks to bank here, you probably commute to work via private helicopter.

Hungary has a confidential bank account for Westerners that pays seven percent interest but Hungary is not the place for your money if you have relatives who live behind the Iron Curtain or who work in the U.S. defense industry. If you are seriously interested in hiding some of your assets overseas, do yourself a favor and read "*Investing Without Borders*," by Adrian Day, Alexandria House Books, Alexandria, Va.

One final word: don't expect free Michael Jackson tickets or trading stamps when you open your overseas bank accounts as most foreign banks tend to be both stuffy and conservative much like the English bank portrayed in the movie "*Mary Poppins*."

If you have really big bucks to hide, I would suggest that you invest

overseas real estate

at least some of it in overseas income producing real estate. On the island of Jamaica you can purchase a high class villa on the beach for $125,000 and rent it out year round for $350 per week. An additional advantage is that if you do get busted and lose all your assets in this country, you still will have a haven to lay low in while planning that big deal which will recoup your losses.

The following real estate firms are honest, ethical and recommended for the novice considering an overseas real estate purchase: Private Islands Unlimited, 17538 B Tulsa St., Grenada Hills, Calif. 91344 (private islands and exotic Caribbean properties); Knight, Frank and Rutley, 19 Hanover Square, London, England W1 (United Kingdom property); and Cromptons, Thompson St., Suva, Fiji (South Pacific property.)

Ever since childhood, most of us have been fascinated by the idea of burying or digging up hidden treasure. When I was nine years old, I buried my collection of Batman comic books and some chocolate Hersey bars in order to avoid them being confiscated by my parents for the duration of Lent.

When I dug up this stash three weeks later, the comics had reverted to an earlier pulpy state while the Hersey bars had melted in their wrappers. The moral of this tale is to use common sense if you chose to protect your

BUDIMALS PRESENTS: FALL REPORT 85

WOW, HAVE THOSE FEDERAL BOYS 'BEEN BUSY... LAST YEAR FOR EXAMPLE THE DEA GOT A FEW FARMS IN NEW ENGLAND... THIS YEAR IN VERMONT ALONE THEY HAVE GOT OVER 3 TIMES THE AMOUNT THEY EVER CAUGHT.. (15,000 CULTIVATED FEMALES.).. THE CROP IS WORTH 125 MILLION TO 200 MILLION THIS YEAR... SEEMS REPRESSION DOESN'T WORK...THE CROP GETS BIGGER NOT SMALLER EACH YEAR...

OH MY... IT'S WINTER '86 ...WHERE DID THE FALL GO?

LOTTSA TAXES JUST SITTING THERE..

REPRESSION IS DRIVING UP THE PRICE... AVERAGE WHOLESALE $2000 - $2600 @ lb. AVERAGE RETAIL 3000 - 4000 @ lb. (OF COURSE THESE ARE THE BEST "ROTHCHILD" FLOWERS...)

SAY... BIG STATES LIKE CALIFORNIA... HOW ABOUT $2 BILLION DOLLARS ...RIGHT... AN AGRICULTURAL VENTURE WORTH 2 BILLION... ...WOW..

HECK, ED MEESE 'N THE BOYS CLAIMED THEY GOT OVER 300,000 PLANTS...

assets by burying them.

For my money, the various PVC-constructed mini-survival vaults are the way to go for burying goods underground as they are laboratory tested to withstand any element from worms to nuclear radiation! For the price of some good sinsemilla you can purchase a nifty little vault which will hold $10,000, a small handgun and enough diamonds to buy a split level house in suburbia, If you would like more information on these vaults you can write to: Survival Sports, PO Box 18206, Irvine, Calif. 92713-8206.

Another method of protecting your assets is to hide them on your property or in a public place. If you choose this method you must be extra careful in the selection of your hiding place as narcotic officers are familiar with all of the traditional stashing ploys, i.e. hollowed-out books. When I was in college, an acquaintance of mine used an abandoned private cemetery as a safe haven for his property. The only problem with this particular scam was that he had to drive 20 miles out of town in order to get to his stash. It is entirely possible to select a suitable storage depot for your property on public land much closer to home.

If you are a well-heeled doper with assets of historical or artistic value you might consider having the government itself help protect your property against police seizure! To do this you merely loan out your valuable assets to an institution such as a library, school or museum with the stipulation that it is given on loan only. Although this limits you in the amount of contact you have with your property, you can rest assured that it will not be seized if your pad is ever raided. If you do go this route just make sure that the institution displaying your property lists it as an anonymous donation and that they understand that it is only given to them on loan.

For most of us however, such exotic methods of hiding our assets will be of no use. In most cases you will have to hide your assets either at home or in a public place on your own. Using your imagination, you can think up many bizarre stash locations. Just make sure that your property is not adversely effected by its storage location like my comic books and candy bars were.

For more information on how to hide things, I recommend that you send $2 to: Loompanics Unlimited, PO Box 1197, Port Townsend, Wash. 98368, and ask them for their main book catalog which lists hundreds of books on such subjects as the art of stashing, home security, false I.D., etc.

Remember though, the best protection against thieves of all sorts is a low profile. So play it smart and keep your big mouth shut!

resources and references

Drug Agent's Guide to Forfeiture of Assets. U.S. Government Printing Office, Washington, D.C. 20402. $9.50 SN 027-004-00035-1. This book is the D.E.A. agent's "bible" on how to seize a doper's assets.

How to Launder Money. Loompanics Unlimited, PO Box 1197, Port Townsend, Wash. 98368. $8.00. If it is clean, it can't be seized. No further comment necessary.

Advanced Investigative Techniques for Private Financial Records. $10.00 Loompanics Unlimited. This book explains the inside secrets of America's homegrown gestapo, the Intelligence Division of the IRS. Must Reading!

How to Hide Almost Anything. $5.95 Loompanics Unlimited. This do-it-yourself carpentry guide has become a classic in its own time.

Search! $6.95 Loompanics Unlimited. If read backwards this treasure hunting manual will explain how cop's minds work during a drug search.

organizations

International Documentation Commission, 1300 Connecticut Ave. #307, Washington, D.C. 20036. This private organization is capable of providing special Laissez-Passer documents which are recognized as valid passports by Ecuador, Zambia, Kuwait, and Marititus.
Ueberseebank, A.G Limmatqai 2-K, CH-8024, Zurich, Switzerland. If you insist on maintaining a Swiss bank account this small private bank would be just your cup of tea.
Bankhaus Deak, Postfach 306, Rathausstrasse 20, A-1010, Vienna, Austria. This well established Austrian bank is safer than any Swiss bank because Austria and the United States do not have any formal bank disclosure treaties.
Bank Leu, Box N3926, Nassau, The Bahamas. This Swiss bank has a branch in the Bahamas which welcomes American accounts. $10,000 minimum.

Kurt Priebe is a free-lance writer from Washington state. This article was first published in Vol. 5, No. 1, page 30.

"Do not listen to what the critics may say with respect to it (hashish). They want to keep you away from it. Disobey any old censor!" —al-Is'irdi`

The Chemical People:
Poisoning Amerca's Airwaves

By Oliver Steinberg
Recently, Public Broadcast System television stations aired a series of special shows entitled, "The Chemical People." This extravaganza, with its accompanying sponsorship of "community meetings" to publicize the broadcasts, was part and parcel of a politically inspired campaign of anti-drug hysteria.

It was no accident that Nancy Reagan was involved in promoting "The Chemical People" and also performed as the hostess for one of the segments. Nancy Reagan's appreciation of the political mileage to be gained from the "drug abuse" bogeyman was noted back in 1980 by the *New Yorker* magazine's ace reporter Elizabeth Drew. And it wasn't long after the Reagan victory in the election before Mrs. Reagan found it helpful to work the "Reefer Madness" routine for all it's worth.

Nancy Reagan's initial months as the First Lady were noticeably rough for her public image, and the bad press was rubbing off on the whole Reagan administration. Nancy's $16,000 gowns and her expensive new White House china inspired little admiration and a lot of scorn among the public. In light of her present "crusade" cynics may recall that Nancy's first significant social decision was to bring hard liquor back into the White House, whence it had been banished by the previous occupants.

Nancy's lifestyle of conspicuous consumption promised to become political poison for the then new administration, so she began to look for some way to divert the critics. She tentatively adopted the cause of the preservation of historic buildings, but that didn't deflect the negative headlines.

While Nancy was busy dispensing Baptist sobriety from the mansion at 1600 Pennsylvania Avenue, many other Americans were likewise enjoying popular recreational drugs— both legal and illegal varieties. Use of contraband and drugs had indeed become so widespread that even some conservative commentators like Paul Harvey were suggesting the legalization of marijuana.

Marijuana is already one of the nation's top cash crops, and it would be a substantial source of revenue if legalized. This is alarming to the narcotics police and bureaucrats for whom marijuana has always been a ticket to easy street, and whose continued careers depend upon its illegal status.

the gimmick

The stage was set when Nancy Reagan, looking for a gimmick that would go over with the media, stumbled upon the narcotics bureaucrats who were seeking a political patron to shore up their own racket. Nancy was already aware of the profitability of a Neanderthal public posture on marijuana, so she forthwith announced her own special anti-drug campaign. In an opportunistic ploy for a better public relations image, she struck political paydirt.

The news media traditionally have never refused to take the bait when politicians offer them "drugs." They grab their blinders, don their cloaks of hypocrisy and ignorance, and lead the charge to save the populace from itself. Although the ranks of contemporary journalists are filled with more boozers, potheads and snowbirds than any other profession besides show business, they take the bait just as gullibly as ever.

the war on civil liberties

As we have seen, Nancy Reagan's role as a born again crusader has been effective as a media circus to drown out criticism of her insensitive habit of squandering money on baubles, while millions are unemployed. But beyond that little trick, her crusade has been very handy for advancing one of the unpublicized goals of her husband's administration, namely, the destruction in law and in fact of the civil rights of the American people.

This goal was implicit in the Heritage Foundation blueprint which the Reagan squad adopted as their game plan for establishing an unprecedented condition of state supremacy in America. The anti-drug campaign is central to implementation of the Heritage Foundation report.

While civil libertarians have been preoccupied with fighting the smothering blanket of official secrecy which Reagan has set up throughout the federal government, administration strategists have taken advantage of the media taboo on open debate over drug policy in order to undermine the basic principle of our free society.

Guided both by their own ideology and by suggestions such as the Heritage Report, the leaders of the Reagan administration clearly intend to nullify the basic principle that the government derives its powers and privileges from the consent of the people. In the American future, as they are building it, our civil rights will only be flimsy privileges granted by the government, subject to revocation upon the president's whim and inclination.

A pattern already exists where every attempt to enforce the misguided policies of drug prohibition has handed greater and greater power to the government. From the "no-knock" law of the Nixon Administration to the recent court decisions which have gutted the Fourth Amendment, the imagined evils of "drug abuse" have served as an excuse for magnifying the government's power to pry, to snoop, to spy, and to invade and control the personal lives of ordinary citizens.

The so-called "War on Drugs" is the ideal smokescreen for this subversion. The unofficial mouthpiece for the Reagan government, *US News & World Report*, extolled the creation of a totalitarian apparatus in this enthusiastic promise of things to come, back in 1981:

"Nancy Reagan's new campaign opposing drug abuse is only the opening salvo in a massive White House offensive against narcotics. By 1984, officials intend to have in high gear a drive to enlist youngsters, parents, teachers, police and others in an all-out war against the multi-billion dollar illicit drug-industry."

Buoyed by Nancy's high profile sponsorship, the Drug Enforcement Administration (DEA) and its satellite pressure groups began to orchestrate a campaign for new and broader prohibition statutes, and for new ways and means of applying and enforcing existing prohibition laws.

They persuaded hundreds of municipalities and many states to outlaw so called "drug paraphernalia." Traffic in look-alike caffeine pills was prohibited, even though all ingredients of the pills were patently legal substances. In addition, a century old law which forbade the use of military forces to engage in civilian law enforcement was repealed, in the name of War on Drugs. Immense computer files are being accumulated, filled with all kinds of unverified accusations against citizens supposed to be drug users or traffickers.

The whole spectrum of "controlled substances" prohibition laws bespeaks a sinister trend. Such laws can really only be enforced by

the prohibitionist mentality

giving government agents the authority to monitor and suppress the private behavior and personal lives of ordinary, average people. This fact should be contemplated by people who do not use illegal drugs, as well as those who do. When the rights of any particular citizens are obliterated, then the rights of all are in jeopardy. If the Reagan regime's "War on Drugs" continues unopposed, it will lead directly to a police state. Traditional American values of personal freedom, personal privacy and Constitutionally guaranteed liberty will all be wiped out.

That is the inevitable conclusion of the prohibition approach. Perhaps it is even a pleasant prospect for the prohibitionist mentality. That's the kind of mentality that is narrow, fearful, insecure, and intolerant. It is the result of a psychological unwillingness to accept the responsibility for making one's own decisions. Instead, the all-powerful State will make all decisions, and the individual will only have to know how to obey.

Besides fearing potential "loss of guidance" in themselves, the advocates of prohibition typically project their own morbid fantasies onto some other element in society which they perceive as alien or threatening or inferior. Therefore it is scarcely surprising to learn that the socioeconomic roots of drug prohibition are sunk in the muck of racial and ethnic bigotry.

Marijuana prohibition, in particular, is an example of a policy rising directly out of appeals to racial prejudice, combined with remarkable scientific ignorance. The spirit animating the marijuana prohibition laws was perfectly expressed by a Montana newspaper, reporting on legislative deliberations back in 1929:

> There was fun in the House Health Committee during the week when the marijuana bill came up for consideration. Marijuana is Mexican opium, a plant used by Mexicans and cultivated for sale by Indians. 'When some beet field peon takes a few rares of this stuff,' explained Dr. Freed Fulsher of Mineral County, 'he thinks he has just been elected president of Mexico, so he starts to execute all his political enemies. I understand that over in Butte, where the Mexicans often go for the winter, they stage imaginary bull fights in the 'Bower of Roses' or put on tournaments in favor of 'Spanish Rose' after a couple of whifs of marijuana.' Everybody laughed and the bill was recommended for passage.

Laws ostensibly passed for the public welfare actually served another purpose. The petty vice or social habit of an unpopular, powerless group was made the scapegoat to be blamed for genuine social and economic problems. In retrospect, the concealed motive is unmasked, as Dr. L.S. Brown, Jr., remarked in the *Journal of the National Medical Association:*

> Upon examining the motivation behind the pressure from the South-western states, one finds that the marijuana issue was used to obtain stricter federal barriers to Mexican immigration so that these states might be able to rid themselves of an unwelcomed manpower surplus in regions devastated by unemployment.

For the past 50 years, over and over again, the supposed detriments of marijuana have been periodically reinvented. When earlier blatant pandering to prejudice went out of style, or when "scientific evidence" of marijuana's evils was debunked, the prohibitionists switched their arguments and shifted to brand new excuses to justify the fundamentally unjustifiable marijuana laws.

The continuing sideshow of drug scares and drug persecution does indeed divert public attention from the politicians' foibles— not only from petty outrages like Nancy Reagan's expensive gowns, but from chronic failure to solve real problems in employment, education, and public safety and health.

the sideshow

This is easily demonstrated by the barrage of sensationalistic news stories which by their sheer volume in the last couple of years would prove the continued use of "drugs" as a political scapegoat. Professional athletes and celebrities ranging from entertainers to governors and congressmen have been singled out for hysterical accusations and condemnation, without the slightest pretense of fairness and often without any evidence of alleged depravity ever coming to light. But still, the witch-hunt atmosphere prevails.

Of course, liquor prohibition failed to keep people from drinking alcohol, and drug prohibition has utterly failed to keep people from using illegal drugs such as marijuana.

Instead of admitting failure and looking for a rational, intelligent policy toward drug use, those with a vested interest in perpetuating prohibition are instead whipping up this national propaganda assault, typified by the "Chemical People" programs. It is to the discredit of the Public Broadcasting System that its network is being used for this kind of brainwashing. It is a perversion of their responsibility to maintain non-partisanship and objectivity.

Newspapers, magazines, and commercial radio and television, all get enormous amounts of money for advertising those lethal (albeit legal) drugs, alcohol and tobacco. Their motive in presenting one-sided stories about outlawed drugs is transparent— they are protecting their established sources of income.

Public television's enlistment in the Reagan anti-drug crusade makes less sense than the journalistic prostitution practiced by the commercial news media. Perhaps PBS was motivated more by ignorance than malice. Whatever the reason, it is disappointing to see how recklessly they have embraced advocacy journalism in its extreme incarnation as "The Chemical People." PBS has discarded even the simplest standards of fair play, intelligent investigative reporting and objectivity.

The opposing point of view has had no chance to be heard. I urge PBS to provide equal time and resources to the people who dissent from this witch-hunt. I ask those who read this article and agree with it, to speak out and challenge the news media, both public and commercial, to live up to their slogans of impartiality and objectivity. I challenge the news media to do their job as they ought to— fairly presenting all sides of this controversial issue of marijuana prohibition. That is how they treat comparable political issues such as gun control or abortion. If the media refuse to listen to alternative points of view about this, they will discover too late that they have been exploited and manipulated for the worst possible cause— the subversion of individual freedom and the imposition of state-dictated conformity in behavior.

In this age of advanced technology, such governmental invasion of people's personal lives and thoughts will be ubiquitous and irreversible. The nightmare world of George Orwell's *"1984"* will arrive right on schedule, unless the media quit acting as touts for the narcotic bureaucracy, the chemical dependency treatment industry, and demogogic politicians.

The drug prohibition campaign is a dual menace: it provides a scapegoat instead of a solution for genuine problems, and it serves as a disguised way to strip American citizens of those inconvenient old 18th century relics— personal freedom and individual rights.

First printed in Vol. 4, No. 4, page 3.

An Interview With George Farnham

George L. Farnham, 29, graduated in 1976 with a bachelor's degree from Washington University; and with a LL.D. from George Washington University Law School in 1979.

Farnham joined NORML in June, 1977 and was named national director in January of 1982. He served in that position until August 1983.

Farnham authored a chapter on marijuana law reform in the book, "Lobby for Freedom in the 1980s," which was published in April, 1983. He has also written numerous other articles on the marijuana law reform movement.

In the following interview, a week after his unexpected resignation as director of NORML, Farnham gave his insight on the future of marijuana law reform, the economic effect of the marijuana industry and what the government is doing to eradicate it.

Tips: Your association with NORML has come to an end. What led up to your departure?
Farnham: My association with NORML as national director has come to an end, but I plan to take an active role within the organization in the future.

It will be interesting to see how NORML evolves and whether the trends that were started in time that I was on the staff as national director will be continued. I believe they will; we reversed a lot of the financial difficulties that the organization experienced when I took over.

Tips: Will NORML come out with estimated dollar figures for the size of the domestic crop?
Farnham: NORML has received a tremendous amount of publicity from the domestic marijuana estimates that we released in 1981 and 1982 on a statewide basis.

Those figures will be compiled again this year (1983), I have already done a lot of the preliminary work. I probably will be working with the remaining staff members to release the statistics in early November.

There are fascinating trends on this year's market. Some are continuing past trends, while some are new ones. More and more people are growing marijuana. Last year NORML estimated that there were 200,000 individuals that were green collar workers, who grew as a primary source of income and another two million personal use growers.

Tips: How fast is the marijuana industry growing?
Farnham: Those figures will probably increase by 20 to 25 percent this year as the number of individuals growing marijuana for both profit and personal use continues to increase. They are growing increasing amounts of marijuana. The outdoor plots are continuing to decrease in size while growers are growing multiple plots so the total number of plants increases also.

The most interesting trend and the one that has really caught on, is the movement to indoor cultivation. Hundreds of thousands of people are growing marijuana indoors under artificial lights. This avoids many of the problems associated with outdoor cultivation such as rip-off artists, animals eating the marijuana and, of course, law enforcement, with the overflight problems.

moving indoors

Tips: Do you think that outdoor growers will be a rare breed?
Farnham: There will still be a lot of outdoor marijuana. What is happening this year, for the first time, is that the majority of the marijuana consumed in this country will have been grown here. NORML's estimates in 1981 of domestic production was 20 percent and in 1982 the figure was evaluated at 35 percent.

This turnaround of the market is phenomenal, because as recent as 1977, only one percent of the marijuana crop was produced in this country and most of that was inferior. Then in 1978, with the paraquat panic from the Mexican program, we saw the first billion-dollar figure in production.

Tips: Do you think that the authorities will resort to unconstitutional methods to eradicate marijuana even if it means not arresting anyone, just to get the marijuana off the market?
Farnham: We are seeing some states such as Hawaii and Kentucky, which have extremely large marijuana crops, take the philosophy that they aren't interested in actually arresting individuals as in destroying the marijuana. If they destroy the pot then they have destroyed the income of the grower for that year.

It is so difficult and time consuming to get a conviction for a marijuana grower. They feel that it is better to destroy a greater number of crops than to concentrate on just the larger crops and going after only several individuals.

Ironically, in some areas, marijuana arrests are on the decrease, while the amount confiscated is on the increase. This tactic varies from state to state and from county to county. There is no doubt that the government has and will continue to use unconstitutional means to eradicate domestic marijuana.

If they do arrest someone under unconstitutional circumstances, they don't give back the marijuana once the person gets the charges dismissed against them. It is this economic hardship that the government views as a sufficient deterent in terms of overall marijuana production.

There has been such a tremendous failure in law enforcement in terms of trying to eradicate marijuana from the marketplace. I don't think using illegal and unconstitutional means will help law enforcement in even lowering the amount of marijuana being consumed, much less eradicating it.

In 1937, when the government first outlawed marijuana with the Marijuana Tax Act, there were 50,000 marijuana users in the country. This law was supposed to eliminate marijuana use. Now most estimates are that there are 35 million marijuana users in this country, which is 700 for every one that existed in 1937. I think that figure shows the failure of 46 years of marijuana prohibition if use has increased 700 fold.

the typical grower

Tips: All kinds of people are getting into growing marijuana. It is not just your stereotypical "hippie."
Farnham: Actually it is a cross section of society that grows marijuana. If I had to generalize, the average grower is in his or her late 20s to late 30s with a high level of education. Some are Vietnam veterans. We are not talking about the scum of the earth as the DEA would like us to believe.

These people are otherwise law abiding individuals who have little or no problems with the law throughout their life. The only crime that they commit is that they grow marijuana. The only difference between marijuana smokers and non-marijuana smokers is that the marijuana smokers smoke marijuana. I think that can be said of the marijuana growers. There is not much difference between a marijuana grower and an average American citizen.

violence

Tips: The media likes to pick up on the potential violence involved with the marijuana industry in this country. Compared to the violence in society in general, there does not seem to be that much violence in the marijuana industry. Have you heard of that much violence in various parts of the country?
Farnham: There is a problem with potential violence in the industry.

Considering that it is an industry worth over $10 billion a year, the level of violence is remarkably low.

Violence in the marijuana industry exists mainly where rip-off artists steal a crop that someone has worked on for six months or more. The violence is not directed towards the law enforcement people but against the rip-offs who steal many people's only source of income.

The only law enforcement officer that was killed on a marijuana raid of a domestic marijuana farm was in Kentucky where the officer was not in uniform and the grower thought that he was a thief. Even though marijuana cultivation is a felony, it is not a serious crime as compared to assaulting a police official. Even though there has been a lot of guns confiscated on raids, considering the amount of people who own guns throughout society, it is not that much out of proportion.

The law enforcement people like to hype the violence with reports of pungi sticks, Siberian tigers, tripwires and booby traps. I have yet to hear of anyone injured as a result of these means of protecting fields.

So basically, it is the DEA hyping the violence and it is not nearly at the level that the DEA would like to have everyone believe. It is not true that every grower is seven foot two, armed with a Uzi submachine gun. It is a figment of the DEA's imagination, when they make the growers out to seem more organized and violent than they are. It is the DEA trying to cover up on their own incompetence

official corruption

Tips: What are your estimates of the level of corruption of law enforcement involved with marijuana?

Farnham: We started keeping files a couple of years ago on police officials across the country who had been arrested for either smuggling, selling or taking bribes involving illicit drugs. We have dozens in our files and I am sure that there are hundreds of officials who have been charged with corruption, which means the actual numbers are probably well in the thousands.

It is a serious problem, which the DEA, FBI and others ignore. It always has been a problem with illicit drug transactions because of the large amounts of money involved. J. Edgar Hoover was notorious for years in not having the FBI involved in drug investigations because of the threat of corruption. That was the primary reason that there was a Bureau of Dangerous Drugs and why we have the DEA.

There is not a murder enforcement administration or a robbery enforcement administration, drug enforcement is the only exception to a specific enforcement agency. It is primarily because of the FBI, under the Hoover administration, refused to get involved in drug investigations.

Reagan now has the FBI involved in drug investigations and we saw the first FBI agent indicted on drug charges. It is extremely rare for an agent to be arrested on a corruption charge but now that they are involved in drug ivestigations we are seeing it.

We saw one of the DEA's top agents, with 17 years on the force, go down on a marijuana smuggling charge. It is a gray area as to which side they are on. Very often the people who are on the public payroll to fight drugs are smuggling drugs into the country. It is a serious problem, one that will always exist as long as marijuana is illegal. A major benefit from legalization would be the elimination of police corruption.

Tips: Do you think that traditional organized crime is involved in the domestic marijuana industry, and will they get more involved as marijuana production moves into the warehouses?

Farnham: DEA and some members of Congress have been stating that organized crime is involved in domestic marijuana production. I think that it is absurd to believe that, in terms of the traditional sense of organized crime. There is obviously an organization on a loose level between the people who grow it and the people who bring it into the big cities, who are called brokers.

I don't think we will see traditional organized crime get involved on a large scale. It is usually too bulky and time consuming for them. Generally they will stay into the heroin, cocaine and other illicit drugs which are smuggled in from foreign countries.

They generally get involved where there is a lot of money. As we are aware, of the 200,000 commercial growers, the average yearly income is not that large. Most growers take in $20,000 to $40,000 per year. It basically is middle class income.

The marijuana growers who make millions, that the DEA likes to talk about, just do not exist. There is probably not one individual who will make a million dollars growing marijuana in this country.

On the other hand, there will be an amazing amount of individuals who will make a million dollars smuggling marijuana or cocaine into this country.

The overall dollars compared to the efforts involved are not that great for consideration by organized crime.

Tips: Do you think that the marijuana issue will grow and that there will be politicians who take sides such as they do with the women's rights and minority rights issues?

organized crime

'time is on our side'

Farnham: Time is on our side more than anything else. The politicians elected average age is decreasing across the country. Younger politicians are acquiring positions of power. People who have grown up smoking marijuana or have friends who smoke marijuana are getting into political office and it is only a matter of time before the marijuana issue matures and will be seriously debated among the politicians of our country.

I think in the future we will have elected officials coming out and saying that they have smoked marijuana and possibly that they still smoke marijuana.

Tips: Do things look bleak on the marijuana front?
Farnham: I don't necessarily think things look bleak now. I am still optimistic. There is a tremendous amount of work to be done. Overall, we may lose more battles than we win. Time is on our side, we will eventually win the battle.

Above all else, we know we are right and the government is wrong. I expect to wear the government down before they wear me down.

First printed in Vol. 4, No. 2, page 32.

NORML's Plan to Legalize Marijuana

By Kevin B. Zeese

NORML's goal is to change marijuana laws. We favor two alternatives: legalizing the personal cultivation and possession of marijuana by adults or regulating and taxing marijuana as a legal commodity. To reach these goals we must educate the public and compel the government to confront the marijuana issue in a realistic way. NORML will accomplish these reforms by providing information to the public and the media, and by encouraging local citizen action at a grass roots level. When we are successful on the local level, we will then approach the issue on a national basis.

NORML is supporting efforts at the state and local levels. NORML played an important role in the campaign of the Oregon Marijuana Initiative (OMI). Our supporters donated thousands of dollars to OMI, our activists, led by Jeanne Lange, NORML's Special Projects

the grass roots path to a national truce

Coordinator, went to Oregon to help with the campaign. NORML lawyer Alan Silber, along with Oregon attorney Michael Rose, challenged the state's fraudulent signature count. We continue to be supportive of OMI's efforts and are planning to coordinate similar efforts nationwide.

The marijuana issue is reaching a critical point in Oregon and Northern California. A growing proportion of the population in these areas are beginning to feel the economic impact of marijuan production. Marijuana police are becoming more militaristic and abusive. Now people see that as long as the marijuana trade is kept illegal it will have negative impacts on their community. Violent poachers are drawn to easy prey in growing areas. Police use illegal methods such as roadblock searches, warrantless searches of private property, aerial dragnets and intimidation.

Police state tactics include aerial spraying, search and destroy programs, and seizure of property which affect the entire community, not just farmers. The escalation of violence between farmers, poachers, and police will help bring about law reform. Finally, marijuana farmers are beginning to realize that prohibition is not good for them either. The violence and other risks are not worth the extra profit.

NORML is challenging the government in court. We currently (1985) have active lawsuits against paraquat, CAMP and aerial surveillance. In addition to challenging abusive law enforcement programs, we are also fighting police excesses and abuse. This litigation serves the additional function of highlighting law enforcement abuse and educating society about the threat current marijuana laws create.

At the same time NORML is educating the public about the economic impact of marijuana. Our annual marijuana crop report makes national headlines each year. As a result, people are realizing that marijuana is challenging corn as the nation's most valuable farm crop. We are expanding both our educational and courtroom activities.

NORML is encouraging state and local activists. You know better than we do what is best for your community. NORML will do what it can to support you. In Northern California, we are encouraging local referenda to curtail the use of the National Guard and helicopter searches. If your state or local legislature will listen, we will support your legislative activities with informational materials and expert witnesses. The bottom line is we cannot make it happen from Washington, D.C. You must make it happen where you are. All we can do is coordinate a national campaign and provide as much

police state tactics

'Washington is not the starting point, but the finish line'

legalization

support as possible.

This is not to say that we are going to ignore Congress here in Washington. We plan to increase our efforts in Washington as efforts increase around the country. But political power comes when you demonstrate that you have voter support and financial support. Washington is not the starting point but the finishing line. To be successful, we need to register more voters, get involved in local political activity and show political power at the grass roots level. Broad-based, grass roots efforts are not only the key to changing laws locally, they are also the key to a national truce in the marijuana laws.

While NORML represents the views of a large percentage of marijuana consumers and supporters of marijuana law reform, we cannot speak for everyone. For example, this magazine is important as a spokesman for marijuana farmers. It is needed to balance the inaccurate law enforcement stereotype of farmers as wealthy violent people who don't care about their community, with the more accurate view which is essentially the opposite.

Similarly, Sandee Burbank's group, Mothers Against Misuse and Abuse (MAMA), presents the view of parents concerned about how their children and families are hurt by the drug abuse industrial complex and by prohibition policies. We need more spokesmen and more viewpoints to get our message across.

We learned from experience that national campaigns are built from the bottom up. Like building anything else, the foundation is critical. The broader our base, the larger and stronger we will be.

Marijuana will definitely be legalized. Every year there are more marijuana consumers. Currently, there are over 30 million marijuana consumers. Ninety percent are over 18 years old and eligible to vote. There are more marijuana consumers then there are people over the age of 65. We would be a powerful political force if we would just stand up and be counted. When marijuana consumers get politically active, and are tired of being treated as criminals, the laws will change. If you are not registered to vote, register and start voting to change the laws.

Our biggest problems are apathy and the feeling that we cannot change the laws. Most marijuana consumers find marijuana easy to get and find the risk of getting caught to be minimal. However, statistically, this is misleading. Last year, 52 people were arrested every hour for marijuana offenses. The use of urine tests to find marijuana consumers is expanding. Last year three million people faced a urine test or loss of employment and over a 100,000 lost their jobs based on a urine test result. A national military police force is being created to combat marijuana cultivation. Over 30 states brought their National Guard into marijuana law enforcement in 1984. Don't wait for your rights or liberty to be abused. Get active now.

Soon everyone, not only marijuana consumers and farmers, will find their pocketbooks and children are being hurt by prohibition. The government loses $15 billion each year it doesn't tax marijuana. Instead it spends billions on law enforcement. Since marijuana is illegal, the government has no way to regulate age restrictions and ensure purity. This can only be done when it is legalized. During the past 15 years, a marijuana user has been arrested every two minutes, yet marijuana continues to be readily available, especially to our youth.

Anyone who says that prohibition protects children is lying or ignorant. Surveys of students show that 90 percent find marijuana easy to get. It is easier for them to buy marijuana than alcohol and more adolescents use marijuana on a daily basis than use alcohol. However, we continue to waste money on law enforcement rather than educating our children about drug abuse. People should be upset that prohibitionists are using their children as pawns in the public relations campaign to keep marijuana illegal.

When I started working at NORML, the organization's problems seemed insurmountable, just as ending prohibition seems difficult today. But we solved NORML's problems and we can change the law. Sure there will be setbacks like the State of Oregon's lawless actions in preventing a vote on OMI in 1984. That merely turns up the heat on a pot that is already boiling, just as CAMP and other militaristic law enforcement programs will increase the incentive to change the laws.

In 1970, virtually every state treated possession of marijuana as a felony, today only Nevada does. In addition, 11 states have decriminalized marijuana and 29 other states have enacted conditional discharge to allow expungement of records for first offenders. Everyone expected marijuana laws to change quickly so it wasn't necessary to build a broad-based national campaign. Instead, we relied on major contributors to fund our efforts. Unfortunately in 1978 when NORML's founder Keith Stroup left, the major donors left with him, and we had a tremendous deficit left from the decriminalization campaign of the 1970s.

In 1980, when I began working as NORML's Chief Counsel, our debt was over $100,000 and our annual income had shrunk to less than $200,000. For a while it didn't seem like NORML would survive. There were many, serious discussions about closing NORML down

'Anyone who says that prohibition protects children is lying or ignorant'

and going bankrupt. Instead, we decided to stay the course and today we are in the best financial shape we have been in since the late 1970s. Our debt is below $15,000 and our budget will expand by 50 percent this year (1985). We are now able to put money into programs and expansion rather than into into debt reduction.

It took a great deal of sacrifice by numerous individuals for NORML to get to this point. Staff and office overhead were cutback. Staff members took pay cuts while others became volunteers. Lawyers and others were forced to increase their financial support as grass roots activists struggled to do something with nothing. Whenever we wanted to file a lawsuit, put on a conference, or do some other project, the staff had to skip paychecks or delay them.

However, even during this period of cut-backs and sacrifices, NORML remained the only effective force challenging extreme marijuana policies. Most recently NORML, along with the Civil Liberties Monitoring Project, successfully sued to stop the abuses of the California CAMP program.

NORML is also suing on a national basis to stop similar abuses around the country resulting from the DEA's nationwide marijuana eradication program. Last year NORML and a coalition of environmental groups, filed the lawsuit which stopped the Reagan Administration's planned nationwide paraquat spraying program dead in its tracks. We have also stopped the marketing of an over-the-counter urine test for marijuana use, challenged the legality of aerial searches and challenged the use of urine tests in the military as well as in civilian employment.

We were the first and possibly the only group to hold a criminal defense seminar focusing on the defense of marijana cases. NORML has also supported efforts to legalize marijuana nationally by drafting model legislation and by supporting legislative hearings in three states during the last three years. We did all of this while struggling with a tremendous financial burden.

The sacrifices paid off. NORML's budget is now expanding as are our efforts to change the laws. One thing is for certain: NORML will not go away until marijuana is legalized. We will continue to harass and pester prohibitionists and, when necessary, sue the bastards until they listen to our arguments and change marijuana policy.

Don't get me wrong. NORML still has to improve its financial situation and people working at NORML are still making sacrifices to ensure the organization's growth. We have nowhere near the budget we need to accomplish our goals. In 1978, at the end of the campaign that decriminalized marijuana for one-third of the population, NORML's budget was over $500,000. Even though we are leaner and more efficient today, we will need a larger budget because opposition is better funded and well-organized, and simply because it is more expensive to do business in 1985. With broad based, grass roots support we can be successful. Please work with us in accomplishing these goals.

Kevin Zeese served as the National Director of the National Organization for the Reform of Marijuana Laws (NORML) from 1983 to 1986. He served as NORML's Chief Counsel from 1980-1983.

First printed in Vol.5, No. 2, page 53.

We Refuse to be Dominated

by Patrick Baysinger

I was cheerfully following Bob Kelly's column in the local Cox publication, The Tempe Daily News. He wrote a diary of his travels across America. Kelly seems witty enough (and an Irishman in the bargain!).

I was flabbergasted when I read of his arrival in his old hometown of New York City. In the July 1 issue, he reports: "On 42nd and Fifth Avenue, a young man walked up to me. He was around 22 and very clean-cut. He looked me right in the eye and breathed one word.

"Marijuana?" he asked.

"No, thank you," I said and kept walking.

"But I wanted to go back. I wanted to slap him upside his young head. I wanted to shake something loose.

"Len Bias isn't cold yet, I thought, and this dummy is looking either to push or be pushed upon. There's a word for that level of intelligence, but they won't let me use it. It starts with dumb."

I guess I was supposed to understand that Len Bias' death from free-basing cocaine and the subject of marijuana are somehow related. I was supposed to make that leap of simplified faith advanced by Nancy Reagan and the party line regulars— the worn-out reefer madness mentality. I see daily delusions like this, living in the largely conservative, Republican, Phoenix Valley, but it never ceases to amaze me.

Typical of this "Alice in Wonderland" hysteria is the *Arizona*

Alice in Wonderland

Republic editorial of June 26, 1986, which states, in part:

"The Drug Enforcement Administration's endorsement of spraying the herbicide paraquat to kill marijuana crops on state and private lands raises anew an old argument...The bottom line, it would appear, is determining which is the most effective means (of killing marijuana crops), if proper precautions are taken. Marijuana is a health hazard whether tainted with paraquat or not, and smokers use it at their own peril.

"So whatever else, let us spray..."

'So whatever else, let us spray'

It is like trying to explain something to a small child, who desperately refuses to face the truth. Read my lips, pilgrim. Marijuana doesn't kill. Its harmful effects are exaggerated, using the sleaziest distortions of the facts, by those in power who need to advance the reefer madness mentality to assure votes. They are hideously corrupt.

Cocaine can kill.

When the truth is told, the two are as different as night and day, despite the brainwashing we are subjected to.

Does rational reasoning exist in the, "War on Drugs?"

The Portland, Oregon daily *The Oregonian*, quotes a doctor involved in ground-breaking research on marijuana during the 1960s. At the widely unreported 1986 NORML conference, he told a Portland audience he believed the drug would be legalized within three years of his research.

"The research showed that marijuana was a relatively mild intoxicant," according to Dr. Andrew Weil, who said the studies were conducted at Harvard Medical School. "It seemed to me that all you had to do was get out this information and then everything would change. I quickly learned— and I think this was the most important lesson— that this is not an area of rationality."

Speaking at the recent NORML conference, Weil, an Arizona doctor and author of *"Chocolate to Morphine"* appeared with Dr. Norman Zinberg, a professor and researcher at Harvard Medical School, in a discussion on marijuana and health issues.

no evidence

Zinberg said much of the research that was critical of marijuana was severely flawed, and that many of the purported ills of marijuana use would not stand up to rigorous scientific examination. He said there was "little or no evidence" that marijuana causes psychological damage.

Visitors to a Scottsdale junior high earlier this year found the school plastered with graphic posters featuring a photo of a hideously deformed baby's head, accompanied by the grim legend, "Marijuana Birth Defects: What the Pushers Don't Tell You."

An article reporting this appeared last May in the valley's alternative newspaper, *The New Times*. The article said that, "Donna Campbell, school board president of the Scottsdale Unified School District, stifled a chuckle when the poster which she had not seen was described to her."

The paper quotes Campbell: "I don't think any of the board members advocate going back to the old scare tactics of the '60s. As far as I know, they didn't work very well back then, and I suspect that they wouldn't work any better today." Later in the same article, a therapist at Terros, a local nonprofit center for drug and alcohol rehabilitation, offered his tongue-in-cheek views: "I have a personal bias that telling the truth is highly desirable and that scare tactics are not the most productive way to go. I personally think it's an oversimplification to say that the upheavals of the '60s and early '70s among young people were a function of the fact that they'd been lied to by their parents. Parents have been lying to their children about Santa Claus, the Tooth Fairy and a whole flock of other things for centuries."

In response to the Oregon Marijuana Initiative, Oregon Governor Vic Atiyeh said in an Associated Press story: "We now know that marijuana is harmful. Marijuana leads to harder drugs," the governor said, while also linking marijuana to child abuse and incest.

Holy Smokes!!!

The current hopeless stalemate cannot continue to be perverted for political coziness, as it now is. The fact is that marijuana prohibition is a screaming failure. The amazing fact that it exists at all is because it serves the interests of the neo-Puritan/tobacco monopoly currently in power. It would seem our legislators and law enforcement professionals would have known their prohibition history lesson, but their education seems severely deficient. Once again, the taxpayers are asked to throw good money after bad by supporting the current futile actions designed to suppress and eliminate the use of marijuana.

As the true enemy of liberty and justice, Nancy's Orwellian nightmare of reefer madness is recognized and ridiculed by tens of millions of Americans. Our youth, not subject to the old-fashioned brainwashing wrought upon previous generations, is continuing the tradition that crashed like a tidal wave in the '60s, which bridged Cannabis from the minorities to the 'burbs and out of the closet forever.

The craziest part of this entire sordid chapter of American history is, marijuana cultivation is only a crime because it's illegal. It's not like rape or murder. Of course, murderers and rapists don't risk

a screaming failure

forfeiture of land and property as do the growers.

There are legal drugs far more dangerous and plenty is spent to brainwash us into using them and risking premature death and destruction; nine U.S. teenagers are killed daily in drunken driving accidents — not to mention the 300,000 premature deaths each year from tobacco. A person who uses tobacco twenty times a day is not defined as a drug abuser. A person who uses marijuana as seldom as once a month can now be targeted as a drug abuser.

Nancy Reagan, in *The Oregonian*, July 9, 1986, is quoted in part: "I implore you to be unyielding and inflexible and outspoken in your opposition to drugs."

The Oregonian has been curiously quiet about the local, historically significant referendum effort.

unyielding and inflexible opposition

On the July 21, 1986 *USA Today* editorial page, the paper's position reads in part, as follows: "Maybe it's time we listed the names of all the victims illegal drugs have killed."

I suggest taking it one step further. Let's separate out and list all the tobacco victims, the alcohol victims, the cocaine victims and so on. Let's include the marijuana victims, too. That'll be the shortest list, because, of course, there will be no names on that list. Let's then list the 400,000 annual marijuana arrest victims and ponder the damage pot laws have done to families and careers.

It is widely reported that the results of legalization in Amsterdam have brought about both a drop in usage and a market crash in the price of the weed. In the discriminating saloons near the police station in Amsterdam, one can choose from several varieties of fresh hashish, openly sold for $1.50 a gram. In a free marketplace, it's no big deal. The result of Reagan's scorched earth policy in the United States is that Cannabis is now a multi-billion dollar a year domestic crop, not even factoring in the unknown tonnage imported from south of our borders.

Nancy's hysterical crusade for ignorance and intolerance of smoking materials, declared in a racist lynch mob atmosphere of the 1930s, has had an unexpected boomerang effect in her greatly failed "War on Drugs."

What has happened is that the totally outrageous equal penalty for marijuana and cocaine has caused a surge in cocaine supplies and a predictable explosion in availability of cocaine and a precipitous drop in the price. Thanks in large part to the errant policies of our government, our junior high youngsters can now buy single doses of crack, with ten times the addictive power of powdered cocaine, for a five dollar bill.

The most dramatic recent example of the government's "witch

hunt" mentality occurred recently in an article entitled, "Kids with Adult Addictions", released in July 1986 by the Scripps Howard News Service.

The dreaded gateway drug, marijuana, is mentioned once and only once. The backhanded bashing of marijuana, that favorite whipping boy, is typical of the current hysteria. The article quotes Wanda Yarboro, principal of the Martin County High School in Florida: "Yarboro said that there is some truth to the old warning that marijuana can lead to heavier drugs. 'What happens these days,' she said, 'is that one kid will lean over to another one at a party with an offer: 'If you're tired of getting high by a slow beer, try this.'

"The 'this' being offered is likely to be cocaine."

Thus is the clear connection between reefer sadness and stronger drugs. Hooray for Hollywood!

We arrive at the last gasp circle of wagons; the worn-out myth that marijuana starts youngsters on the road to addiction. The honest truth is tobacco and alcohol are the first psychoactive substances youngsters are likely to experience. It's an inconvenient truth. As you can plainly see in the Scripps Howard article, the witch hunt for a whipping boy is reckless enough to propagandize with outright McCarthyist lies.

It's a clear case of being led by fossils. The New Right thought they could drive up the price to wipe out pot. Instead, they created an eleven digit a year domestic industry. The New Right coalition in this country is an ostrich in the middle of a social revolution. The current laws are worse than ineffective; they are counterproductive. They even have a reverse effect to what they wish to achieve.

McCarthyist lies

Reagan, Bush, Meese, Helms and the rest of the neo-Puritan zealots should be made to realize there is blood on their hands. The deaths of Len Bias, Don Rogers and countless thousands of others are directly the function of the preposterous, unwarranted hysterics regarding the health risks versus the criminal penalties of marijuana.

It's an easy enough progression for the mind of a young person to assume if parents and authorities lie about marijuana, then they are probably lying about crack and smack. The best example I can think of is the recent revelation released with government blessing, that smoking one joint a day for a year was equal to the lung damage caused by 20 years of tobacco smoking. Let's see— 20 times 20— I guess the 400 year old lungs I'm wearing haven't heard about that study, since they serve me quite well during my hour-long aerobic workouts thrice weekly. Youngsters learn by early high school that reefer madness is senseless and the last dirtiest secret of our great nation— one of the few left after the social revolution of the '60s.

Unfortunately, crack and smack can kill. Reality is not the black and white scenario the Reaganites would have us believe.

It is time to recognize and admit the failure of pot prohibition and correct the enormous costs of an absolutely failed policy. It is quite simply a bankrupt policy dictated by the tobacco monopoly and moneyed elite, at the expense of freedom for tens of millions of otherwise law-abiding Americans.

In the end, Reagan's ideas of federalism may serve effectively as the means to end the prohibition of pot. Whether state, county, or citywide referendums are used, we will see relief from the outrageously draconian existing laws. At first, this will occur in well-known hotbeds of liberalism, such as New York, Humboldt County, San Francisco, Ann Arbor and Madison.

Just as the civil rights movement gradually spread, so will rational thought regarding the money spent to save us from ourselves. Declared in the racist lynch mob atmosphere of the "reefer madness" '30s, eventually pot prohibition will be relegated to a greatly deserved footnote in history.

I was tempted to mention here the one-way air fare to Amsterdam. I decided not to because I don't think we freedom-loving Americans should have to give up our citizenship to attain freedom of choice in smoking materials.

'I don't think this is Kansas'

Who among us remembers the very short-lived TV show, "Turn On" in 1968? After 15 minutes, for fear the show might glorify psychedelia, the screen went blank and a voice came on and told us the rest of the show would not be seen. The network was spared further inquisition with the written agreement the fifteen minutes never be shown again. Of course, it won't be ... Toto, I don't think this is Kansas.

The random urine testing of athletes may also bring about significant changes. Already, numerous athletes have suffered permanent damage to their careers and lives. The laws unquestionably have done them much greater damage than enjoying an occasional joint.

Meanwhile, the moral crusade rages on. W.F. Buckley, in a recent speech here in Tempe, estimated that over $1 billion has been spent in the war on drugs. The result is widespread disbelief and readily available crack, PCP and designer drugs in any major city in the United States.

Last election day, an Oregon initiative to legalize marijuana was defeated by a 73 percent to 27 percent margin. Far from being an overwhelming defeat, as Nancy and her forces would like to assert, it was the beginning of the end of marijuana prohibition.

In 1988, the ballot proposition will probably limit the number of plants and increase the age limit from 18 to 21 thus picking up a percentage of favorable votes. Combine this with present day high schoolers as new voters and older voters dropping out of the picture, and you have the recipe which should provide a few sleepless nights for Ronnie and Nancy!

What a fine example of democratic self-determination this battle is becoming. The pro-marijuana forces were banned from radio and television ads, harassed from pillar to post while Ed Meese urges all federal prosecutors to fight the ballot measure in violation of the Hatch Act.

A fundamentalist prosecutor from Alaska was the designated spokesperson and wrote the definitive argument against the proposition, which was printed in *The Oregonian*. He was not very sophisticated and used the typical, "reefer madness" lunacy and in a debate asserted that, "Enforcing the nation's drug laws is more important than catching murders ..." It was not liberty's finest hour.

The vote assured the multi-billion dollar annual marijuana cultivation movement is alive and well. Despite being legally disabled far worse than any other minority, including child molesters and murderers, the 30 million or so American potheads will certainly not be beaten. People who grow their own pot risk felony convictions, forfeiture or real property and assets large fines and long prison terms, all for the benefit of the tobacco devils who whisper sweet nothings in our president's ear.

Reagan has plenty of reason to be nervously looking over his shoulder. The populist candidate for U.S. Senator from New York, Mark Green, who frequently voiced his intent to legalize marijuana if elected, was narrowly defeated. If a pincer movement occurs from the East and West, can the heartland be far behind?

pincer movement

With the 80 percent a year inflation in Mexico and the devastation of the family farm in the United States, many people go hungry. Hungry bellies like cash crops. The bottom line is, feeding a family is a lot more important than the moral imperatives of the Reagan agenda. It's a simple enough task to grow resinous buds in small patches, camouflaged by other plants. In Hawaii, growers plant in sugar cane fields; in the Midwest, cornfields and hollers are favorites; in the South, rich river bottoms yield record amounts each year. In the West, Californians and Oregonians have progressed to bountiful indoor hydroponic crops. Good ol' boys who believe liberty extends to growing one's choice in smoking materials are in every state of the Union. Reagan's naive policies mean each plant is worth hundreds, if not thousands of dollars. It is truly a lost crusade and a shockingly

a lost crusade

expensive one at that.

Instead of disseminating objective information on the health consequences of marijuana usage, the government stubbornly clings to futile prohibitive laws which mock the very freedom we were promised as idealistic students in the classroom. The current marijuana laws encourage usage and supply of much more dangerous crops, such as cocaine.

I guess what I liked most about the recent Fourth of July celebration in Tempe was the presentation of early patriotic American flags. One of them, the second earliest one presented, reminded me why the Americans beat the British in the American Revolution. It summed up the attitude of tens of millions of us who are virtually political exiles within our own country.

It said, simply, "We refuse to be dominated."

First printed in Vol. 6, No 3, page 63.

"Dixi et salvavi animam meam (I have spoken and saved my soul)" —Karl Marx

Editor's Note:
The following are selections from Tippy Talks, *Sinsemilla Tips'* advice column during the magazine's first two years. They are included here for historical purposes only. The publisher assumes no responsibility for injury, physical or psychological, incurred by any person or persons trusting enough to follow Tippy's advice on anything.

Dear Tippy:
It is another year and another crop. The question is, when will it all end? It used to be that my growing was incidental to the rest of my life, but now I wonder. Lately, my sex life has been affected by THE WEED!

It seems that any time I am with a partner and the petting gets passionate, my plants come to mind. This wouldn't be so bad but my visions are that my plants are in need of water and wilting and at that moment I begin to wilt. Have you ever dealt with such a problem and are there any counselors who specialize in this type of situation?
   Yours truly,
   Horney

Dear Horney:
A similar case comes to mind. It was a fellow I knew in India who turned to religion and celibacy during stressful growing times. Once the crop was in, he debauched. Maybe you should try foreplay in your patch, keeping an eye on the plants during sex, or use sex aids!
   Tippy

Dear Tippy:
I am worried. Pot growing has always been a mellow experience for me with plenty of love and sharing. This time around, it is different. I have dreams, violent ones where my total self hates all who want my

patch.

I bought a gun this spring and fear that if someone fucks with my plants I'll shoot. I was raised in New York. I came to Oregon to be with brothers and sisters who care and now I am like the creeps that I fled from in the city. I have no skills except pot cultivation and weaving. I need the money marijuana provides for me. The gun is with me all of the time which puts off old friends.

What if I shot someone? What if I kill someone? Where will I bury them? Is there any help for me?

Fearfully yours,
Paranoid

Dear Paranoid:

This is a common problem these days. The money is good for an experience, in fact, so good that the lifestyle is addicting. Your only hope is to get rid of the gun and plant more patches so if one or more gets raided, you have an "insurance policy". Try reading *Reader's Digest* for relaxation.

Tippy

Dear Mr. Talks:

I am perplexed. A friend of mine is apparently allergic to marijuana, of all things. He goes into a sneezing and coughing fit whenever he is around the stuff. Since we always have rather large amounts of the herb around, the problem is chronic whenever he comes to visit. Do you know of any natural remedy for this problem?

Yours,
Perplexed

Dear Perplexed:

I knew a family in New Jersey who had the same problem. They found a cure that was inexpensive and painless. They mixed a solution of half infant formula (Nestle's) and half Pepsi-Cola with a pinch of powdered pot and gave it in an enema form as many times a day as possible. The results were positive, the friend never suffered from the allergy again and is now addicted to heroin.

Tipper

Dear Mr. Lips:

Are we in a jam! My teenage daughter has become a born again Christian and joined a fundamentalist church that doesn't tolerate the use of any drugs, including marijuana. She threatens to turn us in for making our living growing the stuff.

I fear that she will blow our cover as worm farmers and tell the preacher, who is the sheriff's brother. I have nothing on the pastor to blackmail him with. What shall I do?

Scared

Dear Scared:

Open your eyes. Surely the holy man likes to fish ... give him all of the worms he needs and if that doesn't work, join the church yourself and give as much money as you can to the cause. That will keep his mouth shut.

You might have to enlarge your operations next year, but that is the cost of security. As for the child, I would give her a good lesson in economics!

Rev. Tippy

Dear Tipper:

We are a religious sect living in the boonies with little money and great faith. Due to our vows against alcohol we have chosen marijuana as our sacrament. Have you any knowledge of this act and is it practiced elsewhere? Or has religion ever been used as a defense in a pot case?

The Elite-Age Prophets

Dear Brethren:

I know of one such group who resided in Colombia. When they were busted, the local church hierarchy saw to it that the followers were crucified. You had better watch what you do. There are too many unemployed carpenters looking for work.

Tippy

Dear Tippy Tops:

It is rumored around here that the Japanese have developed synthetic indica buds that come off of the line looking like manicured Hawaiian. Do you know anything about this and does it taste as good as they say?

I.M. Natural

Dear I.M. Natural:

This is all true and the real kicker is that the price per ounce is around twenty dollars. The U.S. government has agreed to import some of this pot for distribution on the West coast. This is an experiment to try and destroy the domestic market.

And yes, this poly-pot is not a joke. It tastes great, looks swell and knocks you right out the front door of your Toyota.
Tippy

Dear Tippy:
Do you have any solutions for an irritating phenomena caused by indoor grow lights in my bedroom. It seems that my hair and fingernails grow at an alarming rate. I wake up in the morning and my eyebrows hang down to my cheeks, and my nose hairs choke me. Worst of all, my toenails have to be cut out of the bedsheets. I have tried covering my body with protective clothing when working and sleeping under the halides. That is not a solution. What can I do?
Lots O. Hair

Dear Lots O:
I suggest you try a complete body electrolosis or drinking a mild solution of Nair and broadleaf herbicide before bedtime. Better to be safe than sorry!
Dr. Tippy

Dear Tip the Scale:
I'm still having trouble with poachers and rip-offs. No matter how far I go back into the hills, they get me. What can I do?
The Wanderer

Dear Wandering Lost Soul:
Have you seen our latest poster? It reads:
DANGER: YOU ARE ENTERING AN EPA TOXIC WASTE
ZONE. ONLY AUTHORIZED PERSONNEL WITH
PROTECTIVE CLOTHING ALLOWED BEYOND THIS POINT.
These posters are available for $100 each from the EPA headquarters in Washington, D.C. all proceeds go toward the EPA toxic waste superfund.
Good Luck!
Tippy the Mutant

Dear Mr. Tippy Tops:
I am a wheat farmer in central Kansas. The two hippies down the road from me said that I should write to you. You see, I got all this marijuana growing up in my north 40. Yep, acres of it, left over from WWII. The German U-boats were disrupting shipments of hemp from abroad, so the Ag boys gave us some seed and we grew it for hemp fiber. Mighty tough fiber, too! Wish I had a pair of overalls made out

of hemp. Soft as cotton, wears like iron.

Anyhow, I got acres of it growing wild. Do you want some? I could bail it up with my John Deere and store it in my barn with the alfalfa. Do you think I could get $1,000 a pound like the hippies down the road get for theirs?

Yours Truly,
Unruh Decker

Dear Unruh:
Sorry, but $1,000 a pound sounds a little over priced. Try mixing it with your alfalfa and feeding it to your livestock and see what they say!

Tippy

Dear Tippy:
What would you suggest to a person who smokes all his dope before he can sell it?

Smokey

Dear Smokey:
Take two aspirin and go to bed.

Tippy

BACK ISSUES

Vol.1 #1,2,3,4 & Vol.2#2 — OUT OF PRINT

Vol.2 #3 $1.50* — Tippy Talks, Cloning and Mother Plants, Farmer In the Sky on Halides, Cooking with Pot, 1981 Review of West Coast Crop, Gardening Without Soil, Spies In the Skies and More!

Vol.2 #4 $1.50* — Plant Breeding with Robert Clarke, How to Grow an Outdoor Spring Crop, Hydroponics, Growers' Co-ops, The Professional Connoisseur, Fight Spider Mites Naturally, and More.

Vol.3 #1,2,3— OUT OF PRINT

Vol.3 #4 $3.00 *— More Information on Spider Mites and How to Fight Them Naturally, Sinsemilla Seed Production, Cloning Methods, Introducing Bat Guano, Humbolt County News, Lighting Selection, More Interviews with Growers, More Pot Politics and other Miscellany!

Vol.4 #1 $3.00 — Report on the Latest Technology For Indoor and Outdoor Growers, Late Planting Tips, Container Soils, Designer Packaging Labels, NASA and U-2 Spying For Pot Crops, Farmer In the Sky on Indoor Methods, Humbolt County Review and More!

Vol.4 #2 $3.00 — New Indoor Cultivation Tips, The Media and Pot Raids, Wild Magic Mushrooms Free For the Picking, Sinsemilla Tips From the Field, Green Collar Worker Survey, Hawaiian Sinsemilla Tips, Farmer In the Sky's Indoor Report and More!

Vol.4 #3 $3.00 — More Info on Bat and Bird Guano, Farmer In the Sky Indoor Report, Foliar Feeding, Indoor Sinsemilla Tips, Artificial Lighting Report, Introducing Light Tracking Systems, Ozark Sinsemilla Report and More!

Vol.4 #4 $3.00* — Water Conservation, Economics of Outlaw Agriculture, Farmer In the Sky Indoor Report, More on Bird Guano, DEA's Eradication Program and More!

Vol.5 #1 $3.00 — How to Build Cheap Hydroponic Systems, Back Issue Compendium, Remote Sensing by the Government, Introducing the Bush Doctor, How to Organize and Plan a Harvest Festival, Air Layering For Clones, View From Back East, Smart Organics, Soil Building the California Way and 48 pages More!

Vol.5 #2 $3.00 — Cervantes' Hightech Report, 1985 Grower Survey, Electrical Safety, The Bush Doctor on Aphids, Farmer In the Sky, Ed Rosenthal on Genetics, Marijuana Information Explosion, CAMP Attack, How to Make Domestic Hash and 64 pages More!

Vol.5 #3 $4.00 — Short News Tips, Question and Answer Column, More High Tech by Cervantes, The Bush Doctor on Mold, Farmer In the Sky, Plant Breeding, Doctor Hydro, Mary Jane's How to Video on Indoor Growing, More Yield For No More Money, Sky Narc Talks, Midwest Techniques, Basic Primer on Cultivation and 72 pages More!

Vol.5 #4 $4.00 — Cervantes' Hightech Report, Farmer In the Sky, Bush Doctor on Damping Off Disease, Doctor Hydro, Question and Answer Column, The Breeding Corner with Chief Seven Turtles, Humbolt County Review, Smart Investments For Growers, Results of Grower Survey, Keep Plants Small and the Buds BIG, Citizen Observation Group of California, Workaday world on the Big Island, Marijuana Land Forfeiture, Goods and Services Directory and 88 pages More!

Vol.6 #1 $4.00 — Readers' Letters, Bush Doctor on Fungus, Guerilla Gardening, The Outdoor Strategy, Farmer In the Sky, Carbon Dioxide Enrichment Methods, Doctor Hydro, Computer Automated Growing, Humbolt Gold, Pioneers on the High Frontier, Question and Answer Column, Rethinking the War on Drugs and 88 pages More!

Vol.6 #2 $4.00 — Readers' Letters, Bush Doctor on Spider Mites, Indoor Growing For Beginners,

Farmer In The Sky, More Humbolt Gold, Legal Defense For Indoor Growers, New Product Review, More on Rockwool, Management of Indoor Growing Operations, High Tech, Dr. Hydro on Macro and Micro-Nutrients, Just Ask Tips Gardening Advice and Much More!

Vol.6 #3 $5.00 — Indoor Growing For Beginners, Case Studies For New Growers, Legal Tips, Electrical Tips, Safe Lighting Practices, New Product Review, Reader's Rights, Bush Doctor, Farmer In Sky, CO2 & Brewing, Humbolt Gold, Aerial Surveillance and Much More!

Vol.6 #4 $5.00 — Alternative Methods of Harvesting, Hybrid Breeding, Environmental Dynamics In the Grow Room, Basement Farmer, History of Marijuana, Basic Brownie Recipe, Low Profile Growing, Electrical Tips, Humbolt Gold, Before Ruderalis/Reagan and After Ron/Ruderalis, Bush Doctor In Nepal and More!

Vol.7 #1 $5.00 — Beyond Close Cropping, Indoor Growing with Raised Beds, Notes From the Great Outdoors, CAMP's '86 Report, NORML's 1987 Convention, Marijuana In America, Early Flowering Hybrids, Legal Tips, Electrical Tips, Humbolt Gold and Much More!

Vol.7 #2 $5.00 — Holland: Marijuana Breeder's Mecca, Ed Rosenthal's Tips on Training Plants, Outdoor Camouflage, FDIC Notes, Bush Doctor on the A-maize-ing Corn Borer, The 17 Essential Elements, Dr. Indoors, Nipsey and Tipsey, Farmer In the

Sky on Bulbs, Irrigation, Fertilizers, Etc., Legal Tips, Report From the Emerald Triangle, Electrical Tips-testing Ballast Setups and Silencing Electrical Generators, Humbolt Gold, and More!

VOL.7 #3 $5.00 — Just Ask Tips, Growing the S.S.S.C. Way, The History of Cannabis Plant Pathology, Bush Doctor on the Taxonomy of Organisms associated with Cannabis, Life with the Phototron II, Electrical Tips, Property, Privacy and Penalities: the Risks for 1988, Nipsey and Tipsey, The Great Outdoors, Humbolt Gold, Homegrown, and more!

Since 1969, enough Americans have been arrested for possession of marijuana to empty the states of:

Oregon
(pop. 2,633,149)

Nevada
(pop. 944,038)

Idaho
(pop. 800,493)

And the cities of:

Fresno, California; Amarillo, Texas; Santa Fe, New Mexico; Spokane, Washington; Pueblo, Colorado; Redding, California; Salt Lake City, Utah; Casper, Wyoming; Flagtaff, Arizona; and Berkeley, California

In fact, about 6 million people have been arrested for the possession of marijuana in the last two decades—one every minute and a half. And the government has promised to step up the pace. If you agree with millions of other citizens that enough is enough, it's up to you to get involved.

Join the National Organization for the Reform of Marijuana Laws today by sending $25 in membership dues, or write or call for free information:

**NORML, 2001 S Street NW, Suite 640,
Washington, D.C. 20009
— 202-483-5500 —**

New Moon Books

MARIJUANA RELATED BOOKS:

SINSEMILLA TIPS MAGAZINE	
(one-year subscription (4 issues)	$20.00
BEST OF SINSEMILLA TIPS	17.95
MARIJUANA HYDROPONICS	14.95
MARIJUANA BOTANY	12.95
JUST ASK ED	16.95
INDOOR MARIJUANA HORTICULTURE	14.95
HOW TO GROW HERB HYDROPONICALLY	7.95
INDOOR MARIJUANA CULTIVATION	5.95
INTERNATIONAL HANDBOOK OF MJ	9.95
HOW TO GROW THE FINEST MJ	9.95
MJ GROWERS GUIDE (SMALL ED.)	5.95
MJ GROWERS GUIDE (LARGE ED.)	14.95
COOKING WITH CANNABIS	2.95
SUPERMOTHERS COOKING WITH GRASS	1.50
SINSEMILLA TECHNIQUE	14.95
MARIJUANA LAWS OF THE WORLD	10.95
THE PRIMO PLANT	4.50

WEED-ADVENTURES OF DOPE SMUGGLER	9.95
DR. ATOMICS MARIJUANA MULTIPLIER	2.95
MARIJUANA AS MEDICINE	8.95
MARIJUANA POTENCY	10.95
INDOOR SINSEMILLA	9.95
BIGGER & BETTER HYDROPONIC GARDEN	5.95
PRACTICAL CO2 ENRICHMENT	3.50
HOW TO USE BAT GUANO	3.50
MARIJUANA GROWERS HANDBOOK	14.95
CANNABIS ALCHEMY	5.95
MARIJUANA GROWING TIPS	12.95
M. J. CULTIVATORS HANDBOOK	14.95
HOW TO GROW MJ UNDER LIGHTS	7.95
ROCKWOOL IN HORTICULTURE	42.95
SECRET GARDEN	12.95
MARIJUANA BEER	6.95
CASH CROPS	8.00
OUTLAWS IN BABYLON	6.95

MUSHROOM RELATED BOOKS:

MAGIC MUSHROOM FIELD GUIDE	9.95
PSILOCYBIN PRODUCER'S GUIDE	1.50
PSILOCYBE MUSHROOMS & THEIR ALLIES	12.95
POISONOUS & HALLUCINOGENIC MUSH	7.95
THE MUSHROOM CULTIVATOR	24.95

OTHER BOOKS OF INTEREST:

CHOCOLATE TO MORPHINE	8.95
THE NATURAL MIND	7.95
PSYCHEDELIC ENCYCLOPEDIA	12.95
HIGH TIMES MAGAZINE	
(monthly, per issue)	3.95

VIDEOS:

MARY JANE HOW TO	39.95
CALIFORNIA SINSEMILLA	39.95
GANJA SAURUS REX (COMEDY 100 MIN.)	39.95

NAME

ADDRESS   STATE   ZIP

VISA/MASTERCARD #   EXP. DATE   /

PUBLICATION(S) REQUESTED: COST:

SUBTOTAL

PLEASE ADD $2.50 PER BOOK FOR SHIPPING AND HANDLING

TOTAL ENCLOSED

NAME

ADDRESS   STATE   ZIP

VISA/MASTERCARD #   EXP. DATE   /

PUBLICATION(S) REQUESTED: COST:

SUBTOTAL

PLEASE ADD $2.50 PER BOOK FOR SHIPPING AND HANDLING

TOTAL ENCLOSED

NOW WHAT?

For more information on how to get what you need to set up your own indoor or outdoor garden, send now for New Moon Publishing's information packet. Each packet contains complete product information on a wide variety of of goods—fertilizers, lighting, drip systems and hydroponic supplies, books and more—for today's high-tech gardener. Included is a comprehensive list of major retail and mail-order suppliers in the United States and Europe.

Just send $3.00 Check or Money Order to:

Farm and Garden Supplies Directory
New Moon Publishing, Inc.
PO BOX 90
Corvallis, OR 97339

For Visa or Mastercard Orders, Call: 503-757-8477